OLIVER CROMWELL

King In All But Name

1653–1658

He is a King but will not put on a crown fearing, perhaps, that the glittering of state, together with the lustre of his own person, should be too dazzling and glorious.

The Unparalleled Monarch: or the Portraiture of a Matchless Prince Exprest in some Shadows of His Highness My Lord Protector
(London, 1656)

By the same author

The Court of Oliver Cromwell

Superpower Britain

The Civil War in the Midlands, 1642–1651

OLIVER CROMWELL

King In All But Name
1653–1658

Roy Sherwood

SUTTON PUBLISHING

First published in 1997 by
Sutton Publishing Limited · Phoenix Mill
Thrupp · Stroud · Gloucestershire · GL5 2BU

British Library Cataloguing in Publication Data

A catalogue record for this book is available from the British Library

ISBN 0-7509-1066-6

TM   ALAN SUTTON™ and SUTTON™ are the
trade marks of Sutton Publishing Limited

Typeset in 11/12 pt Erhardt.
Typesetting and origination by
Sutton Publishing Limited
Printed in Great Britain by
Butler and Tanner, Frome, Somerset.

For Doreen

Contents

List of Illustrations ix

Picture Credits xi

Preface xiii

1 *More Than Sovereign Authority* 1

2 *With Sound Of Trumpets, In Most Solemn Manner* 7

3 *Soaring Grandeur* 26

4 *More Soaring Grandeur* 43

5 *Gold And Silver Brave* 57

6 *We Have A Crown Made* 69

7 *Monarchy Asserted* 80

8 *Protector Royal* 91

9 *Much Mirth With Frolics* 108

10 *Tempest And Foul Weather* 120

11 *Moses My Servant Is Dead* 130

12 *The Last Act Crowns The Play* 143

13 *A Great Show* 155

14 *Farewell! A Long Farewell To All My Greatness!* 165

Notes 169

Bibliography 185

Index 195

List of Illustrations

Jacket illustrations: front, Oliver Cromwell's second investiture as Lord Protector, after Ellis Silas (1883–1971); *back*, design for the badge to be worn by the Protector's bargemasters and watermen.

1. Olivarius Primus, by William Faithorne (1616–91)
   in Louis de Gand, *Parallelum Olivae nec non Olivarii*, 1656   3
2. Her Highness the Lady Protectress, attrib. Sir Peter Lely (1618–80)   5
3. Westminster Hall   8
4. Protectoral proclamation   14
5. Signature of Oliver Cromwell as Lord Protector   14
6. Banqueting House, Whitehall   22
7. Dutch silver medal of Cromwell   24
8. Palace of Whitehall, by Wenceslaus Hollar (1607–77)   27
9. John Hingston, Cromwell's Master of the Music   29
10. Hampton Court Palace   31
11. Great Hall, Hampton Court   32
12. Caesar on his Chariot, by Andrea Mantegna   34
13. His Highness's heralds, from *A Book of the Continuation
    of Forreign Passages*, 1657   35
14. Spotted woman, from 'The Artificiall Changling' in
    A View of the People of the Whole World, 1654   37
15. View of Westminster, by Wenceslaus Hollar   39
16. Great Seal of the pre-Protectorate Commonwealth, from Wyon,
    Great Seals of England   44
17. Great Seal of the Cromwellian Protectorate, from Wyon   44
18. Great Seal of Elizabeth I, from Wyon   44
19. Great Seal of Charles I, from Wyon   44
20. Arms of the Cromwellian Protectorate   46
21. Proclamation displaying the Protectoral arms   47
22. Henry Cromwell   54
23. Jewelled pendant bearing the head of Oliver Cromwell   60
24. Poor Knights of Windsor, from Elias Ashmole, *The Institution,
    Laws & Ceremonies of the Most Noble Order of the Garter*, 1672   62
25. Arms of the Artillery Company, from William Barriffe, *Military
    Discipline; or the young artillery-man*, 1661, British Library 717.g.34   66

26. Christiana Cavendish, Dowager Countess of Devonshire, from
Henry Drummond, *Histories of Noble British Families*, 1846   67
27. Cromwell refusing the crown, after Herbert Maguire (1821–95)   88
28. Coinage of the pre-Protectorate Commonwealth   94
29. Cromwellian coinage   94
30. Cromwell's second investiture, after Ellis Silas   98
31. Coronation Chair   100
32. Cromwell's second investiture, from *A Further Narrative of the
Passages of the times in the Commonwealth of England*, 1658   102
33. Letters patent for a Cromwellian hereditary peerage, from Noble,
Memoirs of the Protectoral House of Cromwell   105
34. Design for the badge to be worn by Cromwell's bargemasters and
watermen, Public Record Office SP 18/156, fol. 153   107
35. Mary Cromwell   108
36. Robert Rich, second Earl of Warwick, by Daniel Mytens (1590?–1642)   110
37. Andrew Marvell   117
38. Colonel Philip Jones, Comptroller of his Highness's Household   122
39. Frances Cromwell, by John Michael Wright (1625?–1700)   127
40. John Maynard, his Highness's Sergeant   128
41. Elizabeth Claypole, by John Michael Wright   133
42. Richard Cromwell, from *Some Farther Intelligence of the Affairs
of England*, 1659   137
43. Proclamation of Richard Cromwell as Lord Protector   139
44. Great Seal of Richard Cromwell, from Wyon   141
45. Signature of Richard Cromwell as Lord Protector   141
46. Cromwell's lying in state, from *Some Farther Intelligence*   149
47. Cromwell's funeral effigy standing in state, British Library 1093.c.51   152
48. Standards and banners carried in Cromwell's funeral procession,
from Prestwich, *Respublica*   159
49. James I's catafalque, from Nichols, *Progresses*   162
50. Proclamation by Richard Cromwell ordering the dissolution
of Parliament   166

Picture Credits

Preface

Oliver Cromwell as Lord Protector is frequently described as being a King in all but name without much in the way of a coherent, detailed explanation of precisely what this means. This book aims to correct that omission by demonstrating some of the ways in which the embodied paradox and bundle of contradictions that was Cromwell's rule constituted a monarchical regime in the generally accepted sense of the term, that of a crowned head.

We already know that the Protectoral household provided Cromwell with a regal setting (see my *The Court of Oliver Cromwell*). What *Oliver Cromwell King In All But Name 1653–1658* demonstrates is the extent to which the Protector actually functioned as a sovereign prince and the degree to which he was recognised as such both by his own countrymen and foreign observers. A chronological approach has been adopted in order to reveal the progressive restoration of regal institutions and practices and with them Cromwell's assumption of the prerogatives of a King. Revealed too are the rising tide of royal pomp and pageantry, the growing splendour of Protectoral court life, and some of the ways in which the return to 'normality' represented by the new monarchical government was mirrored in society in general. At the same time the persistently voiced notion, originating very early on in the Protectorate, that Cromwell would ultimately accept the title of King is documented. Parliament's formal offer of the crown in 1657 and the ensuing kingship debate is fully re-addressed to show that the Protector demurred only in respect of the *title* of King not the office and that as a consequence the Protectorship was made conformable to the kingly dignity, transforming Cromwell from a de facto into a *de jure* King while retaining the title of Protector. This was, however, a compromise arrangement and evidence is presented which suggests that had death not intervened Cromwell would have gone on to formalise completely his already regal status by adopting the title of King, an omission that played its part in the eventual collapse of the Cromwellian Protectorate royal.

In writing this book I have confined myself solely to teasing out and interpreting what might be termed the regal aspects of the Protectorate and have purposely not attempted a wider interpretation of the Cromwellian regime. Contemporary printed sources, state papers, ambassadorial reports, diaries and private correspondence have been extensively quoted from in order to capture something of the authentic voice of the period. Spelling and punctuation have, however, been adapted to modern usage. Dates throughout are old style but with the year taken as beginning on 1 January.

As always with a work of this nature a very considerable debt is owed to others. First and foremost my thanks are due to my wife, Doreen, for her immeasurable practical assistance and unerring support. I am also extremely grateful to John Goldsmith, County Museums Officer, Cambridgeshire County Council; translators Peter Fisher (Latin/Greek), Michèle Hagard (French) and Michael Taylor (Swedish); the staffs of the British Library, Cambridge University Library, The London Library, National Library of Wales, Public Record Office and Willingham Library; and Roger Thorp, Jane Crompton and Clare Bishop of Sutton Publishing.

Roy Sherwood
Cambridge
1997

CHAPTER 1

More Than Sovereign Authority

During the afternoon of Friday 3 September 1658 a fifty-nine-year-old man died in the Palace of Whitehall, which, in the seventeenth century, was the principal residence of the monarch and the centre of royal government. There followed one of the most spectacular and expensive state funerals the country had ever seen and it was modelled in almost every detail on that of King James I thirty-three years earlier. In accordance with royal custom all the symbolism and ceremonial of the obsequies were attached to and revolved around a life-size effigy of the deceased, the body itself having already been interred in Henry VII's Chapel, the Chapel of the Kings, in royal Westminster Abbey. The effigy was magnificently attired in an imperial robe of royal velvet, girded with a kingly sword, crowned with a richly ornamented imperial crown and furnished with an orb and sceptre. But the man they buried 'with more than regal pomp in the sepulchre of our monarchs'[1] in 1658 did not bear the title King, for this was Oliver Cromwell, head of state, as Lord Protector, of what was nominally the Commonwealth, or republic, of England, Scotland and Ireland, and the Dominions and Territories thereunto belonging: King in all but name.

Less than two decades had passed since the beginning of the Civil War that had resulted in an end to kingly rule with the execution of Charles I and the establishment of the English Commonwealth in 1649. By the end of 1653, however, acephalous republican government was at an end. A written constitution, the Instrument of Government, was drawn up by one of the republic's leading Generals, John Lambert, and other senior military commanders. This decreed that henceforth 'the supreme legislative authority of the Commonwealth of England, Scotland and Ireland, and the Dominions thereunto belonging, shall be and reside in one person, and the people assembled in Parliament; the style of which person shall be, "The Lord Protector of the Commonwealth of England, Scotland and Ireland"'.[2] And the man who would rule as Lord Protector was the one-time relatively obscure East Anglian squire who had emerged from the maelstrom of the Civil War and its aftermath as the most powerful figure in the land, Oliver Cromwell, Lord General, or Commander-in-Chief, of the Army of the

Commonwealth. Ironically, the Instrument of Government was based on the abortive proposals put to Charles I in 1647 by Cromwell and others as the framework for a post-civil war settlement which would have allowed the King to retain his throne. Indeed, the Instrument of Government itself is believed to have originally contained the title of King but Cromwell turned it down.

The title with which Oliver would rule, that of Lord Protector, had a fairly long pedigree. Historically it had been given to those acting as regents during the minority, absence or incapacity of the sovereign. Once the exigence had passed the Protectorate was expected to give way to monarchical rule. These Lords Protector of the Realm or Kingdom, who were usually relatives of the monarch, might be temporarily invested with regal authority in order to ensure that royal government continued uninterrupted but they were not themselves sovereign princes. Obviously, Cromwell was not a Lord Protector in the historic sense of the term. He was Lord Protector of what was at least nominally a republic, not a kingdom, and although he would later claim that he had 'no title to the government of these nations, but what was taken up in a case of necessity, and temporary, to supply the present emergency', he was in fact made Lord Protector for life. He was also a sovereign prince. 'Man', it has been said, 'is an embodied paradox, a bundle of contradictions' and this is an equally apt description of Cromwell's rule. But out of the embodied paradox and bundle of contradictions that was his regime what clearly emerges is that not only did Cromwell's Protectorate in effect represent a restoration of monarchical rule but also if it was intended to make way for anything it would ultimately be to Oliver as King. It was perhaps inevitable, therefore, that the spectre of the one past Lord Protector to become King would receive an outing, with comparisons made between Richard III and Cromwell. Richard was Lord Protector during the minority of his nephew, Edward V, but had overridden the title to the throne of Edward and his younger brother, the Duke of York (the Princes in the Tower), to claim the crown for himself.[3]

But Cromwell was already a King in all but name, even though his sovereign power was shared with Parliament and limited by a Council of State. And this regal status, indeed more than regal status, was attested to by the Venetian envoy in London immediately after Oliver had come to power: 'Such are the principal contents of the Instrument of Government that for all practical purposes it makes him [Cromwell] King, giving him indeed more than sovereign authority, and although England has had Protectors before she never made them as absolute as this.' The extent of the power of 'Old Noll', as Cromwell was popularly known, was even alluded to in a near-contemporary riddle, the answer to which is a rainbow:

> Purple, yellow, red and green,
> The King cannot reach it nor the Queen;
> Nor can Old Noll, whose power's so great:
> Tell me this riddle while I count to eight.

Appropriately Cromwell would be addressed as his Highness Oliver, Lord Protector of the Commonwealth. Hitherto his Highness had been the style afforded Kings of England, his Majesty being adopted by Henry VIII and then

OLIVARIVS PRIMVS

W. Faithorne fec:

Portrait of Oliver Cromwell from a contemporary panegyric in which it was said of Cromwell that hitherto 'divine Providence has allowed no monarch of any nation to rejoice in the name of Oliver, and in consequence he is Oliver the First in every respect'. As such Cromwell's style and title would be his Highness Oliver, Lord Protector of the Commonwealth of England, Scotland and Ireland, and the Dominions and Territories thereunto belonging.

used together with his Highness until the reign of James I, during which his Majesty became the fixed form of address. The French ambassador in London, Antoine de Bordeaux, was therefore only partly right when he reported of Cromwell that 'he is given the title of *Royal* Highness and is to live in the palace of the King, of whom several officers wished him to take the title'. Nevertheless, the style afforded Oliver was sufficiently regal as it was and this was shared by his wife, Elizabeth, who would be known as her Highness the Lady Protectress.[4]

That, as Lord Protector, regality became Cromwell will become self-evident. But anecdotal evidence would seem to suggest that regality had hovered about Oliver from an early age, since his days as a seventeen-year-old Fellow Commoner at Sidney Sussex College, Cambridge, in fact. In a notebook containing anecdotes and memoranda relating to his contemporaries, the Royalist and antiquary, Richard Symonds, recorded that 'in a play at Cambridge called *Lingua*, he [Cromwell] acted the part of Tactus, and stumbled at a crown, and took it up and put it on, and 'twas [a] fit, and asked if it did not become him'. A similar story was related by one of Cromwell's earliest biographers, Samuel Carrington, in his 1659 panegyrical *History of the Life and Death of his most Serene Highness Oliver Late Lord Protector*. Oliver, Carrington tells us, was 'educated at the University of Cambridge, where, as it is reported, a public representation being to be performed, he that was to represent the King's part falling sick . . . our Cromwell was said to have taken the part upon himself, and so well employed the little time he had to get it by heart as it seemed that it was infused into him . . . whereby he represented a King with so much grace and majesty as if that estate had been natural unto him.'[5]

A third of a century and more later histrionics had given way to something more real. In 1651 Cromwell, now Lord General of the Army of the Commonwealth, had sealed the security of the fledgling republic with his victory at the Battle of Worcester, thereby putting paid to Charles II's attempt to gain his executed father's throne. Soon afterwards the Lord General called for a meeting 'with divers members of Parliament and some chief officers of the army' proposing to them that now Charles I was dead and his son defeated it was necessary to come to a decision regarding a permanent political settlement. At the subsequent meeting the debate centred on whether the nation should remain 'an absolute republic' or have 'a mixed monarchical government'. According to state functionary Bulstrode Whitelocke, whose account this is, Cromwell for his part felt 'that a settlement with somewhat of monarchical power in it would be very effectual' and posed the question, if this be the choice then in whom should the power be placed? In the main, recounts Whitelocke, the soldiers were opposed to anything that included monarchy, while generally speaking the lawyers supported the notion of a mixed monarchical government. The lawyers' most favoured candidate for the throne was Charles II's youngest brother, Henry, Duke of Gloucester, still in the country and at eleven years of age 'too young to have been in arms against us or infected with the principles of our enemies'. A Royalist source would give this as Cromwell's own preference, with himself as Protector, but there were those who would actually have Cromwell as King.[6]

Cromwell's wife, Elizabeth, who, as her Highness the Lady Protectress, shared her husband's regal style.

In his *Apologetical Narration*, published a few months after the debate, which had ended without resolving anything, Leveller John Lilburne spoke of 'new sycophants' surrounding the Lord General who 'made it their work to solicit officers of the army . . . to get them to declare General Cromwell King of England' and 'that such a thing hath been and still is in present design by him'. Indeed, if Bulstrode Whitelocke is to be believed, in November 1652 Cromwell was confidentially sounding him out on the possibility of a restoration of the monarchy with Cromwell himself as King. Whatever the veracity of these accounts one thing is certain, a 'settlement with somewhat of monarchical power in it' was eventually arrived at and with Cromwell as monarch, albeit with the title of Lord Protector. Nevertheless 'he is a King', enthused the unknown author of a panegyric entitled *The Unparalleled Monarch*, 'but will not put on a crown fearing, perhaps, that the glittering of state, together with the lustre of his own person, should be too dazzling and glorious'. As it happened the glittering of the state associated with kingship became attached to Cromwell without a crown, a process that would begin soon after his formal investiture as Lord Protector on 16 December 1653.[7]

CHAPTER 2

With Sound Of Trumpets, In Most Solemn Manner

Cromwell's investiture as Lord Protector would take place in the Gothic splendour of Westminster Hall, part of the medieval Palace of Westminster which had once been the seat of royal government and was still the meeting place of the English Parliament. It remained so until fire destroyed the palace in 1843, the hall being the only substantial building to survive the conflagration. Pregnant with history, ancient Westminster Hall (the original structure was already half a millennium old when Cromwell was born) had been the scene of some of the most momentous events in the annals of the nation, including the trial of Charles I, separated in time from Cromwell's investiture by a little under five years. As testimony to the collapse of Stuart fortunes the hall was now decorated with a triumphal display of captured Royalist colours. Just as significant, in fact highly so, Westminster Hall was where the 'secular' enthronement of monarchs by peers and bishops took place prior to the coronation proper in Westminster Abbey, a ritual which was supposed to symbolise that the sovereign was the elected choice of the people.[1]

At about one o'clock on the appointed day his Excellency Lord General of the Army Oliver Cromwell was taken the short distance from the Palace of Whitehall, the centre of both royal and republican government, to Westminster Hall to be invested as his Highness the Lord Protector. The coach in which Cromwell travelled was accompanied by his mounted Life Guard and, on foot, 'many of the chief officers of the army with their cloaks, swords and hats on'. Soldiers also lined the half-mile or so route. Preceding Cromwell were other coaches carrying government officials, members of the judiciary in their state robes, what was to become his Highness the Lord Protector's Council and the Lord Mayor and aldermen of London in their scarlet gowns accompanied by civic functionaries. On their arrival at Westminster Hall this assemblage of military men and state and civic dignitaries arranged themselves about what had once been a royal throne, 'with costly footclothes and most rich cushions', set at the southern end of the building. As Cromwell entered the hall he was preceded by Major-General John Lambert carrying the sword of state. Oliver, dressed in 'a black plush suit and cloak' with a gold band around his hat, stood to the left of the throne, or chair of

Historic Westminster Hall where the pre-coronation 'secular' enthronement of monarchs had traditionally taken place and where Cromwell was invested as Lord Protector on 16 December 1653.

state, while the articles of the Instrument of Government were read out one by one, a process which took over half-an-hour. Cromwell, his right hand raised and allegedly shaking 'extremely and notoriously', then took an oath, a preamble to which explained how he had been prevailed upon to assume the protection and government of the country, not by officers of the army alone but also by several other 'persons of interest and fidelity in this Commonwealth'. He then swore to uphold the constitution and 'govern these nations according to the laws, statutes and customs, seeking their peace and causing justice and law to be equally administered'.[2]

'Thus', in the words of the Venetian envoy's startling observation of the event, 'by universal consent and in most solemn and conspicuous manner he [Cromwell] found himself created Protector of the whole kingdom.' But it was as Lord Protector of the *Commonwealth* of England, Scotland and Ireland that Oliver was invited to take possession of the throne, which he did with his head covered while everyone else present was bareheaded. Next, 'the military officers and other functionaries, hat in hand, did him homage in the obsequious and respectful form observed towards the late Kings'. General Lambert knelt before the newly installed Lord Protector and presented him with a sheathed sword which Cromwell exchanged for his own, signifying the transition from military man to civil ruler. The custodians, or Lords Commissioner, of the Great Seal of the Commonwealth then delivered up to Cromwell the purse containing the state seal and the Lord Mayor of London did the same with the City sword.* Seal and sword were immediately returned to their bearers by the Lord Protector, 'in token of his authority', with the exhortation to use them well. After a short speech by the new ruler the whole assembly processed out of the hall, 'which was thronged with people', and returned bareheaded to Whitehall where Cromwell was expected to reside and 'exercise sovereign authority'. The procession now included four Sergeants-at-Arms each carrying a mace before the Lord Protector. One carried the mace of the City of London, whose Lord Mayor rode in the boot of Cromwell's carriage with the City sword, and the others those of the Protectoral Council, the High Court of Chancery, and Parliament.[3]

This 'new invented ceremony', as the Royalist historian, the Earl of Clarendon, called it, had not been a coronation of course and one contemporary description of the 'solemnisation of the General's Protectorship' as being 'performed with no less state and magnificence than any former Kings have used' was something of an exaggeration. But beneath the soaring hammer-beam roof of Westminster Hall, with stone statues of past monarchs in their elevated niches as mute witnesses, some of the ritualism traditionally associated with the making of a King had most certainly been observed. Indeed, even as Cromwell entered the hall the trappings of kingship were already in evidence. The sword of state which preceded him had customarily been borne upright before monarchs on state occasions as a symbol of sovereign power and authority and the 'royal presence'.

*This would have been the 'Pearl Sword', a gift, it is thought, from Elizabeth I to the City.

Royal sword bearers, however, were usually powerful peers whereas Cromwell's was not. But in the context of the Cromwellian Protectorate Major-General John Lambert, who was a member of the Council and one of the most senior officers in the army, amounted to pretty much the same thing. As for the investiture itself, Oliver in his pledge to 'govern these nations according to the laws, statutes and customs' and so forth had sworn something akin to past sovereign princes in their coronation oaths. And his being invited to take possession of the throne was obviously a deliberate enactment of the monarch's traditional pre-coronation 'secular' enthronement in Westminster Hall. Also very much in accordance with the conventions relating to monarchy was the removal of their hats by those present while Oliver kept his on. This was at a time when the custom was for men to wear their hats indoors, even in the presence of women, but not in the presence of a King, who would himself remain covered. Even the presenting of the sheathed sword to Cromwell could be said to have represented the sword bestowed, along with the other insignia of office, on monarchs at their coronation as a reminder that a sovereign's primary duty is to be the people's protector.[4]

But the ritual which most symbolised the reality of Cromwell's position was undoubtedly his return, after they had been delivered up to him, of the Great Seal and the Lord Mayor of London's sword to those responsible for their safe keeping. This truly was, as one report of the investiture described it, a token of the Lord Protector's authority because the power which these symbols represented had now devolved upon the new ruler and was therefore his to dispense. The Great Seal, affixed to state documents as proof of authenticity, was the supreme emblem of civil authority, authority now vested in the office of Lord Protector. Although at this point the seal in use was still that of the pre-Protectorate Commonwealth and therefore uncompromisingly republican in its design (see Chapter 4) it had nevertheless reverted to what it had once been: 'The key to the realm, the only instrument by which on solemn occasions the will of the sovereign can be expressed. Absolute faith is universally given to every document purporting to be under the Great Seal as having been duly sealed with it by the authority of the sovereign.'[5]

That other token of Cromwell's authority as Lord Protector, the return of the City sword to the Lord Mayor of London, possesses more significance than it might at first appear. The City of London was a semi-autonomous kingdom within a kingdom whose Lord Mayor (at least two of whom can be numbered among Cromwell's ancestors), Courts of Aldermen and Common Council mirrored the sovereign, Lords and Commons. Like a sovereign the Lord Mayor even had a sword borne before him as a symbol of his power and authority and the mayoral presence. This was a privilege granted by the monarch, for whom the City of London's support, financial or otherwise, could prove crucial. Richard II (reigned 1377–1399) had even been cynically dubbed the 'Londoners' King' by the nobility because he owed his throne more to the burgesses of the City than to them. And although not at first inimical to Charles I a change in municipal government on the eve of the Civil War determined that London would support Parliament in the ensuing struggle with disastrous consequences for the King. Just as the Corporation of London would go on to recognise the republic, those with lingering monarchist sympathies having been displaced, so too were they now recognising the Cromwellian regime. By surrendering his sword to Cromwell the Lord Mayor of London was demonstrating his acceptance of the new ruler's ultimate authority over the City. The sword's return therefore symbolised the granting of the Lord Mayor's own powers by the sovereign, in this instance the Lord Protector at whose investiture the Lord Mayor exercised the same ancient prerogative that his predecessors had at coronations – to stand with the great officers of state and in the immediate vicinity of the throne.[6]

One last act in this ceremonial making of a Lord Protector took place on Cromwell's return to Whitehall: he and his entourage attended an 'exhortation', delivered by one of his Highness's chaplains, Nicholas Lockyer, which could be described as the equivalent of a coronation sermon. Again the venue was not without significance being the Whitehall Palace Banqueting House, Inigo Jones's Renaissance-style masterpiece completed in 1622. Like the Palace of Westminster, Whitehall Palace was destined to be destroyed by fire, only much earlier, in 1698. And like Westminster Hall the Banqueting House would be the only substantial building to survive. Providing a classic illustration, if ever there was one, of history's tragic little ironies, the ceiling above the Lord Protector's head as he listened to his court chaplain was decorated with the painting by Rubens depicting a deified James I, arch-exponent of the Divine Right of Kings. It had been commissioned by his son, Charles I, to boost the esteem of his royal House, now replaced by the Protectoral House of Cromwell.

Something that distinguished Protectoral from previous royal ceremonial was the presence of a mounted Life Guard in the investiture procession. Cromwell was the first English ruler to have a standing army and therefore the first to possess a regular professional regiment drawn from it as a personal bodyguard. He had qualified for a Life Guard when he was made Lord Lieutenant of Ireland by the fledgling English republic in 1649. A contemporary description of this guard, together with an account of the new Lord Lieutenant's journey to embarkation at Bristol, provides a revealing, and perhaps to some a contradictory, insight into the character both of Cromwell and the republican regime. The guard consisted of '80 gallant men . . . in stately habit', all of them gentlemen and many with the rank of Colonel. 'It's such a guard as is hardly paralleled in the world.' This splendid band was to add considerable lustre to the then Lieutenant-General Cromwell's already glitteringly stately progress from London to Bristol, which for style and grandeur befits the popular image of the grandest of Royalist grandees, if not a King: 'He went forth in that state and equipage, the like hath hardly been seen, himself in a coach with six gallant Flanders mares, whitish grey, divers coaches accompanying him and very many great officers of the army . . . with trumpets sounding almost to the shaking of Charing Cross had it been now standing.'[7] (The cross was destroyed by Parliament in 1647 as an idolatrous object.)

The guard that accompanied Cromwell to his investiture was his Life Guard as Commander-in-Chief of the Army of the Commonwealth. And it was this, the Life Guard of his Excellency the Lord General, that returned with him afterwards to Whitehall as his Highness the Lord Protector's Life Guard of

Horse. The guard commander, like the composition of the guard itself, remained unchanged. This was Colonel Charles Howard of the noble House of Norfolk. A former Royalist, Howard had purged himself of his 'delinquency' and gone on to serve the Commonwealth with distinction. He fought under Cromwell against Charles II, the son of his former master, at the Battle of Worcester, in which he received wounds he still bore as Captain of the Protectoral Life Guard. Future British monarchs would follow Cromwell in utilising a part of the regular standing army as a mounted Life Guard. It was added to the only permanent guards hitherto available to the sovereign, the Yeomen of the Guard and the Band of Gentlemen Pensioners, versions of which would also be made available to Cromwell, as both a protection and a potent symbol of sovereignty (see Chapters 3 and 5).[8]

Just as such symbols of sovereignty were very much in evidence from early on in the Protectoral regime so it was with the customs traditionally associated with monarchy. As was usual at a King's accession and on his coronation day Cromwell's investiture was commemorated by the ringing of church bells and the lighting of bonfires, one of the Inns of Court, the Inner Temple, expending 8s. 10d. on such a bonfire, 2s. 10d. more than it spent on that for Charles I's coronation. And three days after his investiture Cromwell, by order of his Council, was formally proclaimed Lord Protector in all the cities, boroughs and market towns throughout the land with, if one official account is to be believed, 'great solemnity and rejoicing', everyone of whatever quality and condition being strictly charged and commanded to conform and submit themselves to the government so established. At Leicester the sum of 13s. 4d. was 'paid to the several sextons of the several parishes for ringing on the day the Lord Protector was proclaimed'. In London (with the Lord Mayor and aldermen in attendance) and Westminster the formalities were enacted 'with sound of trumpets, in most solemn manner', at the places where royal precedent dictated that, by order of the sovereign's Council and with solemnity and trumpet fanfare, a new monarch be proclaimed.[9]

On this last occasion officers of the College of Arms were also present, providing another royal parallel. Comprising Kings of Arms, Heralds and Pursuivants, officers of the College of Arms perform a number of quite disparate functions. As well as tracing genealogies and dealing with grants of arms and matters of precedence they are also court officials responsible for overseeing state occasions, such as coronations and funerals, and proclaiming war, peace and the accession of a new monarch. Although part of royal households their posts nevertheless obtained under the republic, being occupied by those officers who had deserted the King and gone over to Parliament in the Civil War or by Commonwealth government appointees. Their grants of arms and genealogical functions continued as before and they officiated on ceremonial occasions, such as the funerals of state dignitaries. A new responsibility, however, was the cataloguing and safe keeping of captured Royalist colours. They continued to wear the traditional tabard as ceremonial dress, harking back to the medieval origin of their offices, but instead of being quartered by the royal arms their tabards were now emblazoned with the arms of the Commonwealth. These arms comprised two shields side by side, one containing the cross of St George for England and the other a harp for Ireland.* In these 'rich coats' did officers of the College of Arms attend the proclamation of the nation's new ruler, giving the occasion that additional regal air in spite of the avowed republicanism manifested in the manner of their dress. Oliver was also proclaimed Lord Protector in that other capital city of the Commonwealth, Dublin, but apparently 'not so soon, and not as cheerfully, as he was in the north'. At the same time 'the new Lord Protector', it was said, 'observed new and great state and all ceremonies and respects were paid to him by all sorts of men as their Prince'.[11]

In an appropriately prince-like manner the articles of the constitution under which Cromwell would rule were 'published by his Highness the Lord Protector by special Commandment' and printed by the Commonwealth's official printers, now designated 'Printers to his Highness the Lord Protector', which, in sentiment at least, approximates to 'Printers to the King's most Excellent Majestie' of the previous reign. And Oliver's first proclamation as Lord Protector followed royal practice by authorising all persons holding office at the time of the change in government to continue 'until his Highness's further direction'. (The previous two monarchs, James I and Charles I, had used the words 'till his Majesty's further direction'.) 'The Protectorate of Cromwell', observed the Venetian envoy in London, 'becomes increasingly authoritative, and his assumption of supreme power makes hourly progress. All edicts and proclamations are issued by his sole order with the advice of his Council.' By such an edict it was also decreed that the law would no longer be administered and justice dispensed in the name of 'the Keepers of the Liberty of England, by Authority of Parliament', which was how the pre-Protectorate Commonwealth government described itself, but once again in the name of the ruler as a single person, 'the Lord Protector' taking the place of 'the Lord the King'. There would not, however, be a parallel reversion to the curiously English form of bastardised Latin used as a language of the law. This had been abandoned in favour of English in the early days of the Commonwealth as Latin had been seen as smacking too much of popery. Furthermore, barristers belonging to what was at this time the highest order of counsel at the English Bar, known as Sergeants-at-Law (since superseded by King's or Queen's Counsel), and who had once been crown appointees now owed their appointments to the Lord Protector.[12]

Soon Protectoral proclamations, orders and declarations would be headed not simply by the Commonwealth coat of arms, as had hitherto been the case, but also with the decidedly regal device of the letters O and P (Oliver Protector), one on each side of the arms of the Commonwealth, just as, for instance, the letters C and R (Carolus Rex) had been placed one on either side of the royal arms. Likewise, official documents requiring Cromwell's signature would be signed in royal style 'Oliver P'. Included in the very early Protectoral proclamations, orders

---

*Although annexed by the republic in 1652 the 'ordinance for uniting Scotland into one Commonwealth with England' was not promulgated until April 1654, after which it was decreed that 'the arms of Scotland (viz Saint Andrew's Cross) should thenceforth be borne with the arms of this Commonwealth'.[10]

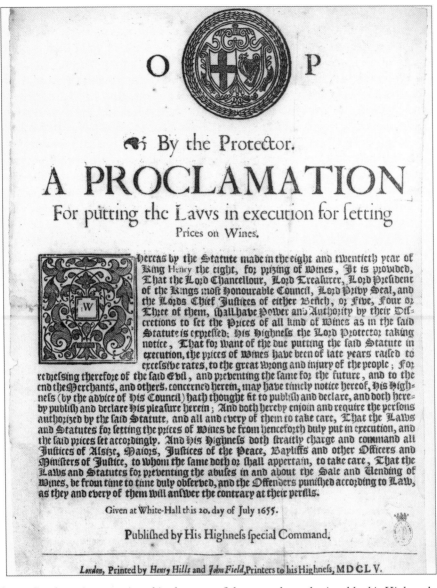

Above: *Proclamations were issued in the name of the new ruler and printed by his Highness's printers. The decidedly regal device of the letters O and P (Oliver Protector) accompanied the Commonwealth arms.*

Below: *Likewise, Cromwell signed official documents in royal style Oliver P.*

and declarations was a new treasons act, another ordinance with decidedly regal connotations. This replaced the Engagement, an oath of allegiance to the republic introduced in 1650 and imposed on all English men of eighteen and over. The form of the Engagement was: 'I do declare and promise that I will be true and faithful to the Commonwealth of England as it is now established, without a King or House of Lords.' Couched in identical language to its royal counterpart the Protectoral treasons act gave out that among those offences deemed treasonous was to 'compass and imagine' the death of the Lord Protector and to deny by whatever means his right to rule. The Cromwellian regime would have felt very much in need of an ordinance such as this. Even as the Protectorate was being proclaimed it came under attack. Two preachers, Christopher Feake and Vavasour Powell, were arrested and brought before the Protectoral Council for speaking out against the new government from the pulpit. They were later released. There was, after all, as yet very little they could justifiably be held for. A third preacher, John Simpson, had maintained publicly that the Protector's rule would not last above six months, something that he swore had come to him through divine inspiration. 'He is considered mad and has therefore been pardoned', recorded the Venetian envoy, 'but if he persists in his abuse of the present government he and all his imitators may expect severe punishment.' With the new treasons act the Cromwellian Protectorate now possessed the same means to inflict severe punishment on its enemies as previous royal governments had.[13]

News of the change in government was formally conveyed to the representatives of foreign powers by the Master of Ceremonies acting as a link between ambassadors and the government. The chief function of the Master of Ceremonies was, however, arranging the receptions and entertainment of ambassadors and organising diplomatic ceremonial, now called protocol, which in the seventeenth century was governed by an incredibly complex body of rules and procedures. Like the officers of the College of Arms the Master of Ceremonies had been a member of the royal household whose post would continue to exist under the republic. The Master of Ceremonies since the republic's inception in 1649 had been Sir Oliver Fleming, sometime one of Charles I's ambassadors and coincidentally a cousin of Oliver Cromwell. There is one important difference worth mentioning between the royal office of Master of Ceremonies and that under the Commonwealth. In former times the Master of Ceremonies supplemented his income with gifts of money from ambassadors. But the republican government obviously strove for higher standards because it expressly forbad the acceptance of such gratuities, regarding the practice 'as dishonourable to the Commonwealth'. Because of the nature of the post Sir Oliver Fleming found himself unable to function without these pecuniary advantages and remain solvent. He was therefore constrained to petition the government for an increase in his basic salary. For its part the government agreed to put the proposal before Parliament so that neither Sir Oliver, nor others who came after him in the office of Master of Ceremonies, 'may be under the temptation of doing things dishonourable'.[14]

Within days of being informed of the change in government ambassadors began, one by one, to be received by the Lord Protector whom they congratulated, in the name of their respective governments, on his 'new authority'. As was commented upon at the time these audiences did not conform to the practices of the pre-Protectorate Commonwealth, when ambassadors were received by a committee drawn from members of the government, but followed 'the usage of the late Kings'. The Protector, surrounded by his Councillors, received the ambassadors in one of the rooms of the ex-royal Palace of Whitehall. During the audience both Oliver and the ambassador kept their hats on while everyone else remained uncovered. This was the ambassador exercising the wholly exceptional and jealously guarded right as the representative of his, usually royal, master to stay covered in the presence of a foreign sovereign prince. Afterwards the ambassador was conducted out of the Protectoral presence by 'three of the Privy Councillors in waiting' with Cromwell, by 'not moving a step to reconduct him', acting very much the King. Reporting on such audiences the Venetian plenipotentiary observed that 'from the style adopted . . . the assumption by Cromwell of the state and prerogatives of royalty becomes daily more manifest'. For security reasons though everyone being received by the Protector was 'narrowly scanned' and not all ambassadors' attendants were admitted into the Protectoral presence, which required passing through no fewer than four closed doors. These relatively private congratulatory receptions would be followed some time later by public audiences organised by Sir Oliver Fleming, who would continue in the post of Master of Ceremonies throughout his kinsman's rule. It was at these receptions that any confusion which may have arisen in the ambassadors' minds as to the precise nature of Cromwell's 'new authority' was to be dispelled.[15]

The inhabitants of the capital had their own foretaste of this less than two months after Cromwell's investiture as Lord Protector. Although the investiture ceremony had not been without its royal ritualism and symbolism it was nevertheless rather short on regal splendour. It certainly did not set the scene for the rising tide of royal pomp and pageantry that would follow immediately afterwards, beginning on 8 February 1654 when the City of London entertained 'in a very magnificent manner' the newly invested ruler 'to the end he might have the greater veneration from the people', as had been the custom after a monarch's coronation since time immemorial.[16]

This same honour of public symbolic acceptance of the regime had also been extended to the government of the pre-Protectorate Commonwealth, the Lord Mayor and Corporation of London's 'ready obedience and good affections to the Commonwealth' taking the form of a sumptuous banquet held in June 1649 soon after the republic had been formally proclaimed. It was held in the grandest of all the meeting places of the City's livery companies, Grocers' Hall. The livery companies were so called because of the distinctive livery worn by their members on special occasions. They had evolved from the medieval craft guilds and played a significant role in City government, the Grocers exercising at this time a long-held leadership in the capital's affairs. Present at this event were the Council of State of the Commonwealth, the Speaker and members of the House of Commons, as well as representatives of the army and judiciary. This naturally included Lieutenant-General Oliver Cromwell who was both a member of the government and the second most senior officer in the army of the republic. In the latter capacity he was soon to be despatched to Ireland, one outcome of which would be that the City could re-assert its rights to the not inconsiderable interests it had in that part of the Commonwealth. The day after the banquet the City gave some indication of the esteem in which it held the army's chief commanders by presenting the Commander-in-Chief, Sir Thomas Fairfax, with 'a large and weighty basin and ewer of beaten gold', and his second-in-command, Cromwell, with 'a great present of plate, value £300, and some 200 pieces of gold'. Two years later, in 1651, Cromwell, by then Commander-in-Chief of the Army, would be entertained in his own right by the City as the victor of the Battle of Worcester. After the lavish entertainment General Cromwell went to Woolwich where he launched a new frigate to add to the republic's growing naval might, naming her *Worcester*.[17]

With another change in government it was Protector Oliver's turn to receive the public formal recognition of the City of London, to which he set forth 'in as great a pomp and magnificence as befitted a person invested with so eminent qualities, and as one who, having reaped so many laurels, had newly restored peace and tranquillity unto three distracted kingdoms'. The words are those of Samuel Carrington and they appear in his panegyrical biography of Cromwell. Carrington's description of the event tallies in almost every essential particular with other, less effusively eulogistic, accounts. State dignitaries, the Life Guard and other soldiers, including 'field officers bravely mounted', accompanied the Protector on the journey from Whitehall to the City as they had done for his investiture. This time, however, fourteen trumpeters and 'his Highness's heralds with rich coats adorn'd with the Commonwealth arms' went before the Protector's coach, which was now attended by two pages 'bareheaded in sumptuous apparel' going before on horseback and 'twelve footmen in rich liveries' and velvet caps. The coach, or 'chariot of state', was drawn by 'six beautiful horses' adorned with rich trappings, which, according to the irrepressible Carrington, 'by their lofty gate, seemed to glory in their drawing so victorious a Hercules triumphing over so many monsters'. But 'his Highness, who always preferred the little ornaments of the soul before those of the body, was only clad in a dark-coloured suit and cloak'.[18]

When this splendidly regal procession reached Temple Bar, which marked the boundary between Westminster and the City of London, it halted. There to greet Cromwell was the Lord Mayor of London together with civic dignitaries, all in their ceremonial finery. The City Recorder 'saluted' the Lord Protector 'with an excellent speech containing several expressions of joy, fidelity and obeisance and of good hopes for his prosperous and happy government'. Having thanked the Recorder, Cromwell alighted from his coach and exchanged his sober cloak, which, like his suit, was musk-coloured, for a rich riding coat embroidered with gold lace. This was not without its purpose. Virtually unrelieved sober attire may have matched the solemnity of the Protector's investiture seven weeks earlier but this was no longer appropriate. As Ilse Hayden tells us in her *Symbol and Privilege: The Ritual Context of British Royalty*: 'King's have rarely been indifferent to the power inherent in clothing. Indeed, what a King wears can even be an instrument of rule, dazzling his subjects, increasing his majesty in their eyes and thus securing him in his right to rule.' Now resplendently attired, Cromwell mounted a horse, equally as resplendently adorned with rich trappings, for the journey through the City. At this point the Lord Mayor delivered up his sword to Cromwell who 'speedily' returned it. Thus was enacted a royal ritual dating back to the late fourteenth century. By always stopping at the boundary in this way on their visits to the City of London monarchs were showing due respect for the rights and privileges of the City. While the surrendering of the City sword by the Lord Mayor symbolises, as it had at Cromwell's investiture, the monarch's ultimate authority over this petty state within a state. The custom had once been that monarchs retained the sword throughout their visits to the City. But Charles I began a new custom of accepting and then immediately returning the sword. Cromwell was therefore following the precedent set by his immediate royal predecessor. It should be said that during the pre-Protectorate Commonwealth period the Speaker of the House of Commons took part in the same ritual. But he did so as the representative of the acephalous English republic, not as head of state.[19]

After the Temple Bar ceremony the Lord Protector rode to Grocers' Hall amid the clamour of bells from the London churches ringing out in his honour. Before him rode the Lord Mayor, bareheaded as a symbol of 'the respect and obedience of the City', carrying the sword, drawn and upright, symbolising the citizenry of London's 'fidelity and resolution to spill their blood in the defence of the peace of the state and for the preservation of the life and new dignity of his Highness'. The route was bedecked with the bunting of the twenty-four livery companies whose members stood in their finery behind blue cloth-covered rails which had been placed on both sides of the streets. At Grocers' Hall the City Recorder made a speech in which he compared rulers to 'heavenly bodies, much in veneration but never at rest' because 'they are not made for themselves, or their glory, but for the safety and good of mankind'. He went on to draw attention to the affection, manifested in 'the solemnity of this day', which the citizens felt towards the new ruler. But 'they leave it to other nations to salute their rulers and victorious commanders with the names of Caesars and Imperators and, after triumphs, to erect for them their triumphal arches. . . . Their end, this day, is not any such outward pomp or glory [the lavish reception put on for Cromwell obviously notwithstanding], but that those who have been delivered together might rejoice together, and express their desires that the civil sword might be as prosperous for public ends, in the hand where it is placed, as the military sword hath been in the same hand.'[20]

His Highness was then 'royally entertained', the Lord Mayor sitting on his right and Henry Cromwell on his left, the rest of the table being occupied by the Protectoral Council and officers of the army. After 'a sumptuous banquet' the Protector exercised his prerogative as sovereign by knighting the Lord Mayor, Thomas Vyner, who became one of the first to be so honoured under the new monarchical regime. Clarendon summed up the significance of Cromwell bestowing this knighthood, and indeed the day's events generally, very succinctly: 'The City of London invited their new Protector to a very splendid entertainment at Grocers' Hall, the streets being railed, and the solemnity of his reception such as had been at any time performed to the King; and he, as like a King, graciously conferred the honour of knighthood upon the Lord Mayor at his departure.' In this particular instance Clarendon chose not to display his Royalist partisanship; not so the diarist John Evelyn: 'In contradiction to all custom and decency the usurper Cromwell feasted at the Lord Mayor's on Ash Wednesday, riding in triumph through the City.' While Samuel Carrington also left little doubt where his loyalties lay by relating how the Lord Protector 'left all the City filled with an admiration of his heroic virtues and with a general satisfaction of his candour and generousness, their hopes being laden with acclamations and good wishes'. But not all in the City were filled with admiration. In his account of this glittering event Royalist Richard Symonds concludes with: 'At his [Cromwell's] return by Arundel House, he being in a coach which was rich, all gilt, one threw a stone of six pound weight upon his coach.' More in hope than in anger, though, another contemporary writer chose London's lavishly staged public symbolic acceptance of Cromwell as ruler as the point to put a period to his brief history of Britain since the death of the late King or, as he himself put it, 'from the end of one monarchy to the beginning of another, under which (if it pleases the wise disposer of all things . . . to grant us peace both at home and abroad) . . . I may live to see happy days'.[21]

And it was peace abroad that was the subject uppermost in most minds at the first of those public audiences given early in March 1654 by the new regime to representatives of foreign powers because those attending were the ambassadors from the seven states which constituted the Netherlands republic, or United Provinces, with whom England would sign a peace treaty a month later. They were followed at the end of March by the French ambassador who also desired 'a firm peace to be settled with England'.[22] The procedures for these and all subsequent receptions were identical in almost every detail to those followed by Cromwell's royal predecessor, Charles I, a mark of whose character was an extreme punctiliousness in his observance of the formalities of diplomacy. Indeed the Protectoral regime seems to have observed the whole gamut of royal diplomatic protocol practically to the letter.

On first arriving in England at Gravesend, literally their first port of call, ambassadors had customarily been welcomed by the Master of Ceremonies in the sovereign's name. They were then transported by water to one of the royal palaces, Greenwich House, where they temporarily resided before being taken in the royal barge to the capital, usually landing at Tower Wharf. Here they were met by a peer of the realm and then escorted in the King's coach by courtiers and civic dignitaries to their official residence where they would be welcomed yet again, usually by the younger son of a peer. Prior to an audience with Charles I ambassadors had been entertained at the King's expense in the house of a royal functionary, Sir Abraham Williams, within the precincts of the Palace of Westminster before being conveyed in the King's coach to Whitehall. A public audience would then take place, either in the Whitehall Palace Presence Chamber or the more magnificent Banqueting House, as protocol dictated, before a private interview with the King in the Withdrawing Chamber.

Conscious of the need to observe diplomatic niceties the pre-Protectorate Commonwealth had retained as much of this protocol as was relevant to a republic without a head of state. The justification was that with 'a new government now established in a more just and equal way . . . princes, looking upon their common interest, will apprehend the prosperity of the Commonwealth' which 'may prove an allurement to their people to shake off the yoke (whereof there are some symptoms in several parts) and to imitate so laudable an example'. Ambassadors were still welcomed at Gravesend by the Master of Ceremonies, stopping over at what was now the ex-royal palace of Greenwich House before being conveyed to Tower Wharf in the former King's barge, richly turned out but no longer adorned with the royal arms but with those of the new republic, as was the livery of the bargemen who rowed it. Thereafter they rode in a red-upholstered coach specifically provided for the conveyance of ambassadors, the coachman and postilion, like the bargemen, wearing livery which incorporated the arms of the Commonwealth. Even Sir Abraham Williams's house continued to be used for the pre-audience entertainment of ambassadors, at the state's expense. But the audiences themselves, which, as has already been said, were held with a committee drawn from members of the government, no longer contained the elaborately ritualistic public element.[23]

Under the Protectorate the royal diplomatic protocol of past times was to be fully restored, as was foreshadowed by those congratulatory receptions for foreign ambassadors at the beginning of Cromwell's rule. One significant part of this involved the nature of the transport put at the disposal of ambassadors. The royal great barge of Charles I, commandeered by the pre-Protectorate Commonwealth government as a barge of state principally for the conveyance of the representatives of foreign powers, was once more in the possession of the nation's ruler as the barge of his Highness the Lord Protector and rowed by his Highness's watermen. Likewise the land transport put to the same use was the Lord Protector's appropriately grand state coach drawn by six greys 'in gallant equipage', most probably Oldenburgs, a breed still in use as coach horses by the Royal Mews. In befittingly royal mode the driver and postilion wore the livery of the Protector, as did the footmen who accompanied the coach. There was even a Master of the Horse, a senior court official responsible for overseeing the sovereign's stables, the post being filled by Cromwell's son-in-law, John Claypole, who was married to Oliver's second daughter, Bettie. Claypole's duties would also have involved him in the care of the horses sent to Cromwell as gifts by admirers, usually foreign princes, and in his father-in-law's attempts to establish the Arabian breed of horse in England. An additional monarchical touch to Protectoral diplomatic receptions was that ambassadors were now formally welcomed to the country in the Protector's name and 'entertained nobly at the Protector's charge'.[24]

But most significant of all was the resumption of those elaborately ritualistic public audiences not seen since the previous reign, beginning with the receptions given for the Dutch and French ambassadors in March 1654. As royal precedent dictated these were held in the Whitehall Palace Banqueting House which was hung with 'extraordinary rich' tapestries like it had been for the public audiences given by Charles I. The reception for the Dutch ambassadors, one for each of the seven states which constituted the United Provinces of the Netherlands republic, was reported in some detail and complied in all respects with long-established royal forms. Present were 'divers' lords, knights and gentlemen, together with officers of the army. People packed both the body of the room and the galleries (a report of another, much later, reception tells of the galleries being filled with ladies). Those who could not get in thronged the courtyards outside. At the upper end of the room, surrounded by carpets, there was a railed-off area, also carpeted, in which had been placed 'a chair of state, very rich' for his Highness the Lord Protector and other chairs for the ambassadors. This 'theatre' had always played an important role in promoting the cult of sovereignty and Cromwell was evidently prepared to exploit it to the full. Elaborately staged public receptions for ambassadors had the additional value of pointing up the power and prosperity of the nation that the ruler represented while at the same time demonstrating that this same ruler enjoyed the recognition of his fellow sovereign princes.[25]

The Lord Protector made his entrance into the Banqueting House by way of 'the privy door'. As he did so the men present removed their hats. His Highness raised his hat to the assembled company and stood to the left of the chair of state, king-like with his head covered. Surrounding the Protector, having followed him into the room, were members of his Council, the Secretary of State, John Thurloe, and the Protectoral Master of the Horse, John Claypole, who, by waiting attendance on Cromwell in this way, was performing one of the ceremonial duties of his royal counterpart. A lane was made for the seven Dutch ambassadors to approach the Protector from the other end of the room. As they did so they doffed their hats three times as they would to a King with Oliver returning the salute. On reaching the Protectoral presence the ambassadors gave a low bow. One of them then delivered a speech to which Oliver made reply. Apart from 'putting off their hats to salute each other upon some words of protestation or affection' neither the Protector nor the ambassadors removed their headgear during the speeches, the ambassadors thereby exercising their prerogative to remain covered before a foreign sovereign, something which that most punctilious of monarchs, Charles I, insisted was only at his prior invitation. The scene was as glittering as it was remarkable. Here, in glory, was Oliver Cromwell standing in the very stead of Charles I and in the room through which this 'King by Divine Right' had walked on his way to his execution on the scaffold erected outside one of the Banqueting House windows. It goes without saying that the extraordinariness of this turn of events did not pass without comment. After his own public audience seventeen months later the Swedish ambassador 'could not look on it without emotion and compassion for the mutabilities of this world'. When the Dutch ambassadors took their leave of the Lord Protector they saluted his Highness three times as they progressed back down the length of the room.[26]

After audiences Charles I had entertained ambassadors with a masque, an extravagantly staged poetico-musical masked dance (hence the name) based on a mythological or allegorical theme. The genre reached its high point with the masques performed at the court of the first two Stuarts. Those written for Charles, which starred the King and his consort in the principal roles, were given a blatantly propagandist slant in order to glorify the monarch and his reign and project an image of power that in reality Charles did not possess. Charles's

The Palace of Whitehall Banqueting House, Inigo Jones's Renaissance-style masterpiece, where Cromwell received foreign ambassadors with the same pomp and ceremony as his Stuart predecessor.

make-believe world produced by these histrionics would be swept away when the storm clouds gathering outside the King's cocooned existence finally burst into the flood of civil war. The outcome would ultimately usher in the rule of Oliver Cromwell under whose regime entertaining ambassadors as Charles I had done was one royal practice that was not revived. There is, however, a single instance of this during the pre-Protectorate Commonwealth when, in March 1653, a masque was performed in honour of the Portuguese ambassador. Entitled *Cupid and Death* and written by one of Charles I's masque writers, James Shirley, this is said to be the only example of the true masque tradition surviving under the Commonwealth.

Cromwell, who had been living in relative obscurity as an East Anglian squire while Charles acted out his fantasies, did not need the artifice of a masque to exalt his power. To foreign ambassadors this was all too real and was the outcome of an aggressive foreign policy which had been inherited from the pre-Protectorate Commonwealth regime and which would continue to be vigorously pursued under the Lord Protector. Some idea of the esteem with which Cromwell was held abroad can be gained from the indignant outbursts of Oliver's enemies. According to Clarendon the Lord Protector 'received greater evidence and manifestation of respect and esteem from all the kings and princes in Christendom than had ever been showed to any monarch of those nations: and which was so much the more notorious in that they all abhorred him when they trembled at his power and courted his friendship'. Sir William Dugdale, scholar, antiquary and one of Charles I's officers of the College of Arms, whose close association with the Royalist cause meant that he was out of favour with, and out of office in, the new regime, sounded off in similar vein: 'Peace with the Dutch and the slavish condition whereunto this monster Cromwell had brought the people of these nations made him not only much idolised here by all his party but somewhat feared abroad, for certain it is that most of the princes of Europe made application to him, amongst which the French King was the first.'[27]

There was even more for Dugdale to wax indignant about when the ambassador of the King of France, whose audience took place immediately after that of the Dutch, addressed the Lord Protector as 'Your most serene Highness'. Thus even more grandeur had been added to Cromwell's already regal style, serene being an honorific epithet given to a reigning prince. As for the ambassador's speech, this was couched in the most complimentary language imaginable, such as: 'His Majesty doth communicate none to any with so much joy and cheerfulness as unto those whose virtuous deeds and extraordinary merits render them more eminently famous than the greatness of their dominions. His Majesty doth acknowledge all these advantages wholly to reside in your Highness.' The French attitude to England's new ruler and the splendour and solemnity that was being re-established under the Protectoral regime was to irritate yet another of Cromwell's enemies, James Heath. As he wrote in his malicious *Flagellum: or the Life and Death, Birth and Burial of O. Cromwell the Late Usurper*: 'A great deal of state was now used towards him [the Protector], and the French cringe, and other ceremonious pieces of gallantry and good deportment, which were thought unchristian and savouring of carnality, introduced in place of austere and down looks.'[28]

Cromwell 'received greater evidence and manifestation of respect and esteem from all the kings and princes in Christendom than had ever been showed to any monarch of those nations', a point crudely made in this Dutch silver medal. The obverse depicts the Protector wearing a laurel crown while the reverse shows the ambassadors of France and Spain competing for Oliver's favour by submitting to gross indignities at the feet of Britannia.

Others, however, saw things differently. The international cosying up to Cromwell and the nation's manifest might generally seem to have provoked an outbreak of what in a later age would be called jingoism. The following extract from a contemporary ballad entitled *Joyful News from England* gives an idea of the attitude in some quarters:

> The noble states of Holland,
>   Ambassadors have sent,
> To England's Lord Protector,
>   worse dangers to prevent
> To have a peace concluded,
>   to which he did agree,
> That bloody wars twixt them and us,
>   forthwith should ceased be.
>
> Also from other countries
>   the messengers do hie,
> Both France and many nations more,
>   with England to comply:
> For fear of disagreement,
>   what after might befall,
> Thus Englishmen from east to west
>   are fear'd, and lov'd of all.

All of which had been commanded from above: 'We see the powers of Heaven/do all our actions guide.' Apparently divine intervention on the nation's behalf was available at Cromwell's personal behest if the following story is to be believed. 'A notorious, obstinate cavalier that had a journey to go from London, who, as soon as he heard of the late fast for rain appointed by his Highness the Lord Protector, sent at once to have his horse ready and called for his boots, for he would be away without delay into the country whither he was to go. And being asked why he made such haste his answer was that he knew there would be great rain and the ways would be dirty because whatever this present power prayed for they had and therefore he would be gone before the rain came.'[29]

CHAPTER 3

Soaring Grandeur

Royal pomp and circumstance, the beginning of another monarchy, the respect and admiration of foreign princes and divinely inspired omnipotence notwithstanding, the Lord Protector was not, at the time of the Dutch and French ambassadors' dazzlingly regal public audiences, living in any degree of state. He and his family still occupied the quarters they had been given after the then General Cromwell's return from Ireland in 1650. These were lodgings next to the Cockpit within the precincts of the Palace of Whitehall. But plans were already in hand for the Cromwells's transference to the infinitely grander surroundings of the palace proper. They had been announced in an official news-sheet seven days after Oliver's investiture: 'Whitehall is being prepared for his Highness to reside in, and the old Council Chamber is being fitted out for his honourable Council to meet in.' Thereafter the government seemed to think it necessary to keep the public informed in some detail, through one or other of their mouthpieces, of the progress being made. One report in particular is noteworthy for the degree of its minutiae. It is dated March 1654:

> The privy lodgings for his Highness the Lord Protector in Whitehall are now in a readiness, as also the lodgings for his Lady Protectress and likewise the privy kitchen and other kitchens, buteries and offices. It is conceived the whole family will be settled there before Easter.

> The tables for diet prepared are these:

A table for his Highness	A table for the gentlewomen
A table for the Protectress	A table for coachmen,
A table for chaplains and	grooms, and other
strangers	domestic servants
A table for the steward and	A table for inferiors or
gentlemen	subservants

On 13 April came further news: 'This day the bedchambers and the rest of the lodgings and rooms appointed for the Lord Protector in Whitehall were prepared for his Highness to remove from the Cockpit on the morrow.' And finally, on the following day: 'His Highness the Lord Protector, with his Lady and family, this day dined at Whitehall, whither his Highness and family are removed, and did this day lie there, and do there continue.'[1]

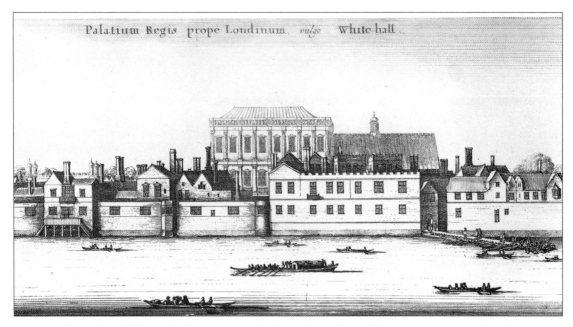

The Palace of Whitehall where, in regal splendour, Cromwell would 'exercise sovereign authority'.

As the process of settling the Protectoral family into the regal splendour of the Palace of Whitehall neared completion the vicar of the north Essex village of Earls Colne was writing in his diary: 'Heard there would be an assembly and that there is speech of an high title for the Protector, *viz* Emperor of the South.' The vicar was the Reverend Ralph Josselin and the entry in his diary is dated 2 April 1654. It has been said that the overall impression gained from Josselin's narrative 'is of a man who became a moderate Cromwellian, very well informed both about national and international affairs [and] closely in touch with events in London'. This must of necessity add some weight to his observations on talk about a change in Cromwell's title. Josselin went on to record other instances of rumour and speculation concerning Cromwell and the crown which would recur continuously throughout the Protector's rule. But the reason for this may not have been entirely due to Josselin's 'moderate' support for the Cromwellian regime and a sustained interest in political matters generally because there was something else equally as relevant which engaged this Puritan cleric's mind, a 'curiosity about current millenarian beliefs'. These current millenarian beliefs were those of the Fifth Monarchy Men and encompassed the notion that the execution of Charles I and the establishment of the English republic presaged the downfall of all earthly monarchies and the inauguration of the rule of Christ with the second coming. The Fifth Monarchy Men saw Cromwell as the man chiefly responsible for the overthrow of that republican government, 'as the perfidious betrayer of the cause of the godly, and the chief obstacle to the inauguration of the reign of King Jesus and his saints'. There was therefore one more group to add to the list of the Cromwellian regime's enemies, which included republicans and the Royalists and Levellers it had inherited from the pre-Protectorate Commonwealth.[2]

Along with the Protectoral family's removal into more appropriate accommodation it was decided that the new monarch should have a household 'modelled on, though not of the same order as, that of the late King'. As the Venetian envoy observed: 'Since his proclamation as Protector he [Cromwell] has changed his style and manner of living as well as his mode of address and audience.' He went on to explain that along with appropriately constituted government departments 'of every description' the Protector was about to form a 'numerous retinue' and household. This, the envoy opined, 'will doubtless increase his popularity and win for him greater respect and obedience'.[3]

A royal household, which Cromwell's would progressively come to resemble, constituted the monarch's below and above stairs servants and office holders. Generally speaking the household below stairs provided most of the necessities of life, such as food and drink. It employed cooks, bottle washers and the like and was headed by the Lord Steward of the Household. The household above stairs, also known as the Chamber and presided over by the Lord Chamberlain of the Household, consisted, in the main, of those whose duties involved ceremonial, entertainment and direct or intimate contact with the sovereign. Those employed in the household above stairs therefore included the Master of Ceremonies, musicians, the Yeomen of the Guard, Gentlemen of the Privy Chamber, Gentlemen and Grooms of the Bedchamber, chaplains, physicians, barge masters and watermen. The household above stairs also encompassed the wardrobe department, which was principally responsible for the furniture and fittings in the state apartments.

The household above and below stairs, together with the stables department, made up what was known as the court, the overall head of which was the Lord Chamberlain who was, of course, also the chief officer of the household above stairs or Chamber. As we have seen the Protectoral stables, with its pages 'in sumptuous apparel' and footmen 'in rich liveries', presided over by Cromwell's son-in-law, John Claypole, as Master of the Horse, had already made an appearance. This was the court in the narrow technical sense meaning, collectively, those who were involved in the monarch's domestic arrangements and gave lustre to the kingly dignity. There was another, wider, application of the term denoting political and other influential figures surrounding the sovereign as well as family and friends. It was, however, customary for certain courtiers to be members of both groups. In this as in most other respects the Protectoral court would resemble the royal courts that had preceded it. Not only that, according to the Venetian envoy, 'the new Protector has summoned to his service all the household of the late King offering them the old terms'.[4]

Among the ex-royal household servants who benefited from the re-establishment of the court were four out of the seven musicians and singers who would become known as 'Gentlemen of his Highness's Musique' in the household of Protector Oliver. These four were previously employed by Charles I and two of

John Hingston, one of the ex-royal musicians to benefit from the re-establishment of the court under the Protectorate. He became Cromwell's Master of the Music as well as organist to the Protector and music teacher to the Protector's two youngest daughters.

them had even held posts under James I. The 'Gentlemen of his Highness's Musique' were joined by 'two lads brought up to music' who sang for the Protector's delectation Latin motets (short sacred choral compositions) by the composer Richard Dering. These same motets had, in all probability, originally been sung in the chapel of Queen Henrietta Maria at whose court Dering held the post of organist. As in a royal court the Protectoral singers and musicians came under the jurisdiction of the Master of the Music. Cromwell's Master of the Music was the organist, composer and viol player John Hingston, who was also organist to the Protector and music teacher to the Protector's two youngest daughters, Mary and Frances. A pupil, so it is thought, of Orlando Gibbons, Hingston, too, had been in the service of Charles I but not as Master of the Music.[5]

One break with tradition was the settling on Cromwell of a set sum of money expressly for the maintenance of his household. Previously the monarch had been expected to 'live of his own' and maintain not only the household and the remainder of the court out of his revenue but also bear all the expenses of government. The Protectoral financial arrangements, embodying the principle of a civil list whereby the cost of maintaining the sovereign's household is separated out from the expenses of government, would become an established practice, but not until the reign of George III. In this regard the Cromwellian regime was therefore more than a century ahead of its time.[6]

Now, midst soaring grandeur, Cromwell could exercise his sovereign authority on a day-to-day basis in a setting befitting his role. Among the first to be exposed to the awe-inspiring experience that this involved were the Mayor and Corporation of Guildford. The occasion, which took place just four days after the Protector had taken up residence in the Palace of Whitehall, was reported in some detail by a government news-sheet:

A declaration and petition from the Corporation of Guildford was brought by the Mayor and four of the aldermen, the steward and the bailiff of that town to Whitehall, where they showed it to one of the Lord Protector's gentlemen and entreated his assistance to bring them where they might present it to his Highness; which gentleman courteously brought them to the gallery where the chair is fixed and desired them to have a little patience till his Highness was risen from Council and they should then have admittance to him. They observed his direction and, after some time of necessary waiting, they were called into the next chamber, which is between the two galleries, and there received by another gentleman of very great and exceeding becoming civility who conducted them where his Highness stood, and some of his heroes [distinguished military men] and divers other gentlemen of quality attending on him, in an handsome and somewhat awful posture fairly pointing towards that which of necessity, for the honour of the English nation, must be showed to him who is their Protector. And Mr Mayor of Guildford, and his company, by what they then observed, and by what some of them had observed heretofore, do declare and say that they are confident that his Highness is pleased with those phylacteries [burdensome traditional observances] and fringes of state (if pleased with them at all) because he must. And that his Highness knows that there is no more in harmless ceremonies of state only than common and weak eyes discern, or have any wise cause to be offended at.[7]

The elaborate manner in which these civic dignitaries had been conducted into the Protectoral presence represented another palpable return to royal practices. As to the suggestion that Cromwell found these regal displays and observances burdensome but necessary, cynics may cavil at this, especially as the self-consciously apologetic report appeared in one of the regime's own official mouthpieces. But the reason given for their existence, 'the honour of the English nation', is fairly stated. It was expected that a country's ruler should be surrounded by as much grandeur as could be mustered. Oliver may indeed have found it burdensome but genuinely necessary. He was, after all, to rail against the deceit of what he chose to call 'feigned necessities, imaginary necessities' four-and-a-half months later in a speech to his first Parliament concerning matters that were infinitely more weighty than the assumption of the mere trappings of monarchy.[8]

The same could be said of Cromwell's occupancy of the Palace of Whitehall and of the fact that the half-a-dozen other ex-royal residences, including ancient Windsor Castle, were also put at the Lord Protector's disposal. Sovereign princes were expected to live in a palace, nay, any number of palaces, just as they were expected to be surrounded by liveried servants and the like. As it happened Cromwell would use only one other of the ex-royal palaces besides Whitehall and that was Hampton Court. Whitehall was an obvious choice because it had not only been the principal dwelling-place of the monarch but was also the centre of royal government. Likewise the government of the republic had, since its inception in 1649, also made use of Whitehall. Indeed,

Hampton Court Palace, the Protector's magnificent out-of-town residence.

some departments of state ensconced there were compelled to remove themselves in order to make sufficient room for the Protectoral family. Residing in the palace mews were aged and impoverished ex-royal retainers not re-employed by the new ruler, together with relatives and dependants of those who had once been in the King's service. These too were given notice to quit, although there is evidence to suggest that these pathetic left-overs from the past were not exactly left destitute.[9]

The alternative Protectoral abode, the magnificent palace of Hampton Court, became Cromwell's out-of-town residence where the Protector was in the habit of spending most weekends, arriving there on Friday and returning to Whitehall the following Monday. This was a security nightmare because of the ever-present threat of assassination. The journey was therefore always made in secret with a strong guard, either by coach or by barge. At Hampton Court the business of government would continue in more congenial surroundings, which involved the weekly transference of the Protectoral family, the court and state dignitaries the fifteen miles from Whitehall. This also involved accommodating the Protectoral entourage at Hampton Court. For example, the President of the Protector's Council was assigned as lodgings what had once been the dressing room of Charles I, while Cromwell's son-in-law and Protectoral court office holder as Master of the Horse, John Claypole, was, together with his family, allocated the accommodation once occupied by Charles I's Master of the Horse, the Duke of Hamilton. From this most luxurious of country retreats Cromwell could indulge his love of hawking and stag hunting. (Among the many gifts sent to the Protector by well-wishers were some hawks from the Prince of East Friesland and a young deer from the President of Providence Plantation, New England.) Here too guests of the Protector were royally entertained as a means of signalling favour. On a

The Great Hall of Hampton Court decorated with the Abraham *tapestries originally bought by Henry VIII and assigned to the Lord Protector.*

visit to the palace the Swedish ambassador and his entourage, after being 'very warmly welcomed and excellently fed', were entertained with music, possibly played on the organ from Magdalen College, Oxford, which Oliver had installed in the Great Hall of Hampton Court. They were then taken stag hunting, following which the ambassador played croquet with his Highness, Bulstrode Whitelocke and Charles Fleetwood. 'The ambassador returned to London that same evening well pleased with the way he had been received, to the annoyance of. many others who are staying here and who marvel at the way in which he [Cromwell] lavishes his hospitality upon us', observed one of the ambassadorial party.[10]

Both Whitehall and Hampton Court had had to be re-equipped and refurbished to provide an environment that corresponded with the grandeur of Cromwell's exalted state. This was accomplished, in large part, by utilising what was left of the late King's personal property that had not already been sold off. In some instances items were actually bought back from their purchasers for the express use of the Lord Protector. These ex-royal effects ranged from humble household and kitchen utensils to expensive carpets and sumptuous bedroom suites. John Evelyn seemed to be rather piqued that a 'very extraordinary' table clock, 'richly adorned' and valued at £200, 'whose balance was only a crystal ball' was 'now in the possession of the usurper' having 'been presented by some German prince to our late King'. But not everything was a royal hand-me-down. Some items were new, like the 'two services of plate for the Protector and his lady', to the value of £3,000 and more, ordered from Thomas Vyner, goldsmith and Lord Mayor of London.[11]

This process of investing Cromwell with at least some of the princely splendour to which his royal predecessors had been accustomed seems to have required that a large number of tapestry hangings be assigned to him. These carried depictions of a whole host of historical, classical and biblical themes and included the immense ten-piece *Abraham* tapestry bought by Henry VIII and which still decorates the walls of Hampton Court as it did in Protector Oliver's day. Responsibility for tapestries and other such household stuff had once rested with the royal wardrobe department. Now they were the responsibility of Clement Kinnersley and his son John, one-time wardrobe keepers to Charles I and now Keeper and Assistant Keeper of the Wardrobe to his Highness the Lord Protector. Also assigned to the Protector were those pictures still remaining after the disposal of Charles I's celebrated collection, said to have been one of the world's greatest. Among them were landscapes, portraits and canvases whose subject matter was both classical and biblical. They encompassed a full-length portrait of King Louis XIII of France and such renowned masterpieces as Titian's *Herodias with the Head of John the Baptist*, the Raphael cartoons of the *Acts of the Apostles* (now in the Victoria and Albert Museum) and Andrea Mantegna's nine-canvas picture cycle *The Triumph of Caesar* which was, during the rule of Protector Oliver, displayed in the long gallery at Hampton Court, as it had been in the reign of Charles I. Like the *Abraham* tapestries Mantegna's masterpiece remains at Hampton Court to this day.[12]

'Caesar on his Chariot' from Andrea Mantegna's masterpiece The Triumph of Caesar, *one of the works of art from Charles I's renowned collection put at Cromwell's disposal. Among the titles rumoured to have been proposed for the Lord Protector was 'Oliver, the first Emperor of Great Britain and the Isles thereunto belonging, always Caesar'.*

One possible interpretation of this particular choice of pictures, some of which were the most valuable (and, incidentally, the largest) works in the royal collection, could be that when it came to art appreciation Oliver Cromwell and Charles I, the greatest art collector and connoisseur ever to sit on the British throne, shared something of the same taste. Charles's role as connoisseur and patron of the arts generally has, however, been interpreted as possessing certain psychological undertones which are difficult to ascribe to Cromwell: 'By collecting pictures and patronising the arts Charles could indulge his personal fantasies, for unlike the world of Parliament and politics he could control that of poets, playwrights and painters where every artistic piper soon realised the exact tune the King called and paid for – sometimes even better than the King himself.' This apart it has certainly been suggested, rather patronisingly perhaps, that the Protector's selection of pictures 'illustrates the acumen of Cromwell in regard to matters which might be supposed a priori to have lain outside the sphere of his knowledge and concern'. But a more plausible, if somewhat prosaic, explanation is that pictures were needed for the necessary adornment of the Protectoral palaces and those reserved for his Highness were simply the most acceptable from among the works of art readily available for that purpose. Either way the point has been made that because of Cromwell valuable art treasures were saved for the nation (or more accurately the royal collection) and for that 'lasting gratitude' is owed the Lord Protector. This, however, is to ignore the possible influence of the Protectress. Oliver's lodgings in Whitehall were, for instance, furnished 'according to instructions from her Highness the Lady Cromwell'. Like much else that is consistently misrepresented about the Cromwellian regime there was, either by accident or design, clearly no less style than would have been displayed by most (and a good deal more than some) sovereign princes of the period.[13]

Certainly when it came to the adoption of royal observances the process was inexorable. The signing of the peace treaty between the Protectoral government and the Netherlands republics at the end of April 1654, for instance, conformed almost precisely to the procedure followed at the ratification of the treaty between the government of Charles I and Spain in 1630. On both occasions the peace was proclaimed by heralds with trumpet fanfare, first at Whitehall and then at the various points where proclamations were traditionally made. Bonfires were lit

'His Highness's heralds with rich coats adorn'd with the Commonwealth arms' proclaiming peace between England and the Netherlands republics in April 1654. Their Highnesses the Lord Protector and the Lady Protectress performed the same honours at the signing of this peace treaty as their Majesties King Charles and Queen Henrietta Maria had done at the ratification of the treaty with Spain in 1630.

before Whitehall and throughout London and church bells were rung to celebrate both events. The Protectoral government's peace treaty with the Netherlands was also marked by salvos at the Tower of London and from ships moored on the Thames. One of the Dutch ambassadors was told by some old merchants that there 'was such rejoicing at the peace that the like demonstrations of joy were not shown at the coronation day of King James nor the last [that of Charles I]'. A banquet was given for the ambassadors concerned. They were brought to Whitehall by the Master of Ceremonies, the Spanish ambassador and his retinue in his Majesty the King's coaches in 1630 and the Dutch twenty-four years later in his Highness the Lord Protector's coaches, and announced by trumpet fanfare. Their Highnesses the Lord Protector and the Lady Protectress performed the same honours as their Majesties King Charles and Queen Henrietta Maria and with the same regal splendour; the wine flowed, the music played while the guests ate and, following royal precedent, a psalm was sung. As a Dutch ambassador commented, on the entertainment given by the Lord Protector: 'In sum all things were done here in great solemnity.' Another comment on the event was that of James Waynwright, the agent in England of the diplomat and merchant Richard Bradshaw. In a letter from London to his master in Copenhagen Waynwright wrote on 28 April 1654: 'Yesterday were the ambassadors feasted at Whitehall in great state by the Protector. In a short time I believe his Highness will be Emperor of Great Britain and King of Ireland.'[14]

What was noteworthy about the banquet given to the Dutch ambassadors by Cromwell was not so much its conformity with royal practice but the manner in which it provided another manifestation of the regal splendour that was attaching itself to the Protectoral regime and with it the proliferation of what had been royal court posts. Present were the newly reconstructed Yeomen of the Guard, the English monarchy's most ancient bodyguard instituted by Henry VII in 1485. Cromwell's Yeomen of the Guard were also known as the Life Guard of Foot, thus complementing the Protectoral Life Guard of Horse. At the banquet they 'carried up the meat', which had been one of the functions traditionally performed by royal Yeomen of the Guard. One difference was that instead of the scarlet uniforms of their Stuart predecessors (who did not, as may be popularly supposed, wear the 'traditional' Elizabethan ruff and beribboned hat) the Protectoral Yeomen of the Guard were dressed in Oliver's own livery, which was a velvet collared coat of grey cloth welted with velvet and silver and black silk lace. This livery, described at the time as being rich and sumptuous, was worn by other of the Protector's servants, the 'pages lacqueys', or footmen, also being equipped with velvet caps when out of doors. In accordance with royal custom the Yeomen Warders of the Tower of London too were dressed in the Protector's livery. Charles II had remnants of the old royal Yeomen of the Guard with him in exile and it is claimed that this represents continuity in the corps' existence. But these yeomen were not able fully to discharge their duties, which were not only that of personal bodyguard to the sovereign but also 'to uphold the dignity and grandeur of the English crown', especially on state occasions. The de facto ruler was currently Oliver Cromwell not Charles Stuart and it was his Highness the Lord Protector's Yeomen of the Guard which would uphold the dignity and grandeur of the regime.[15]

The most celebrated Captain of the Yeomen of the Guard had been Sir Walter Raleigh who held this court appointment on and off under Elizabeth I and into the reign of James I. Cromwell's Captain of the Yeomen of the Guard was another Walter, Walter Strickland, who was a member of the Protector's Council. This was an example of someone belonging to the wider court of political and other influential figures surrounding the sovereign also holding office in the narrower court comprising those involved in the monarch's domestic arrangements and giving lustre to the kingly dignity. Strickland was probably chosen for this post because of his past experience as a diplomat in the Netherlands, first for Parliament in the Civil War and then for the republic. He was therefore able 'like an ape', to quote from the vitriolic outpourings of an anti-government pamphlet, 'to act the part of an old courtier in the new court' as 'Captain of the Protector's magpie, or grey-coated foot guard'. But at least Walter Strickland would not suffer the ignomiy of being escorted to his incarceration in the Tower of London by what had been his own Yeomen of the Guard as had his namesake, Sir Walter Raleigh, after his fall from royal favour.[16]

Even though, in these first months of Cromwell's rule, the tide of royal ritual, ceremony, pomp and pageantry was still on the rise and nowhere near its full flood there was clearly already sufficient state to warrant direct comparison with past monarchical regimes. And that year's May Day celebrations could conceivably have been a reflection of this return to 'normality' after the trauma of the Civil War and the relative austereness of the pre-Protectorate Commonwealth

Spotted woman (1654). Illustrative of a return to 'normality' was the first May Day of Oliver's rule, which was 'more observed by people going a-maying than for divers years past. . . . Great resort came to Hyde Park', where could be seen 'many hundreds of rich coaches and gallants in attire . . . painted men and spotted women.'

regime. The festivities were reported, in what was obviously considered a suitably censorious tone, by an official news-sheet: 'May 1 was more observed by people going a-maying than for divers years past, and indeed much sin committed by wicked meetings with fiddlers, drunkenness and the like. Great resort came to Hyde Park, many hundreds of rich coaches and gallants in attire, but most shameful powdered hair, painted men and spotted women. Some men played with a silver ball and some took other recreation.' Ten days later John Evelyn was complaining to his diary that: 'I now observed how the women began to paint themselves, formerly a most ignominious thing and used only by prostitutes.' At the home of the Catholic Throckmorton's in Worcestershire 6d. was paid out of the household accounts for music on May Day and May Day mummers were given 2s. All of which sounds very much like the so-called Merry England of the so-called Merry Monarch, Charles II. But it is not. This is England under the rule of Oliver Cromwell, over whose head the crown continued to hover, there being 'some talk', so it was reported at the end of May, 'that the Protector will assume a higher title very shortly'. Another, quite separate, report at this time tells of the Cromwellian regime being 'without question upon a deep consultation for some new title, and in their whispers there is one mentioned; "the most puissant Oliver, august Emperor of the British Isles"'.[17]

As spring turned to summer in this the first year of Protectoral rule, Cromwell would himself continue to provide evidence of a reversion to the practices of the past. In July the three custodians, or Lords Commissioner, of the Great Seal (a mixture of new and re-appointees) were sworn in before the Protector's Council, following which Oliver 'after the royal fashion, with great form, delivered the Great Seal to them'. This was still the manifestly republican seal of the pre-Protectorate Commonwealth. A weekly news-sheet in Genoa, however, reported on 1 July 1654 that 'the Lord Protector hath changed the Great Seal of England, setting upon the new one his own effigy on horseback with this inscription: Oliver, the Great Emperor of England, Scotland, Ireland and France, and Protector of the Protestants and of all the Reformed Churches'. The description of Cromwell as protector of the Protestants and all the reformed churches refers to the Protector's championing of the Protestant cause throughout Europe and the succour he gave to those Protestants suffering persecution for their faith. Although the report in Genoa that a positively regal Protectoral Great Seal had been instituted was incorrect at the time it nevertheless showed a remarkable foreknowledge of what would eventually occur (see Chapter 4).[18]

Not reverted to though were the prerogative courts. These were distinct from ordinary courts of law in that the monarch, by means of his Council, exercised his sovereign right and discretionary powers in the adjudication of cases brought before them. But the prerogative courts became a bone of contention between Parliament and the King in the period leading up to the Civil War because of what were seen as abuses of the royal prerogative exercised through these courts of arbitrary jurisdiction. One such judicial body, Star Chamber, had by the perceived 'tyrannical exercise and illegal extension of its power' been used by Charles I to prosecute political and religious dissidents. When Parliament and the King finally fell out Parliament effectively killed off the prerogative courts. They

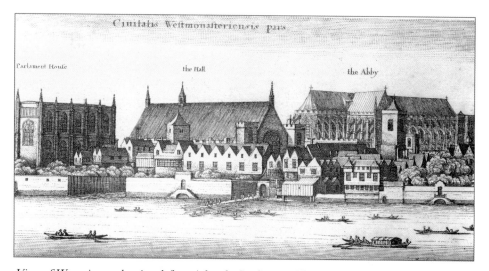

View of Westminster showing, left to right, the Parliament House, where Cromwell opened his Parliaments in the manner of a King, Westminster Hall, scene of his investiture as Lord Protector, and Westminster Abbey, where he would be buried in the Chapel of the Kings.

were never to be restored. One which had served a rather more socially useful purpose than the others, in that it adjudicated in what were in the main poor men's civil actions, was the Court of Requests. This was controlled by Masters of Requests. Posts with this title also existed under the Protectorate but these were horses of another colour, their function being simply to investigate petitions concerning alleged grievances addressed to the Lord Protector as ruler. As such they had no judicial role whatsoever. Cromwell 'appointed certain days every week to receive reports from the Masters of Requests of petitions presented to them, and to give answers'.[19]

At summer's end, in the Essex village of Earls Colne, the Reverend Ralph Josselin again got wind of a change in Cromwell's title. On 31 August he wrote in his diary: 'I heard that the Protector was proclaimed Emperor, but for my part I believe it not thinking the time and season is not yet come for the doing of it.' And the very next day he tells us: 'One called and told me this Friday [1 September] the Protector was to be proclaimed Emperor.'[20] Josselin's first instinct was, however, nearer the mark – it did not happen. Nonetheless, three days later, on 4 September, and eight-and-a-half months after Cromwell's accession, there would be a very public manifestation of a return to past royal practices. On that day, following the first election for fourteen years, the Lord Protector opened Parliament with all the ritual and pageantry of a King, the ceremony being preceded by a sermon in the Gothic splendour of royal Westminster Abbey.

On the majestic short progress between the Palace of Whitehall and the Abbey the Lord Protector's 'rich coach drawn by six horses, in the hinder end whereof he himself sat', was preceded by 'a marshall with his staff' and what were described as some hundreds of gentlemen, together with his Highness's Life Guard and officers and gentlemen of eminent quality. As was the practice on such occasions there were also 'some well affected citizens', namely Protector Oliver's draper and other tradesmen, who walked 'in rank, three and three' with the Protectoral 'domestic officers'. On one side of the Protector's coach walked Captain of his Highness's Life Guard Charles Howard and on the other Captain of his Highness's Yeomen of the Guard Walter Strickland: Howard, of noble birth and an ex-Royalist, and Strickland, the 'obscure gentleman' as Clarendon called him, who had served the Parliamentarian cause as a faithful functionary throughout the Civil War. Both would sit as members of the Parliament which Cromwell was about to open. As courtiers they were among those Members of Parliament who constituted the 'court party' which represented the Protector's interests in Parliament just as the King's courtiers with parliamentary seats had done. Around the coach were liveried footmen and immediately behind it rode the Master of the Horse performing another of his time-honoured ceremonial royal duties by leading the horse of state equipped 'with a rich saddle curiously embroidered with gold and pearl', and behind that was led 'a war horse . . . with pistols at the saddle'. Master of the Horse John Claypole too would sit in this Protectorate Parliament as a member of the court party. The whole procession, which included two more coaches carrying state dignitaries, was, in accordance with royal precedent, escorted by the Yeomen of the Guard and their offshoot, the Yeomen Warders of the Tower of London who customarily shared the Yeomen of the Guard's ceremonial duties at that time. All were in his Highness's livery, the Yeomen of the Guard being reported as 'having new halberts', the combined spear and battleaxe with which their royal counterparts had been armed.[21]

After the Abbey sermon, delivered by one of the Protectoral chaplains, Dr Thomas Goodwin, President of Magdalen College, Oxford, Oliver and members of his Parliament processed over to the Palace of Westminster, ancient and venerable meeting place of the English Parliament, which, for the first time in history, would now admit representatives from Scotland and Ireland. Before the Protector walked Sergeants-at-Arms bearing the maces of the legislature and departments of state as they had done at the investiture. Also borne before his Highness was a purse holding the state seal and immediately in front of Cromwell Major-General John Lambert again carried the sword of state.[22]

Since 1536 monarchs had opened Parliament before both Houses in the House of Lords. But the Lords had been abolished in 1649 soon after the establishment of the republic. Cromwell, therefore, opened his single chamber Parliament in the Painted Chamber, so called because of its thirteenth-century wall paintings. Adjacent to the House of Lords, the Painted Chamber was as pregnant with history as Westminster Hall where Cromwell's investiture had taken place. By tradition it was supposed to have been Edward the Confessor's bedchamber (either that or it was built on the same site) and the place where he died in 1066, fatefully naming Harold as his successor as King of the English on his deathbed. It is also thought to have been the place where Charles I's death warrant was signed. But more significantly in relation to Cromwell opening his first Parliament, it was in the Painted Chamber of the Palace of Westminster that English sovereigns had opened their Parliaments from the earliest times up to 1536. Oliver was therefore reverting to the practice of his more ancient predecessors, for which 'was made two steps to a throne [symbol of rule and authority] or seat for his Highness the Lord Protector'. Cromwell delivered his speech from the throne to the respectfully silent and hatless assembly, opening grandiosely with: 'Gentlemen, you are met here on the greatest occasion that I believe England ever saw, having upon your shoulders the interest of three great nations with the territories belonging to them. And truly I believe I may say it without any hyperbole you have upon your shoulders the interest of the Christian people in the world, and the expectation is that I should let you know (as far as I have cognizance of it) the occasion of your assembling together at this time.' Having delivered his speech the Protector withdrew into the now defunct House of Lords. As soon as the Members of Parliament had gone into the House of Commons Oliver made his way back to the Palace of Whitehall 'privately by water'.[23]

Meanwhile, 'the members being returned to the House [they] unanimously elected for their Speaker William Lenthall, Esquire, Master of the Rolls. It is observable that although Cromwell had already exercised many personal acts of royalty since his advancement to the Protectorate, yet the ancient ceremony of presenting the Speaker to the King for his approbation was omitted to his Highness, so that this officer stood solely upon the election of the House.' Although it has been said that Lenthall 'was reputed to be favoured for that position by the Protector' it makes no matter. What does matter is that this particular, and fundamental, prerogative of kingship – approval of the legislature's choice of Speaker – was one which Cromwell chose not to exercise and marks a significant step in the progress towards a parliamentary monarchy.[24]

Lenthall was elected Speaker of the first Protectorate Parliament 'in regard of his great experience and knowledge of the order of that House and dexterity in the guidance of it', which was something of an understatement. Lenthall had been Speaker of the House of Commons in the Long Parliament when, on that fateful day in January 1642, Charles I had entered the chamber to arrest five of his leading opponents on a charge of treason. Asked by the King if he saw any of them present or knew where they were Lenthall fell on his knees and uttered those immortal words: 'May it please your Majesty, I have neither eyes to see nor tongue to speak in this place but as the House is pleased to direct me, whose servant I am here; and humbly beg your Majesty's pardon that I cannot give any other answer than this to what your Majesty is pleased to demand of me.' But 'his birds were flown' and the King left the House of Commons empty handed to cries of 'Privilege, Privilege'. Lenthall was still Speaker when the Rump of the Long Parliament became the legislature of the English republic in 1649 and it was in this capacity that he represented the Commonwealth at the ceremony marking the City of London's recognition of the regime. Another unwelcome entry into the House of Commons, this time by General Cromwell, put an end to the Rump's sitting and presaged the demise of the pre-Protectorate Commonwealth. Unlike Charles, who had left his armed guard outside, Cromwell ordered soldiers to be brought into the chamber. Nevertheless Lenthall again stood his ground, refusing to vacate the Speaker's chair until compelled to do so. Having already lived in interesting times as Speaker under the monarchy of Charles I and an acephalous republic, Lenthall was again to occupy the office under the New Model Monarchy of Oliver Cromwell. When originally returned as a member of Protector Oliver's first Parliament Lenthall had commented with understandable wariness: 'My intentions were not bent to so public an employment, having been thoroughly wearied by what I have already undergone.' He was, nonetheless, prepared to take his seat and subsequently to be elected Speaker but he did so in a spirit of resigned dutifulness.[25]

It is little wonder that with a palpably royal ceremony on the scale of the state opening of the first Protectorate Parliament speculation about Cromwell accepting the crown would be rife. Perhaps the most fantastical manifestation of this was a rumour said to have been circulating in Cologne at the end of September 1654 to the effect that after the Protector had addressed his Parliament those assembled 'with unanimous consent called his Highness Emperor; and his title they have written thus: "Oliver, the first Emperor of Great Britain, and the Isles thereunto belonging, always Caesar".'[26] In reality Parliament was far more intent on discussing ways of limiting Cromwell's power and enhancing its own than elevating the Protector's title. At the end of December, however, one member of Parliament, the regicide Augustine Garland, 'moved to have my Lord Protector crowned, which motion was second[ed] by Sir Anthony Ashley Cooper, Mr Henry Cromwell and others, but waived – nothing was done in it more'.[27] The Royalist turned Parliamentarian, Sir Anthony Ashley Cooper, was a member of the Protector's Council and Henry Cromwell was Oliver's son, both very much of the Protectoral court party in Parliament, although Ashley Cooper would later switch his allegiance again and join the republican opposition to the Cromwellian regime. This, in the circumstances provocative, move to effect a change in Cromwell's status must therefore have been a government initiative. The Venetian envoy in London thought so, as his highly tendentious report, written up a fortnight later, clearly indicates:

> It is certain that the Protector, with the support of his partisans, recently had it suggested that the convenience and dignity of the nation required that his title should be changed and that of King or Emperor assumed in the Protector's person. At the moment when Parliament was discussing this article, which his Highness had always coveted but which involves high and perilous consequences, some opposition members arrived. Astonished at their opportune appearance and by the force of their arguments, the Protector's satellites were silenced, causing the question to be put on one side.[28]

Cromwell may not have had a crown but on 16 December 1654 the first anniversary of his investiture as Lord Protector was celebrated in a very traditional, and very royal, manner with the ringing of church bells, just as anniversaries of coronations had been on what was known as crownation day. For the occasion the unofficial Protectoral poet laureate, Andrew Marvell, penned his *First Anniversary of the Government Under O.C.* In this commemorative paean to the Protector's rule Marvell has it that to wear the crown is the manifest destiny of Oliver Cromwell, this 'great Prince' who already 'seems a King by long succession born'.[29]

CHAPTER 4

More Soaring Grandeur

Cromwell dissolved the first Protectorate Parliament at the earliest opportunity. This should have been around the third or fourth of February 1655, five months after Parliament's first sitting, in accordance with the Instrument of Government. But by the simple, and arguably devious, device of calculating in Lunar instead of calendar months the Protector was able to accomplish a much desired dissolution on 22 January. Oliver's experience with Parliament was no less fraught than Charles I's had been when the Protector was a member of the parliamentary opposition to the King. Also, according to the ever-vigilant Venetian envoy commenting in early January 1655, the general opinion was that as things stood Cromwell's 'seat will always remain unstable and consequently the form of government also'. Which is why the kingship issue would remain very much alive. It again invaded the rural fastness of Ralph Josselin and laid siege to this Essex parson's imagination, the item in his diary for 8 March 1655 reading: 'This day was a day I had thought of as the bound within which some great action would be, the throning of the Protector really done.' Notwithstanding Josselin's false dawn a combination of speculation, manifest desire and hard evidence suggests that in this, the second year of the Protectorate, Cromwell's acceptance of the crown was not simply a consideration but a very real possibility. Oliver looked set to meet what to Andrew Marvell was his hero's manifest destiny.[1]

To begin with there was to be a new Great Seal to replace the one dating from the pre-Protectorate Commonwealth. Naturally, no sovereign was depicted on the original Great Seal of the republic as had always been the case under the monarchy. Instead, one side showed about a hundred tiny figures grouped around the Speaker of the House of Commons representing the legislature of the Commonwealth in session. On the other side there was a map of England and Ireland, together with the islands of Jersey, Guernsey and Man, and ships in the coastal waters representing the fleet, as though anticipating the brilliant naval feats that would be performed and the 250 years of naval supremacy that would be established during the republican period. There were also two ornate shields, one bearing the cross of St George and the other an Irish harp. The legend around the seal read: IN THE THIRD YEARE OF FREEDOME BY GOD'S BLESSING RESTORED and the date 1651. (This seal had replaced an almost identical one instituted when the republic was established in 1649 – IN THE FIRST YEARE OF FREEDOME.) Traditionally, like the language of the law, legends on royal great seals had been in Latin. But, like the language of the law under the

GREAT SEALS

Pre-Protectorate Commonwealth

Cromwellian Protectorate

Elizabeth I   *Charles I*

The distinctly republican design of the Great Seal of the pre-Protectorate Commonwealth gave way to the manifestly monarchical Great Seal of the Cromwellian Protectorate, which was closer in design to Elizabeth I's than that of the Protector's immediate royal predecessor, Charles I.

republic, the legend on THE GREAT SEALE OF ENGLAND, as it describes itself, was in the language spoken by the majority of the nation that the Commonwealth government claimed to represent – English.[2]

To say that the new Great Seal 'to which his Highness gave his approbation' was as monarchical as the one it replaced was republican would be to plumb the depths of understatement. Like its immediate predecessor it was the work of the foremost engraver of his day, Thomas Simon, soon to be officially confirmed as sole maker of medals and chains to his Highness and the public service as well as chief engraver at the Mint.[3] On one side of this Great Seal of what continued to call itself a republic, Cromwell is shown on horseback in full armour, as had male monarchs on previous royal seals. But there are significant differences. The Protector's royal predecessors were depicted charging into battle brandishing a naked sword in their right hand and they usually wore a helmet with their full armour. Oliver's horse is pacing, not galloping. His sword is sheathed and in his right hand he holds a baton. He is also bareheaded. In the stateliness of the pose there is a close resemblance to Elizabeth I's seal on which the Queen too is seated on a pacing horse with a sceptre in her right hand. The inference of this abandonment of the warlike posture of past Kings, who were either less successful as Generals or had never even seen a battle, is obvious: the Protectorship may have had military origins but in its governance it is civilian.

The other side of the seal was equally as startling. This displayed the newly-approved arms of the Protectorate, which turned out to be virtually the complete heraldic achievement of an English monarch. Over the prince-like shield, fashioned as a royal breastplate, was set the six-barred helmet of monarchy with royal mantling and surmounted by a kingly crown. On top of this there was the royal crest of Great Britain (originally the crest of the Plantagenets), that is a lion passant guardant crowned with an imperial crown. One break with royal tradition was the use, in the quarterings on the shield, of the cross of St George for England and the saltire of St Andrew for Scotland. These were instead of the three leopards for England and the Scottish lion associated with past royal Houses. (The pre-Protectorate Commonwealth seal also used the cross of St George for England but Scotland had not been represented.) The Irish harp, however, continued to represent Ireland, the saltire of St Patrick having not yet been invented. The ancient and hollow pretension that English, and later British, monarchs were also Kings of France, represented on the royal arms by three fleurs de lys, was dropped. A small shield at the centre of the Protectoral quarterings bore Cromwell's own arms of a lion rampant. This was the custom for elected monarchs who would place their own heraldic arms over all those of their dominions. The next British ruler after Cromwell to do this was William III some thirty years or so later. An elected monarch, William placed his own paternal arms of Nassau upon the British royal arms.[4]

The heraldic supporters of the regal Protectoral arms are at one with the rest in their implications, being those most favoured by the Tudor monarchs. One was a lion guardant imperially crowned representing England. The other was a dragon in profile with wings raised representing Wales. This was the red dragon of the last British King, Cadwallader, 'the dragon of the great pendragonship', the

Arms of the Cromwellian Protectorate, which resembled the heraldic achievement of a Tudor monarch.

pendragonship being the office of chief ruler of the Ancient Britons from whom the Welsh claimed descent. The red dragon of Cadwallader was the emblem on the banner of Henry Tudor when he defeated Richard III at Bosworth in 1485 and seized the English crown. Thus was signified the boast of the Tudors that they were descended not from the English King Edward the Confessor, nor his Norman successor, William the Conqueror, but from no less personages than the legendary Arthur and Wales's most celebrated prince, Llywelyn the Great. To some the accession of Henry VII was therefore a fulfilment of the ancient bardic prophecy that a Welsh conqueror will emerge to reclaim the right to rule over England, the land stolen from the Britons by the Saxons. Cromwell too was of Welsh descent. His family's surname had originally been the decidedly Cymric Williams. Cromwell, the illustrious maiden name of Oliver's paternal great-great-grandfather's wife Katherine, sister of the Henrician statesman Thomas Cromwell, had been adopted by the family in the reign of Henry VIII. With Cromwell, a descendant, so it was claimed, of the ancient princes of Powis, now occupying the English throne a revival of those predictions from the realms of myth and legend proved irresistible. In 1657 a Welshman, Thomas Pugh, would publish a pamphlet demonstrating 'his Highness's lineal descent from the ancient princes of Britain, clearly manifesting that he is the conqueror so long prophesied of'. It may very well have been this that the Reverend Ralph Josselin referred to in his diary as 'a book, especially of Welsh prophecies, which asserts that Cromwell is the great Conqueror that shall conquer Turk and Pope'. Although Josselin's 'heart fixed on him [Cromwell] to be most great' he nevertheless confessed to himself that 'this book giveth me no satisfaction but perhaps may set men a-gadding to greater him'.[5]

The precise reason for the inclusion of the red dragon in the Protectoral arms is impossible to say. It could indeed have been a reference to the Protector's ancestry. But then again, as the dragon replaced another mythical beast, the unicorn of Scotland, brought into the royal arms with the accession of James I, it

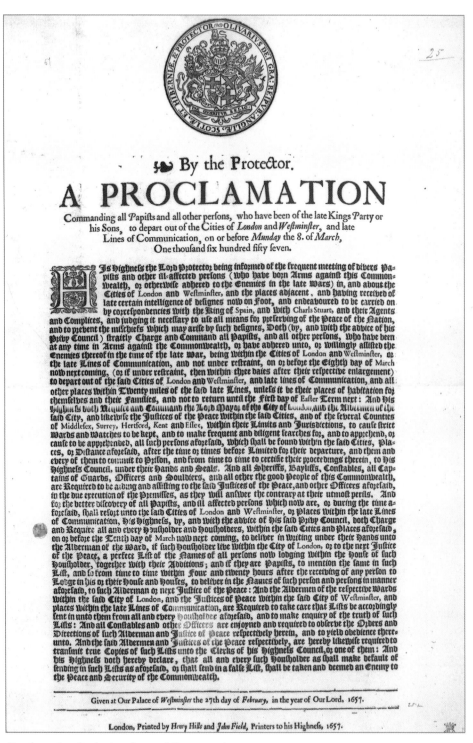

Proclamation displaying the regal Protectoral arms.

could have been a purposeful attempt to obliterate the unhappy associations with the Stuarts by returning to royal supporters last used by Elizabeth I, whose reign in contrast to that of Charles I was seen as a golden age. If the fantastical notion behind a jotting in the notebook of the Royalist and antiquary Richard Symonds is to be believed then perhaps an emblem of the House of York should have been included in the Protectoral arms. The entry reads: 'Cromwell alias Williams his name is and he pretends [to] be by Williams descended of Perkin Warbeck.'[6] Perkin Warbeck was executed for treason in 1499. He had attempted to invade England and claim the throne as Richard IV by pretending to be the Duke of York, the younger of the two Princes in the Tower.

More indications of a return to previous royal convention were provided by the legend around the seal. This was once again in Latin, Cromwell's style and title being presented in singularly regal form as OLIVARIUS DEI GRA REIP ANGLIAE SCOTIAE ET HIBERNIAE &c PROTECTOR (Oliver, by the Grace of God, of the Commonwealth of England, Scotland and Ireland, and the Dominions and Territories thereunto belonging, Protector). Also in Latin was the new motto of this nominal republic, PAX QUAERITUR BELLO, which translates as Peace is Sought through War. The original motto of the Commonwealth had been GOD WITH US and was at all times expressed in English. Now manifestly regal in its design the Great Seal had become in every respect 'the key to the realm, the only instrument by which on solemn occasions the will of the sovereign can be expressed'.[7]

Also instituted at this time was a new Privy Seal (literally private seal). This was affixed to documents that were afterwards to pass to the Great Seal, or to documents of less importance which did not warrant the Great Seal. On the instructions for the legend of the Protectoral Privy Seal 'ordered by his Highness the Lord Protector, by and with the consent of the Council', and again in Latin, even France was included in the territories over which Cromwell ruled, so nearly completely did the style and title of the Protector match those of an English, or British, King. Not carried over though was FIDEI DEFENSOR (Defender of the Faith), although a member of the Swedish Parliament thought it possible that Cromwell wished to 'conserve the title which all English Kings have borne, i.e. to be called "defensor fidei"'. Protectoral court chaplain Hugh Peter had his own highly individual view on the subject: 'The Protector sleeps upon no easy pillow. If 'twas such a matter for King Charles to be Defender of the Faith, the Protector has a thousand faiths to protect.' This was a reference to 'the unprecedented rise and multiplicity of sects', facilitated in no small measure by Cromwell's religious toleration.[8]

There is no doubt whatever that the institution of new seals was linked directly to the possibility of Cromwell accepting the crown. 'A new Great Seal is almost made, with the addition of Scotland to England and Ireland therein with his Highness's portraiture on the other side, which makes people here give out generally that his Highness is to be crowned forthwith', ran a May 1655 report from Westminster. And the seal was regal in design because Cromwell's title was not intended to have remained Protector of the Commonwealth. The Swedish ambassador, Peter Julius Coyet, tells us what it should have been: 'It is certain that upon one side of the Great

Seal his [Cromwell's] title has long ago been made to run Olivarius Dei Gratia Angliae, Scotiae et Hiberniae but it has been left open whether he shall be designated Rex or Imperator.' This is consistent with that, at the time incorrect but nevertheless remarkably prescient, report in Genoa a year earlier to the effect that a new regal-style seal had been instituted on which Cromwell was described as 'Oliver, the Great Emperor of England, Scotland, Ireland and France'.[9]

Rumours of kingship and emperorship had abounded throughout the spring and early summer of 1655. 'I think we may beg his Highness to take the crown' went one May report. This had its echo in a May entry in Ralph Josselin's diary: 'Heard what formerly I apprehended, that Cromwell would be styled Emperor.' Early in the same month Richard Bradshaw in Copenhagen was receiving reports to the same effect from his agent James Waynwright in London. 'We have great hope that his Highness will accept of kingship, which all men desire generally, and by that means we hope to come to a settlement. Our lawyers do press hard for it, and some refused to act in some great places.' The lawyers who refused to act in some great places were a number of state high office holders who objected to an ordinance effecting certain legal reforms. They did so on the grounds that this was the Protectoral government acting where it had no legal power. Therefore for them to execute this ordinance as a law 'could not be justified in conscience and would be a betraying of the rights of the people of England, and too much countenancing of an illegal authority'. Bulstrode Whitelocke and Sir Thomas Widdrington lost their posts as Lords Commissioner of the Great Seal over the issue. Cromwell 'spake to them to lay down the Seal, which they did, and then they were desired to withdraw. And so this great office was voluntarily parted with by them, upon terms of conscience only.' This did not, however, mean a complete end to their service to the Protectoral regime, both continuing in other posts. Later in May James Waynwright reported again to Richard Bradshaw on the matter of Cromwell and the crown. 'We have had a great rumour of having a King. It hath been so long in expectation that the people of these parts begin to despair for the benefit that will arise thereby. Some are of the opinion good and some bad but we ought to acquiesce with what God will have.'[10]

June brought with it further reports. On the first of the month it was said that 'his Highness, sending for the Lord Mayor Thursday last and the judges the next day about business of great concernment, caused many to come down to Westminster in great expectation that his Highness would alter his title. But he being gone to Hampton Court they think it may probably be Thursday next.' This did not happen. Even so reports continued throughout that month of June. One was 'the altering of his [the Protector's] title is much spoken of'. Another was from James Waynwright again. 'There is some alteration in some places of trust but as yet not much. We expected a greater and we hope it will be that his Highness will take some other title . . . either Kingship or Emperor.' And Royalist intelligence circles had been abuzz with speculation concerning a June coronation for Cromwell, 'upon the failing whereof many hundreds have been lost in wagers'. In July Ralph Josselin was still anticipating 'some eminent occasion' relating to Cromwell, adding that 'the noise of his crowning is not as formerly, though nearer it may be than when talked of'.[11]

Not for the first time Josselin's prognostication proved to be wrong. The noise of the Protector's crowning was not as formerly because the plan had already been dropped. The Swedish ambassador when he commented on Cromwell's title for the Great Seal being held in abeyance awaiting the designation Rex or Imperator also remarked that 'deliberations about this having continued for some time, many reasons for and against being urged, it was nevertheless at last resolved to adhere to the title of Protector; and some time ago the vacant space on the Great Seal was filled up'. The ambassador was writing in July and it had been about a month earlier, in mid-June, that the new seal, with Oliver designated as Protector, formally came into use. As was reported on 16 June 1655: 'The old Great Seal is broken and Colonel Fiennes and Lord Lisle sit as Lords Commissioner of the new Great Seal, which hath this circumscription: Olivarius Dei Gratia, Angliae, Scotiae et Hiberniae, &c. Protector, with the arms of England, Scotland, France [*sic*] and Ireland and his own in the midst of them, and on the other side his own effigy mounted on horseback.' This was the new Great Seal of England. Separate Great Seals were made for Scotland and Ireland.[12]

The Protectoral regime may have decided by mid-June against giving Oliver a new title, 'by reason of the opposition of the principal officers who will by no means have an hereditary supreme authority', but that was not the end of the matter. Two months later a petition was raised 'in the name of the freeholders of England desiring his Highness to assume the title of King or Emperor'. Apparently this initiative was far from welcome because we also learn that 'his Highness and Council have since thought fit to give order for calling in and suppressing the said petition'. But the Swedish ambassador, with a diplomat's nose for machination, had his own ideas about this solicitation to the Lord Protector: 'It would seem that the people are not averse to the idea of having a King again; but there are things in the petition which do not please the more prudent and sensible sort, as appearing to confer on him [Cromwell] greater power than any King of England ever had before in direct violation of their fundamental law. It is said that the petition is to be banned by public proclamation; but it is nevertheless impossible not to believe that it is a deliberate manoeuvre by themselves.' The ambassador even sent a copy of the petition to the King of Sweden together with a further expression of his suspicions: 'This is certainly all a device, whose purpose will in time appear.'[13]

A device it most probably was and one which has all the appearance of an attempt to circumvent the obstacles put in the way of the restoration of the kingly dignity by the senior military men. Other, contemporaneous, moves certainly suggest that in spite of everything Cromwell still intended taking the crown. On 10 August 1655, which is the date of the petition, what had been important royal court posts were reconstituted. Protectoral Councillor Sir Gilbert Pickering was made Lord Chamberlain, the highest official in a royal household, and four Gentlemen of the Bedchamber were appointed to attend the Lord Protector in the role of one of a sovereign's most intimate body servants. The lord chamberlainship was, however, shelved almost immediately after its reconstitution, paralleling the shelving of this latest plan to make Cromwell King. Significantly it would re-emerge two years later with the total assimilation of the Protectorship to the kingly dignity and a corresponding assimilation of the Protectoral household to a royal household (see Chapter 10). Unlike the lord chamberlainship the posts of Gentlemen of the Bedchamber were not set aside, indicating that even without the crown the intention was to continue the process of surrounding Cromwell with at least some of the trappings of monarchy. As for that elusive crown, Johan Ekeblad writing from London on 1 September 1655 states that 'all is peaceful here. Some want the Protector to be King but most do not. He himself pays little attention to such discussions since he now has as much power as a King.' On the same day as Ekeblad's letter it was also reported from Westminster that a declaration was being drawn up by 'his Highness and Council . . . showing their dislike of the late printed petition . . . for constituting his Highness King or Emperor'.[14]

But once again this was not to be the end of the matter, as a 5 November 1655 Venetian ambassadorial report demonstrates:

> The supporters and partisans of his Highness are trying adroitly to sound the chief commanders in the army about a change in the present government in favour of the Protector. They point out that with the fall of the late King's head there fell the foundation of the laws and civil life of the community. This disorder needs remedying. The best way would be to raise the Protectorate to the dignity of Emperor of the three kingdoms. This conspicuous title is not ill adapted to the might and power of this state. The Emperor would be elected by the army, in imitation of the ancient Romans, elevated to the throne by the legions and exalted by arms. Cromwell has the courage, character and authority to uphold this high dignity with honour. The forces of England are more respected now than in the past and deserve a more distinguished head. It would bring honour to the army to which would be attributed the elevation and election of this august personage.
>
> These artful insinuations which come from the lips of his Highness's supporters have not generally been well received by the army or by the chief and most influential officers. The first obstacle is that the most influential commanders aspire to occupy his seat themselves after his death and are pleased to see the government established at a height to which they also may aspire some day. Second, that as this is a republic only in name, they fear that the removal of this slight pretence would increase the universal unpopularity and disfavour of the present government. Finally, after condemning monarchical government and utterly destroying it, to set it up again would look like a repudiation of all their past acts and would prove that the sole object of all the persecution of the King was not the public good but private ambition, especially in the Protector, which would become the more manifest from his occupying the position which he had previously attacked and finally destroyed. For this reason I do not think that there will be any considerable change for the moment, but that the government will maintain its present position until a better opportunity occurs.[15]

The 1655 drama of Cromwell and the crown was played out against the backdrop of the ever increasing splendour of the Protectoral court. At the same time, and somewhat paradoxically, there were a number of serious challenges, from both within and without, to the Protector's authority. The challenge to

rity posed by the refusal of two of the Protector's own great
Commissioners of the Great Seal Bulstrode Whitelocke and Sir
ington, to execute an ordinance because they considered
lave exceeded his powers has already been mentioned.
us with this was another, similarly motivated, affair, the George
Chapter 10). Yet another challenge came from a Royalist rising in
of England, which had followed on from a Leveller conspiracy
against the government. Although easily crushed, the Royalist insurrection
resulted in the short-lived division of the country into twelve districts, each ruled
over by a Major-General, in an attempt to prevent similar uprisings in the future.
At the same time a ten per cent tax was levied on Royalist sympathisers.
Cromwell 'began the Protectorate by attempting to reconcile the Royalists but the
force of circumstances drove him more and more to measures of repression. For it
takes two to make a reconciliation and the Royalists showed no willingness to
accept the hand offered them.'[16]

As for the growing splendour of the Protectoral court, in May 1655 Oliver gave
a reception for the new Spanish ambassador, at which there was 'the greatest
assembly of English nobility and gentry present that have been these many years'.
We do not know precisely who these were but the implication is that a new influx
of nobility and gentry had joined those already in regular attendance at court. If
this was so then like salmon returning to their spawning grounds they would have
been responding to a powerful impulse, one which had impelled them to where
power and influence resided. Royal courts had not only been the very hub of
national government they were also the wellspring of patronage and preferment.
While the Protectoral court was undoubtedly the hub of national government it
was not the wellspring of patronage and preferment in the way royal courts were.
But with the assimilation of the Protectorate to a monarchy already in progress
and the very real prospect of a new King, Oliver the First, it would have been
only natural to assume that everything would revert to what it had been. It
certainly seems possible that the Cromwellian court, where, it was said, 'my Lord
Protector has induced the Spanish habit and port [i.e. dress and deportment]',
may have started to become the arbiter of fashion that previous royal courts had
been. Writing to her sister from Covent Garden on 30 June 1655, Alice Clifton,
the Royalist sibling of the politically neutral Earl of Huntingdon, says: 'I have
according to your directions bought the things in the note, most of them from
French shops. For the linen you wrote about, I have sent you the pattern in paper
as it is worn at court.' The presumption is that Alice Clifton was referring to the
Protectoral court and not to that of Charles II in exile.[17]

Evidence of Cromwell's court functioning in the traditional wider context –
displaying to the world the wealth and greatness of the nation and demonstrating
the ruler's magnificence – is provided by the Venetian ambassador to England
designate who reported from Paris on 6 July 1655 that: 'The court of England by
sheer force had made itself the most dreaded and the most conspicuous in the
world. Six ambassadors from crowned heads are now resident there and others
are expected. Pomp has reached such a pitch that the Genoese ambassadors,
Fiesco and Spinola, had each a train of 80 persons.' For this reason the 'new

mission' with which the ambassador had, in his own words, been 'saddled' when he was 'expecting repose, so necessary to my domestic affairs', involved him in 'fresh expenditure and anxiety'. He therefore requested of his masters, the Doge and Senate of Venice, payment of arrears for past services or exemption from the 'fresh burden' of exchanging his ambassadorship at the court of Louis XIV for the anxieties involved in being ambassador to the awe-inspiringly brilliant and prestigious court of Protector Oliver and be allowed to return home: 'I have always considered it my duty to obey and do not now consider the interests of my family or my shattered health, but I beg the state to consider that the London embassy is a conspicuous one, filled by distinguished ministers. I am the first ambassador accredited to England by your Excellencies since the change of government, and the manner of my appearance will be marked. I should risk the public dignity and my personal honour if I did not display due pomp, and that is impossible unless I receive my arrears. When they reach me I will not lose a moment, taking with me six Venetian nobles now at this court besides others from the mainland.'[18]

The awe-inspiring brilliance and prestigiousness of the Protectoral court would have been impossible had Cromwell and his family not risen to the requirements of their new dignity. As is to be expected this provoked nothing but disdain in some quarters, not least among those for whom the Cromwellian Protectorate was as abhorrent as the royal regime they had so recently opposed. Such a one was Colonel Matthew Alured who, 'speaking of his Highness's prodigality in himself, sons and family', alleged that 'it is already come to that height that the lace of one of his son's boot hose-tops cost thirty pounds per yard and the hangings of one of their bedchambers cost fifteen hundred pounds'. Alured further alleged that 'the King did never wear so rich clothing as the Lord Protector did, being embroidered with gold and silver, and there was no apparel good enough to be gotten in London for the Lord Richard and Lord Henry (meaning his said Highness's two sons) to wear. And the said Lord Richard and Lord Henry did keep courts higher (meaning more chargeable) than ever the Prince (meaning the King's eldest son) did and the Lord Protector did expend the Commonwealth's money in making himself such a coach as the King never had.' It did not stop at a coach either. Very suggestive of Charles II, a pleasure boat was rigged out by the navy for his Highness on orders from the Admiralty. Another critic of the Cromwellian court was the Quaker Anthony Pearson who complained of the haughtiness he encountered there, alleging that while he was haranguing a respectfully attentive Cromwell (until he wearied of it) at Whitehall Palace in came the Protector's wife 'and about twenty proud women more and after them at least thirty young fellows, his sons and attendants'.[19]

Lucy Hutchinson, too, had something disparaging to say concerning the Cromwell family's readiness to assume outward manifestations of their elevated status. This extreme Puritan spouse of the regicide but anti-Cromwellian Colonel John Hutchinson wrote of the Protector's wife and children 'setting up for principality, which suited no better with any of them than scarlet on the ape'. She modified her stance a little though when it came to Oliver. 'To speak the truth of himself, he had much natural greatness and well became the place he had

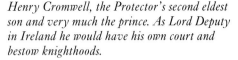
Henry Cromwell, the Protector's second eldest son and very much the prince. As Lord Deputy in Ireland he would have his own court and bestow knighthoods.

usurped.' She does the same for Cromwell's eldest daughter, Bridget Fleetwood, who 'was humbled, not exalted, with these things', and also Richard, whom she describes as 'a peasant in his nature, yet gentle and virtuous, but became not greatness'. But only these three get any benefit from Lucy Hutchinson's modified stance. 'The rest', she says, 'were insolent fools' and singles out for special mention Henry Cromwell and his brother-in-law, Protectoral court office holder John Claypole. These she describes as 'two debauched, ungodly cavaliers'. Here Mrs Hutchinson was using cavalier in its early seventeenth century sense meaning a roistering, swaggering fellow rather than someone who had fought on the side of Charles I in the Civil War. Even in the latter context it had been a term of reproach applied to the swashbucklers on the King's side who hailed the prospect of war. Obviously Henry Cromwell and John Claypole did not come up to Lucy Hutchinson's vision of the Puritan ideal, which was how she saw her husband. But she does, in a backhanded way, attest to the growing image of Cromwell's second eldest son as the most princely of Protectoral princes because the picture she paints of him does represent one popular version of the stereotypical royal prince.[20]

The picture Lucy Hutchinson paints of the Cromwellian regime generally has royal connotations, being very much the accepted image of the reign in which her *Memoirs* were actually written, that of Charles II: 'His [Cromwell's] court was full of sin and vanity, and the more abominable because they had not yet quite cast away the name of God but profaned it by taking it in vain upon them. True religion was now almost lost, even among the religious party, and hypocrisy became an epidemical disease, to the sad grief of Colonel Hutchinson and all true-hearted Christians and Englishmen. Almost all the ministers everywhere fell in and worshipped this beast and courted and made addresses to him. So did the

City of London and many of the degenerate lords of the land, with the poor-spirited gentry.' From her particular standpoint the venom directed at the Cromwellian regime by Lucy Hutchinson was perfectly justified. Her husband had not fought on Parliament's side in the Civil War and signed Charles I's death warrant simply to usher in 'the exercise of tyrannical power', as she saw it, by one of Colonel Hutchinson's fellow Parliamentarians and signatories to that fateful document. But her description of the Protectoral court as a place of sin, vanity and profaneness does not square with the view of another villifier of the Cromwellian regime whose firsthand knowledge of Oliver's court makes him more qualified than Lucy Hutchinson to make a judgement. This was one-time Protectoral physician George Bate who even in his expedient post-Restoration condemnation of his late master felt constrained to concede that Cromwell's court 'was regulated according to a severe discipline; here no drunkard, nor whoremonger, nor any guilty of bribery was to be found without severe punishment'.[21]

Samuel Pepys gives us a further insight into the Cromwellian court, this time *vis-à-vis* that of Charles II. An entry in his diary for July 1667 relates that he met a fellow naval administrator who told him 'the King and court were never in the world so bad as they are now for gaming, swearing, whoring and drinking, and the most abominable vices that ever were in the world – so that all must come to naught. . . . He doth say that the court is in a way to ruin all for their pleasures; and says that he himself hath once taken the liberty to tell the King the necessity of having at least a show of religion in the government, and sobriety; and that it was that that did set up and keep up Oliver, though he was the greatest rogue in the world.'[22] This was at a time when Charles II's reign had already begun to be compared unfavourably with the rule of the Protector, one example of which was the Lord Treasurer's plaintive cry in 1665, also diarised by Pepys: 'Why will not people lend their money? Why will they not trust the King as well as Oliver? Why do our prizes come to nothing, that yielded so much heretofore?'[23]

As if mirroring the political scene, life in the wider world continued to demonstrate that everything did indeed seem to be reverting to what it had been. The autumn of 1655 saw the return of the once-popular Lord Mayor's Shows, magnificent combined land and aquatic pageants based on a specific theme and presented annually at the expense of the livery company to which the newly elected Lord Mayor of London belonged. This was the first show since 1639 and although there had been gaps before in the staging of these events since the first definite Lord Mayor's Show in 1553 none had been as long as this break resulting from the Civil War and its aftermath. The 1639 show, because it was the last before the nation became embroiled in internecine strife, provides another classic illustration of history's tragic little ironies – its theme was 'London's Peaceable Estate'. The 1655 show, whose theme was 'Charity Triumphant', was held on 29 October, which, by tradition, was the fixed day for this event. It seems to have been a relatively low-key affair with only one livery company, the Mercers (dealers in textile fabrics) taking part. The weather was bad too. Nevertheless it represented a restoration of those 'planetary pageants and praetorian pomps' for which London had once been renowned as surely as Cromwell's Protectorate represented a restoration of monarchical rule, a monarchical rule that was now almost two years old. To mark its second anniversary in December 1655 an entertainment was staged at one of the Inns of Court, Middle Temple, at which Payne Fisher, a former Royalist officer who vies with Andrew Marvell for the unofficial title of Protectoral poet laureate, delivered his oration in praise of 'our most serene Prince, Oliver, by the Grace of God the most puissant Protector of England, Scotland and Ireland'.[24]

CHAPTER 5
Gold And Silver Brave

Though for a time we see Whitehall
With cobweb-hangings on the wall,
Instead of gold and silver brave,
Which formerly 'twas wont to have,
With rich perfume in every room,
Delightful to that princely train,
Which again shall be, when the time you see
That the King enjoys his own again.
> Martin Parker (d. 1656?)

But the King to which this contemporary song refers, Charles I, was destined never to enjoy his own again.* Instead fate had decreed the public severing of his head from his body outside the Banqueting House of the Palace of Whitehall. The palace though would be restored to the happy state described in the song without the restoration of the Stuart dynasty. John Evelyn was able to record early in 1656 that 'I ventured to go to Whitehall, whereof for many years I had not been, and found it glorious and well furnished'. And even as Evelyn was confiding these thoughts to his diary steps were being taken to enhance still further Cromwell's already princely surroundings. The grounds of Hampton Court, for instance, which were already graced with such works of art as statues of Venus, Adonis, Apollo and Cleopatra, were receiving even more refinement in the form of a fountain with brass figures by the renowned Florentine sculptor much patronised by Charles I, Francis Fanelli. This had been removed from another ex-royal residence, Somerset House. Also relocated for the Protector's delectation was the organ of Magdalen College, Oxford, which was installed in the Great Hall of Hampton Court. This complemented the organ in the Cockpit at Whitehall. The Cockpit had been converted into an elegant court theatre for Charles I by Inigo Jones with light blue and gold decor and twelve heads of emperors by Titian displayed around the auditorium. Here, in this testimony to Charles I's abiding love of the theatre, Oliver Cromwell, as Lord Protector, would entertain and be entertained.[1]

---

*The song *When the King Enjoys His Own Again*, originally titled *Upon Defacing of Whitehall*, was written during the Civil War to bolster the cause of Charles I. It went on to do like service for his son, Charles II, and later still for the Stuart pretenders to the British throne.

At Whitehall there was far more than simply furnishings, the 'gold and silver brave' of the song, to remind observers of the ex-royal palace as it had once been. If the Mayor and Corporation of Guildford found their visit to Whitehall back in April 1654 awe-inspiring because of the regal pomp and ceremony the Cromwellian regime had already adopted then they would have been rendered speechless by what could have been witnessed two years later. Although in those early days of Oliver's rule royal observances had been followed these were maintained solely by the Protectoral version of the royal Gentlemen of the Privy Chamber (a post held by Cromwell's own great-grandfather, Sir Richard Cromwell, in the court of Henry VIII) who, as part of their accustomed function of waiting attendance on the monarch, had conducted Guildford's civic dignitaries into the presence of their new ruler. Now, Yeomen of the Guard 'in their livery coats, with halberts' were again on duty in the outer chamber (the first of the public rooms) and at the head of the stairs leading up to it, where they would have functioned as their royal predecessors had done by 'suffering no strangers to pass through unless they be known'. They also guarded 'in very handsome order' the rest of the palace rooms and stairways as well as doors and passages.[2]

The outer chamber in which the Yeomen of the Guard stood sentinel was where those waiting to be received by the monarch had congregated before being ushered into the royal presence in what was appositely named the Presence Chamber. Once inside the Presence Chamber visitors to royal courts had encountered more guards. These were Gentlemen Pensioners (now called Gentlemen-at-Arms), a royal bodyguard formed for the sovereign's additional protection by Henry VIII in 1519, some years after the Yeomen of the Guard had been instituted. As their name implies Gentlemen Pensioners were drawn from a higher social order than the Yeomen of the Guard and the suggested origin of the term pensioner is that it was in imitation of the French royal guard who were called *pensionnaires*, that is, those who ate at the King's table. In 1633 Charles I laid down the following criteria for membership of this élite corps: 'The Band of Pensioners having the honour to be our nearest guard, and to have their daily access to our Presence Chamber, we think fit and ordain that from henceforth they be freely chosen by our knowledge out of our best families, and such as have best education, in several counties of our kingdoms, that all our loving subjects of best rank and worth may find themselves interested in the trust and honour of our service.'[3]

When, early in 1656, additional protection for Cromwell was felt necessary this royal institution too was reconstituted. Its members were not, however, known as Gentlemen Pensioners but Ordinary Pensioners, ordinary in this context being an obsolete term meaning staff officers in regular attendance or service. This was because they were drawn from the Protector's Life Guard. Whether they fitted Charles I's criteria for their royal equivalents is open to question, especially in the light of what the Swedish ambassador had to say about the Cromwellian military in a July 1655 missive from Gravesend. 'The army itself consists mainly of a collection of officers who as to a great part of them have been drawn from the common people (the Colonel who is governor of this place is by trade a goldsmith and most others are of the same sort).' Generally speaking though the cavalry were drawn from a higher social order than the infantry. This would have been especially true of the Protectoral Life Guard from which the Protector's extra bodyguard of Ordinary Pensioners were drawn. Their designation of 'Gentlemen of the Life Guard' could be interpreted as evidence of this.[4]

Additional protection for Cromwell at this time also meant that his Highness's Life Guard was subject to reorganisation. Those whose loyalty was in doubt were removed and the strength of the guard was quadrupled to 160, all hand-picked to ensure that it remained steadfast in its role as a mainstay of the Protectoral regime. Splendidly mounted, equipped and attired (they wore both breast and back plates as protective armour) the reconstituted Protectoral Life Guard was by all accounts an imposing sight, as is to be expected of a 160-strong élite corps whose upkeep absorbed an appreciable proportion of the annual expenditure on an army which numbered just over 40,000. Life guardsmen received double the pay of ordinary troopers, who were themselves not exactly underpaid. 'The common soldiers he [Cromwell] binds to himself by the high pay that he gives them, the like of which is almost unheard of . . . so that it is possible to maintain such strict discipline that the country scarcely knows that there is an army in it', observed the Swedish ambassador.[5]

With reorganisation came a new Captain of the Life Guard, Charles Howard being replaced by Major Richard Beke. Beke's appointment followed his marriage to Cromwell's niece, Lavinia Whetstone, and was one of the few examples of what could be described as nepotism by the Lord Protector, literally in this case because the term originally meant preferment of nephews. Another example had been the conferment of the post of Master of the Horse on Cromwell's son-in-law, John Claypole. Of particular interest is the actual wedding ceremony of Major Beke and Cromwell's niece. This equalled in splendour any previous royal court nuptials, having been 'performed at Whitehall in a very pompous and magnificent manner, the Protector and several nobles gracing it with their presence'. One of these nobles was Edmund Sheffield, Earl of Mulgrave, a member of Oliver's Council.[6]

Meanwhile the question of Cromwell and the crown was still at issue. At the end of March 1656 Richard Bradshaw in Copenhagen received from James Waynwright, his agent in London, news that kingship and a new Parliament were conceived of by some to be in the offing. Waynwright, however, was not so sure: 'I do not believe it, tho' I wish . . . it may be.' Count Christer Bonde, who had recently succeeded Peter Julius Coyet as Swedish ambassador, reported, also from London, on the same anticipatory mood: 'Matters of great moment are at present under consideration here, and it is conjectured that they have to do with some alteration in the constitution, and that the Protector is anxious to assume the crown.' The ambassador goes on to describe how he encouraged Cromwell in this since in his view it would greatly strengthen the Protector's government and consequently make it safer for the Swedish King to ally with it. As if in preparation for Cromwell's assumption of the kingly dignity what had hitherto been known as the Council, the Council to his Highness or the Council of State, now became his Highness's Privy Council, the name by which the sovereign's Council had previously been known.[7]

Contemporary jewelled pendant bearing the head of Oliver Cromwell. A similar 'fair jewel with his Highness's picture' was presented by Cromwell to the outgoing Swedish ambassador in 1656. The presentation of such gifts by the monarch was one of the many long-standing royal practices maintained by the Lord Protector.

In May 1656 Cromwell, still without a crown, knighted the outgoing Swedish ambassador, Peter Julius Coyet, and gave him 'a handsome sword with a rich scabbard'. Cromwell had had an exceptionally close relationship with Coyet (they dined, supped and played bowls together) and this mirrored the close friendship that Oliver had nurtured between himself and his fellow Protestant monarch, the King of Sweden. The Protector also presented Coyet with some trinkets worth £600. These were 'a rich gold chain' and 'a fair jewel with his Highness's picture', which was a miniature of Cromwell 'garnished with ten large diamonds and about thirty small ones'. The presentation of such departure gifts to foreign ambassadors by the monarch was traditional. Twenty-five years earlier Charles I had given the Duke of Savoy's ambassador 'a jewel set with diamond . . . having under it the King's and Queen's pictures'. Like so many other long-standing royal practices this was another that Cromwell was obviously prepared to maintain, starting with Coyet, the first such recipient under the Protectorate.[8]

The conferment of knighthoods on foreign ambassadors was also a royal tradition. Cromwell's knights were all Knights Bachelor, that is they were knights of the lowest, albeit most ancient, degree but did not belong to any of the specially named orders, such as the Garter and Bath which were the only ones in existence at this time. Scotland's Most Ancient and Most Noble Order of the Thistle was not placed on a regular foundation until 1687 although its origins were, so it is claimed, indeed 'ancient'. So the creation of Knights of the Garter and Bath was one royal prerogative not exercised by Cromwell. No Knights of the Bath had in any case been created since 1638 and none would be until Charles II's coronation in 1661. Knights of the Garter, however, were created by Charles II while in exile along with Knights Bachelor, paralleling those of Protector Oliver. Charles II's pre-Restoration Knights of the Garter may have been invested by the dispossessed monarch but their installation into the Order had to wait until 1661 because this took place in the Garter chapel, St George's, at Windsor Castle, which obviously was not available to the Order during the Commonwealth period. Windsor Castle was, in fact, one of those ex-royal residences put at Cromwell's disposal as Lord Protector but not used as such by him. The ejection of the canons, minor canons and lay clerks early in the Civil War put an end to Anglican services in the castle's St George's Chapel, services which had been 'esteemed for the beauty exemplified in their singing'. Cromwell could be said to have been a beneficiary of the abolition of traditional choral services in the chapel because one of the King's singers there, William Howes, would go on to perform for the Protector's delectation as one of the 'Gentlemen of his Highness's Musique' in the Protectoral court. The chapel's monuments and pictures were defaced and removed as 'justly offensive to godly men' and the organ destroyed. By the time of Charles I's burial in the chapel's royal vault in 1649 depredation and neglect had taken their toll on this medieval 'royal thank-offering for the kingdom's success in war and internal peace' and 'monument to piety and chivalry', which now stood as a poignant metaphor for the late King's reign.[9]

With Cromwell as King in everything but name and the exiled Charles II King in name only, with no realistic prospect of gaining the throne, the Order of the Garter was to all intents and purposes defunct. And yet one institution, the Poor Knights of Windsor (known today as the Military Knights of Windsor), which had been attached to the Order of the Garter, was allowed to survive. In spite of their name the Poor Knights of Windsor were not necessarily knights as such but impoverished military officers who had been granted a small pension and accommodation in Windsor Castle as a reward for meritorious service, which remains the statutory qualification for a Military Knight of Windsor. The institution had been founded by Edward III in 1348, the same year as the Order of the Garter. Then it was known as the Poor Knights of the Order of the Garter and in exchange for their pensions and living quarters in Windsor Castle its twenty-six members (one for every Knight of the Garter including the sovereign) were expected to attend St George's Chapel daily to pray for the souls of the King and his successors, as well as those of the Knights of the Garter. Such prayers of intercession ceased at the Reformation to be replaced by straightforward daily prayers for the sovereign, his or her successors, and the Garter Knights. At around this time the establishment of the Knights of Windsor was fixed at thirteen, including their governor, to be maintained out of the revenue from lands settled on the dean and canons of Windsor.[10]

This was the arrangement pertaining at the start of the Civil War, during which the Poor Knights found themselves in dire straits. Parliament having effectively abolished episcopacy in 1642 there were no dean and canons to administer the funds necessary for their upkeep, as a result of which it was claimed two very probably died. But the institution would subsequently benefit from being one of those charities that Protector Oliver wished to see continue in being in accordance with the original intention of the founders, which in this instance were his royal predecessors. Accordingly, in September 1654, *An Ordinance for the Continuance and Maintenance of the Almshouses and Almsmen called Poor Knights and other Charitable and Pious Uses* was passed by his Highness the Lord Protector, with the consent of his Council. This authorised the governors of the almshouses of Windsor Castle, which included members of the Protector's Council, the Mayor of Windsor and the Provost and Fellows of Eton College, as Commonwealth successors to the dean and canons of Windsor, to fill vacancies in the ranks of the Poor Knights from those whom they considered the most deserving. These were required to be 'such persons as have faithfully served the Commonwealth as commissioned officers in the army and are now out of commission and incapable of doing service either by reason of age or for want of some limb lost in their service'. There were, however, certain provisions. Candidates must not have acted in any way that was prejudicial to the Commonwealth nor be dissatisfied with the present government and their candidacy had to receive the approbation of the Lord Protector. Provision was also made for 'certain necessary officers' – a minister, weekly lecturer, chapel clerk, sexton, clock-keeper, bell-ringer and porter – together with repairs to St George's Chapel. The establishment would remain at thirteen, including their governor, but with the later addition of a further five paid for out of a private bequest. Obligatory daily prayers for the monarch, the monarch's successors and Knights of the Order of the Garter were replaced by an equally obligatory daily attendance at readings from the Bible.[11]

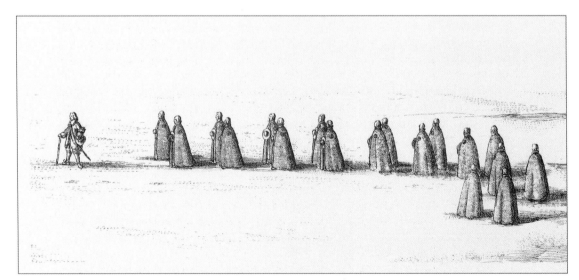

Poor Knights of Windsor processing during the reign of Charles II. Founded by Edward III in 1348 as a charitable adjunct of the Order of the Garter, the Poor Knights was one of those regally established institutions that would continue under the Protector and receive his patronage.

Previously Poor Knights had worn a red gown with a shield bearing the cross of St George embroidered on the left shoulder symbolising their connection with the Order of the Garter. Now a gown of sober grey with the Commonwealth arms taking the place of the cross of St George was the livery for the Protectoral 'continuance' of the royal and ancient institution of the Poor Knights of Windsor. The money to maintain the initial thirteen knights would come from the same source as formerly – the revenue which had obtained to the abolished dean and canons of Windsor and now settled on the governors of the almshouses of Windsor Castle. At the same time other past 'charitable and pious ends and purposes' supported by this income were to be restored. Provision was therefore made for two scholars at both Oxford and Cambridge universities, the relief of the poor of Windsor, preaching in Windsor town and castle and the maintenance of a grammar school, 'his Highness the Lord Protector being jealous to continue and establish all works and foundations tending to the advancement of learning, or any other charitable and pious use or uses whatsoever'.[12]

Like the Poor Knights of Windsor a high office connected with the Order of the Garter also survived into the Protectorate. This was the grandly named Garter, Principal King of Arms who combined the role of chief herald and principal officer within the College of Arms with ceremonial and other duties associated with the Order of the Garter. During the pre-Protectorate Commonwealth and throughout Oliver's rule this office, created by Henry V in 1415, was occupied by Edward Bysshe. Naturally Bysshe performed none of the Garter duties traditionally associated with his office. There was at this time, however, another, some would say the only true, Garter, Principal King of Arms, Sir Edward Walker, who held his title from Charles I. But Walker was sharing Charles II's exile and so his ability to exercise the office was considerably restricted. Bysshe, who was fully able to perform the duties of chief herald and principal officer within the College of Arms, had been a pre-Protectorate Commonwealth appointee, which demonstrates that the establishment of a republic did not necessarily mean a complete break with the past in every sphere.[13]

Other royal foundations also continued in being into the Commonwealth, although direct Protectoral patronage would not necessarily go on to replace royal patronage. Westminster School, attached to the Abbey, was a case in point. Originally founded by Henry VIII this institution actually flourished during the Commonwealth and Protectorate in spite of its known corporate propensity to royalism. The school was now governed by a lay committee instead of the abolished dean and chapter of Westminster Abbey but it was still maintained by revenue from the Abbey's lands and rents. With a fresh regime came enlightenment, one of the first acts of the new, Puritan inclined, governors having been to restore free places for poor scholars. Pupils were still expected to attend services in Westminster Abbey which remained a place of worship but had been cleared of 'monuments of superstition', while services were now conducted by Puritan divines. Otherwise things remained much as they had been – rigid academic discipline leavened with a degree of high living. Even the status of Bishop's Boy and King's Scholar were retained, notwithstanding the abolition of episcopacy and the office of King.[14]

The headmaster, too, quite remarkably under the circumstances, remained the same. The Protectorate coincided with the end of the second and the beginning of the third decade of Dr Richard Busby's long headmastership, which spanned the fifty-seven years from 1638 to his death aged eighty-eight in 1695. Not only was he the school's most celebrated headmaster but the claim to be the most remarkable headmaster of all time has also been staked on his behalf. Busby's severity, however, was already proverbial in the sixteen fifties. Although he dedicated one of his later translations to Busby, one former pupil of Westminster School, the poet and Cromwellian civil servant John Dryden, never forgot his old headmaster's zeal for corporal punishment. Only a few months before his death at the age of sixty-eight he still recalled how 'our Master Busby used to whip a boy so long till he made him a confirmed blockhead'. An unreconstructed High Anglican and Royalist, Busby, nicknamed 'Richard Birch-hard' by another Westminster schoolboy, somehow managed to keep his post in spite of his known sympathies and the fact that he had omitted to take the National Covenant, which was the oath signifying acceptance of ecclesiastical reforms imposed by Parliament in 1644 and a necessary requirement for maintaining such posts as that occupied by Busby. He also turned Puritan enthusiasm for education to advantage. The number of pupils increased throughout the Commonwealth and Protectorate and great noble families began sending their sons there. By the time of the restoration of the Stuarts in 1660 Westminster School had become the most outstanding school in the country. Busby's survival as headmaster was indeed extraordinary. It has been said of him that 'no one called him a time-server; he made the times serve him'. Certainly Busby is one extreme example of the existence of continuity during these turbulent times.[15]

By the summer of 1656 the continuing matter of Cromwell and the crown looked set for a final positive conclusion. In early July the new Swedish ambassador, Count Christer Bonde, reported a conversation he had with Bulstrode Whitelocke, whom he described as 'a person highly regarded in Parliament'. The ambassador learned from Whitelocke 'that he was in favour of his Highness assuming the crown, though Parliament must reserve to itself the rights which pertain to estates in well-ordered kingdoms; and as far as I can gather from one person and another it seems likely that in the course of this Parliament his Highness will become King'. A month later in another of his missives Bonde reports that 'as far as I could gather from my Lord Lambert there is now no general disinclination to his Highness becoming King. All the principal nobility in the country desire it.' Cromwell's poet cousin, Edmund Waller, seems therefore to have caught the mood of the moment with his poem commemorating the capture of a large quantity of Spanish bullion in September 1656, the last seven lines of which are devoted to 'our great Protector' and end with:

> Let the rich ore forthwith be melted down,
> And the state fixed by making him a crown;
> With ermine clad, and purple, let him hold
> A royal sceptre, made of Spanish gold.

Waller was a former Royalist and, according to one assessment of his character, 'an unprincipled politician, whose muse, worthy of a nobler office, was ready to become the laureate of any power in possession'. The lines in Waller's poem referring to Cromwell were omitted in the reprinted editions published after the Restoration.[16]

As if to underscore the fact that the Cromwellian regime was about to be established on a firmer and more traditional footing, the 1656 Lord Mayor's Show demonstrated that the event was now very much here to stay. This was a full-blown affair, paid for by the Skinners' Company (dealers in skins, pelts and hides). Its theme was 'London's Triumph'. The water pageant took the form of a running mock battle between two flotillas of barges as they progressed along the Thames. Passing Whitehall a salvo was fired from the river in salute to the Lord Protector and his Council who were watching the spectacle from the palace. The Lord Protector replied to this mark of respect 'with signal testimonies of grace and courtesy'. Of the land pageants one had a twelve foot high giant 'going before . . . for the delight of the people'. Another depicted lions, tigers and bears in a wilderness setting dancing to the charmed music of Orpheus. The symbolism here was considered to be singularly apt given that the incoming Lord Mayor was a member of the Skinners' Company. An alternative interpretation, also advanced at the time, was that 'as Orpheus tamed the wild beasts by the alluring sound of his melody, so doth a just and upright governor tame and govern the wild affections of men by good and wholesome laws'. The 'governor' here is of course the Lord Mayor of London but as the City was regarded as a microcosm of the country, the very 'heart of the nation' even, then by extension this could also refer to the Lord Protector who was also known by that name. Symbolism apart this particular Lord Mayor's Show, the second during Cromwell's rule, was certainly seen as marking a full and complete restoration to the City of 'those ancient customs of joy and triumph which formerly gave it the title of the most fortunate, plentiful and flourishing city in the world'.[17]

There was a full and complete restoration to the City at this time of something else equally as ancient, the institution now known as the Honourable Artillery Company. This had been founded by Henry VIII in 1537 as the Fraternity or Guild of St George for the practice, by Englishmen 'of good name and fame', of military exercises and training and 'for the better increase of the defence of this our realm'. As such it constitutes the oldest extant unit in the British army with a list of past members which includes John Milton, thus explaining the military knowledge that the poet was able to display in his writing. Traditionally it had supplied officers for the London trained bands or militia, although as a force the company was separate from these military organisations. It was, of course, the trained bands of London which formed the nucleus of the Parliamentarian army in the Civil War. After the conflict, in which some of its members fought on the Royalist side, the company became more or less moribund. In 1655 London's Lord Mayor and Commissioners of Militia had petitioned the Lord Protector for leave 'to revive the power of the Artillery Company for the better disciplining of the citizens, whereby they might, upon any emergency, be enabled to act together for his defence', promising that none shall be admitted into the company but such

ARMA PACIS FVLCRA

The 1661 arms of the Artillery Company. This was another regally established institution of which Cromwell would assume the patronage exercised by his royal predecessors, nominating Philip Skippon as its Commander as Charles I had done.

as were well affected to his Highness. Cromwell agreed and assumed the patronage of the company, which had previously been under the sole control of the crown. He also exercised the hitherto royal prerogative of nominating the commander of the Artillery Company, which was the latest of a myriad names the unit had been known by since 1537. The choice fell on Philip Skippon who had, ironically, been Charles I's choice as Captain in 1639. In the intervening years this stereotypical stout-hearted, honest Puritan soldier became one of Parliament's most outstanding military men in its struggle against this same King. Now he was a member both of the Protectorate Parliament and the Protector's Council. This is why, while he 'was pleased to acknowledge himself Captain of the Company', Skippon nevertheless explained that 'there could not be expected so much from him as formerly there had by reason of such multiplicity of business that lay upon him'. Again, Cromwell had used the power vested in him as Lord Protector to revive an ancient, regally established institution, even nominating, in this particular and peculiar instance, the same person to head it as Charles I had done.[18]

Rumour that Cromwell was also about to succeed to Charles I's crown, and with popular consent, persisted into the autumn of 1656. 'There is talk here of a King but it is no otherwise than the people will have it, not any intent of Parliament nor yet of him [Cromwell]; but I wish it were', opined James Waynwright at the end of November. Such was the state of affairs at this time that even committed Royalists were now apparently prepared to compromise their position. In that same November of 1656 Christiana Cavendish, Dowager Countess of Devonshire, was writing to fellow Royalist and kinsman Lord Bruce

Christiana Cavendish, Dowager Countess of Devonshire, a zealous Royalist who did not scruple to be of service to the Cromwellian regime or to encourage the marriage between her grandson and the Protector's youngest daughter.

to the effect that: 'I am preparing to receive an ambassador, being thought the most accomplished for such good purposes . . . such honour I must receive to increase the fame of Roehampton.' Clearly the dowager countess was only too happy to be of service to the Cromwellian regime by entertaining foreign ambassadors, if only to enhance the social reputation of the family seat. And yet otherwise her Royalist credentials were, and seemingly remained, impeccable. When the Civil War broke out her second son, Charles Cavendish, 'took a commission of a Colonel in his Majesty's cause', to quote John Aubrey, 'wherein he did his Majesty great service and gave signal proofs of his valour'. Cavendish was killed, aged 23, when his regiment clashed with some Parliamentarians near Gainsborough in July 1643. The commander of the opposing force was Colonel Oliver Cromwell. Throughout the Protectorate the Dowager Countess of Devonshire was in the habit of entertaining supporters of Charles II at her house 'to discourse with and persuade them to the most active endeavours for the King's restoration'. To the same end she also kept up a correspondence with prominent Royalists, both at home and abroad. Later, much would be made of this particular noblewoman's zeal in the King's service and the consequent danger she faced from the Cromwellian regime, which was well aware of her activities. The service she rendered to this same regime seems, however, to have been conveniently overlooked.[19]

CHAPTER 6

We Have A Crown Made

On 31 December 1656, Christiana Cavendish, Dowager Countess of Devonshire, again wrote to Lord Bruce: 'Charles Howard has his patent drawn to be a baron. They speak of more nobility, a good presage, I hope, of what has been long expected.' As the creation of hereditary peerages, such as Charles Howard's proposed barony, is an exclusively royal prerogative then the dowager countess's 'good presage . . . of what has been long expected' can only refer to the prospect of Cromwell becoming King. On the face of it Christiana Cavendish would seem to have been hedging her bets in the matter of political allegiance by appearing to welcome the possibility of Protector Oliver becoming King Oliver. But there may have been other considerations. When Cromwell was eventually tentatively offered the crown by Parliament the French ambassador reported that 'the Royalists . . . express great joy at this plan and are convinced that, since the quarrel is between two families, the King's party will be strengthened'. In other words, with Cromwell King the subject of the crown would become a matter between two rival claimants in which the House of Stuart was bound to prevail over the House of Cromwell. There was a distinct advantage to this arrangement, other than a probable restoration of Charles II. As part of the political settlement following the dynastic conflict that was the Wars of the Roses, Henry VII had declared that no one who had given his allegiance to one claimant to the throne should be judged a traitor by another, as had hitherto been the case. Thus, by this 1495 *De facto* Act, those who had given their allegiance to Cromwell would enjoy indemnity from the charge of treason by a rival successor regime, but only if Oliver became King. And this act would actually be cited by the Royalist-cum-Cromwellian peer, Lord Broghill, as one of the reasons why it was necessary for Cromwell to accept the title of King. 'By your Highness bearing the title of King', Broghill argued, 'all those that obey and serve you are secured by a law made long before any of our differences had a being, in the eleventh year of the reign of Henry VII, where a full provision is made for the safety of those that shall serve whoever is King.'[1]

The Dowager Countess of Devonshire's reference to the prospect of Cromwell becoming King squares with a resurgence of speculation to that effect, both at home and abroad, around this time. On 23 December 1656, eight days prior to the dowager countess's letter to Lord Bruce, one of spymaster Thurloe's agents was reporting from Paris: 'Here has for this fortnight past been a whisper at the court that my Lord Protector would take the crown upon him. Just three days ago

Mazarin said in the hearing of a friend of mine that he had very certain information thereof from England.' Thurloe's informant thought the rumours were without foundation but if there did happen to be such a sudden alteration in government then he was confident that 'it would be a condescension on his [Cromwell's] part to the importunity of the Parliament and others who might desire that change to prevent some important alterations which otherwise may happen to the prejudice of the public. . . . Some think it wise and generous, others are but of half that opinion. But all believe the thing, it coming both in letters to the French court and to some of the English.'[2]

The agent in question was Colonel Joseph Bampfield, one of those one-time supporters of Charles I who would go on to serve my Lord Protector with the same zeal that they once served my lord the King, and in a similar capacity. In 1644 Bampfield had been employed by Charles I on a mission 'to penetrate the designs of the two parties in Parliament'. Four years later, with the King's cause now lost, the Colonel was organising the escape from England of Charles's second son James, Duke of York. After the King's execution he was arrested but managed to escape, fleeing to the Netherlands. In 1652 he returned to England and was recruited into the service of the new republic. He was arrested in August of that year and ordered to leave the country, 'a normal procedure when Thurloe wished to infiltrate an agent into Royalist circles'. From 1654 Bampfield was in Paris informing Thurloe of the comings and goings at the royal court in exile. He also sent a lengthy and detailed report concerning factionalism among Charles II's immediate advisers and some inside information on the Gerard Plot. 'Upon this you may rely', Bampfield says of Colonel John Gerard's failed attempt on Cromwell's life early in the Protectorate, 'that the King both knew of it, approved of it, and looked to it as the only and most necessary means to set all his other designs in motion.' The King's 'other designs' were Royalist risings in the south of Scotland and north and west of England. The names of some of those implicated were given, along with a list of other supporters of the King's cause residing in what were now the Protector's domains. This ex-Royalist's reports, some of which were in secret writing using lemon juice, demonstrate outstanding diligence in the service of the Protectoral regime and a conviction that if Cromwell were to accept the crown it would only be out of political necessity.[3]

Within weeks of Bampfield's report and the dowager countess's letter the discovery of more plots to assassinate Cromwell produced a significant development. On 23 January 1657 in the House of Commons John Ashe, member for Somersetshire and a leading Presbyterian, proposed an amendment to the Speaker's address congratulating the Protector on his escape. 'I would have', Ashe said, 'something else added, which, in my opinion, would tend very much to the preservation of himself and us and to the quieting of all the designs of our enemies; that his Highness would be pleased to take upon him the government according to the ancient constitution, so that the hopes of our enemies' plots would be at an end. Both our liberties and peace, and the preservation and privilege of his Highness, would be founded upon an old and sure foundation.' In the event no mention of a change in government was made in the Speaker's speech. Nevertheless the subject of Cromwell and the crown had now been formally, if somewhat tentatively, broached. The French ambassador lost little time in reporting what had occurred in Parliament. 'One of the members', he writes, 'took the opportunity . . . to propose that the government should be returned to its old form under a King and that Parliament should be composed of Lords and House of Commons. Some supported this proposal and others rejected it but the former seemed to be in the majority. The Master of Ceremonies, who came to collect me in the afternoon of the same day to attend an audience, informed me in no uncertain terms, without my having mentioned it, that it was not to be doubted that the proposal would shortly be passed. There seems to be, however, a certain amount of repugnance for it in the army. This is the only matter spoken of at the moment and one which exercises all parties.' Later on in the communiqué the ambassador relates how 'many friends of the Lord Protector cannot see that it would be to his advantage to take the title of King into consideration. However, after the approaches which have come to light, and the speech the Master of Ceremonies delivered to me to that end, it cannot be doubted that he is ready for all the disadvantages that this new title will entail.'[4]

It was obviously news of Ashe's proposal in the House of Commons which prompted Sir Henry Vane (the younger) to observe on 2 February 1657 in a letter from The Hague that 'I did always believe this Parliament would make him [Cromwell] King before they parted'. Sir Henry, whose letter was intercepted by Thurloe, was a convinced republican and one-time close friend of Oliver. He it was who uttered the words 'this is not honest, yea it is against morality and common honesty' when General Cromwell called in the soldiers to clear the House of Commons at the dissolution of the Rump, to which the General retorted angrily 'O Sir Henry Vane, Sir Henry Vane, the Lord deliver me from Sir Henry Vane'. Later Vane would write a tract condemning the Protectorate, for which he was briefly imprisoned. According to intelligence received by the French ambassador Vane was currently in communication with fellow republicans and they intended establishing links with those of like mind in the army with a view to re-establishing the pre-Protectorate Commonwealth after Cromwell's demise. Nearer to home it was reported on 7 February that 'many citizens of London have laid several wagers of late that we shall have suddenly an alteration of the present government but what their meaning is we cannot yet discern'.[5]

Then on 23 February Sir Christopher Packe, a Cromwellian knight and one of the members for the City of London, suddenly stood up in the House of Commons and, apropos of nothing that had gone before, formally presented a Humble Address and Remonstrance:

That your Highness will be pleased to assume the name, style, title, dignity and office of King of England, Scotland and Ireland and the respective Dominions and Territories thereunto belonging, and the exercise thereof, to hold and enjoy the same with the rights, privileges and prerogatives justly, legally and rightly thereunto belonging. God who puts down and sets up another, and gives the kingdoms of the world to whomsoever he pleaseth, having by a series of Providence[s] raised you to be a deliverer of these nations and made you more able to govern us in peace and prosperity than any other whatsoever.[6]

The rumour mills now began to grind a new variety of speculation – not will Cromwell be offered the crown but how soon will his coronation take place. A letter from London to Lord Conway in France informed this Royalist nobleman that 'preparations are making in this country for the coronation of the Protector'. Like an echo, identical intelligence passed in the opposite direction: 'Here we believe the Lord Protector is voted King and suddenly to be crowned', Secretary of State John Thurloe was told in a 17 March 1657 communiqué from Paris. On 19 March Ralph Josselin was diarising some optimistic observations on the proposed settlement: 'Heard that the alteration intended will not be to the prejudice of honest people, the Protector will provide for their interests.'[7]

In such a climate as this it is only to be expected that the spectre of Richard III, first resurrected in 1653 when Cromwell became Lord Protector, was going to receive another outing. And it is hardly surprising that the occasion would be risen to by someone like William Prynne. An extreme Puritan, lawyer and pamphleteer, Prynne had a history of uncompromising recalcitrance reaching back to the 1630s when he published what was perceived of as a veiled attack on Charles I, which cost him dear. Undaunted, he persisted in his diatribes, writing tracts against episcopacy in general and attacking, anonymously, one bishop in particular, the Bishop of Norwich, for which he received further severe punishments. Naturally Prynne supported Parliament in the Civil War but he opposed the trial and execution of Charles I and became as big a thorn in the side of the republican regime, which imprisoned him for three years, as he had been in the side of the late King. Now it was the Protector's turn to receive the attentions of this persistent pamphleteer who said of himself 'the more I am beat down, the more am I lift up'. Prynne's attentions took the form of a tract entitled *King Richard the Third Revived*, published anonymously. It details how Richard, while Protector, was importuned 'to accept the kingship and crown of England' through 'a memorable petition and declaration contrived by himself and his instruments . . . in the name of the three estates of England'. There is no direct reference to Protector Oliver and the Humble Address and Remonstrance offering him the crown but the tract's subject matter and the timing of its publication leave little doubt that this was a veiled comment on current events. If there were any initial doubts they would have been dispelled by Prynne's conclusion: 'It is solid piety, policy and prudence in such an age as this for all considerate, conscientious Englishmen advisedly to remember, read and consider the tragical ends, as well as the successful beginnings and proceedings, of this King Richard and his active instruments to gain and settle the kingship by such politic stratagems.' The Venetian envoy in England was rather more explicit in a March 1657 communiqué. Commenting on the possibility of a Royalist invasion of England from the Continent he drew an exact parallel between Cromwell and Richard III, with Charles II in the role of Henry VII.[8]

After a month-long debate covering all aspects of the Humble Address and Remonstrance the House of Commons voted by 123 to 62 formally to request the Protector to accept the crown. Tuesday, 31 March, in the Banqueting House were the time and place fixed for Parliament to commend to Cromwell the 'new model of a kingly government and to his own person the title and dignity of King', which was contained in a refined version of the Humble Address and Remonstrance, now titled the Humble Petition and Advice of the knights, citizens and burgesses now assembled in the Parliament of this Commonwealth.[9]

The enemies of the Cromwellian regime were decidedly unimpressed by this turn of events. A republican pamphlet published at the time by 'a friend to the Commonwealth and to its dear-bought rights and freedom' forcefully pointed out that because of the choice of some and the expulsion of others this was not a free Parliament, which was perfectly true. When this second Protectorate Parliament had first convened on 17 September 1656 the desire for a less disruptive assembly than the previous Parliament led to about one hundred returned members being barred from taking their seats. Another fifty or sixty of the four hundred and sixty-member Parliament chose not to sit. The exclusion of malcontents was effected without infringing the constitution because article twenty-one of the Instrument of Government allowed the Protectoral Council to peruse the list of returned Members of Parliament and judge whether or not they were qualified to sit. The rule would obtain for the first three Parliaments of the Protectorate only.[10]

Perhaps more telling was the republican pamphlet's 'catalogue and some historical account of one hundred and eighty-two of the members of that unworthy assembly who were either sons, kinsmen, servants or attached to the Protector's interest and fortunes by places of profit, offices, salaries or other advantages which were all paid by the public' to the tune of 'one million, sixteen thousand, three hundred and seventeen pounds, sixteen shillings and eight pence Sterling and upwards per annum'. There is a further list of the 'kinglings', the name the pamphlet gives to those one hundred and twenty-odd Members of Parliament who voted for the proposal that Cromwell should be offered the crown. Five were Privy Councillors, together with the Secretary of State, twelve were the Protector's 'kindred', twenty were army and naval officers 'in pay' and there were thirty-three 'others receiving salaries and lying under other engagements'. This totalled seventy in all. 'The other fifty are Scots and Englishmen of slight, low and inconsiderable principles and will turn any way their master will have them.' The pamphlet's argument against Cromwell as King is both cogent and compelling: 'Let not that lively active spirit that once appeared for God against tyranny and wickedness in the late King's days now die when the same spirit and wickedness is again revived and acting, even by them who were so instrumental in destroying the late royal House for these very things.' Republicans were not, however, alone in their mindfulness. Cromwell would himself express similar views during the ensuing kingship debate.[11]

There had also been vociferous opposition to kingship in Parliament itself. And this from among some of those directly connected with the government. The opposition was led by General John Lambert, a Privy Councillor and arguably the second most eminent political figure after Cromwell. The acknowledged architect of the Instrument of Government, in which Oliver had originally been offered the title of King, Lambert was now displaying disaffection towards the Cromwellian regime. But Lambert was joined in his opposition to the offer of the crown to the Protector by others who did not necessarily share his disaffection, principally

Lord Deputy in Ireland Charles Fleetwood and Colonel John Desborough, both Privy Councillors and respectively Cromwell's son-in-law and brother-in-law, together with the military element in the House of Commons generally.

Evidence concerning the army's role in this matter is contained in what has been described by C.S. Egloff in the Bulletin of the Institute of Historical Research as 'one of the relatively few surviving letters written during the kingship crisis by a participant in the events'. The letter was written by Robert Beake, Member of Parliament for Coventry and a strong supporter of Cromwellian kingship and is dated 28 March 1657, which was three days after the House of Commons had voted to make Cromwell King and three days before the crown was formally offered to the Protector. Beake's letter, writes Egloff, 'provides further evidence that the majority of the House of Commons clearly identified the army (which he viewed as a corporate body and a definable pressure group) as the main obstacle to settlement. Beake regarded the new constitution as the will of Parliament, against which the army's opposition was that of a mere faction which the Protector should not heed. He was keenly aware that the military, defeated in the House, was pinning its hopes on personal appeals to the Protector to refuse the title.'[12]

Such an appeal had been made by a group of some one hundred officers within days of Sir Christopher Packe's proposal in the House of Commons that the Protector should accept the crown. They prayed that Cromwell 'would not harken to the title (King) because it was not pleasing to his army and was a matter of scandal to the people of God [and] of great rejoicing to the enemy; that it was hazardous to his own person and of great danger to the three nations, such an assumption making way for Charles Stuart to come in again'. This prognostication mirrored the belief held by some Royalists that the existence of two rival royal Houses was bound to result in a struggle for supremacy in which the Stuarts were certain to prevail over the Cromwells, bringing about the latter's downfall. The officers were, however, sent away with a flea in their collective ear. Time was, Cromwell told them, when they 'boggled not' at the word King, this being the title originally contained in the current constitution, the Instrument of Government, which he had chosen to refuse. Now they 'startle' at the same title, this 'feather in a hat', which he loved as little as they did. He went on to say how they had made him 'their drudge upon all occasions', from the dissolution of the Rump by military force onwards. Cromwell's conclusion was that 'it is time to come to a settlement and lay aside arbitrary proceedings so unacceptable to the nation'. Similar sentiments were expressed by Robert Beake: 'The soldiery . . . are much disobliged and great discontents there are in their spirits but I hope God will let his Highness see that his interest lies as much in the preservation of laws and affections of his people as in military power, the power that hitherto has ruled us.'[13]

Outside Parliament there was also opposition from the more extreme Puritan element, which made its opinion known through petitions to the Protector. One such 'humble remonstrance of divers churches of Jesus Christ' in Gloucestershire, Worcestershire, Warwickshire and Oxfordshire, voiced their disapproval of the 'present design, noised about the whole nation, to raise your Highness to a greater style and title of regal power, under the pretence of greater honour to your Highness'. They saw in this a plot, hatched by their and the Protector's enemies, to create a division between them and the Protector and the Protector and the army, resulting in the ruination of all concerned, in order to promote 'another interest'. Likewise, nineteen Anabaptist ministers in London expressed their 'deep resentment of, and heart bleedings for, the fearful apostasy which is endeavoured by some to be fastened upon you, upon plausible pretences, by such who for the most part had neither heart nor hand to engage with you and the good people of the nation in the day of straits and extremities, by persuading you to re-edify that old structure of government, which God, you and them had signally born testimony against and destroyed, and assume that office which was once declared and engaged against by Parliament'. While Captain William Bradford of York made a personal plea to Cromwell: 'I beg and beseech your Highness, nay again and again, with tears and prayers I beseech you to consider what you are doing.'[14]

Some of the details of the parliamentary proceedings relating to Cromwell and the offer of the crown are owed to the letters addressed to 'Jos. Williamson' in France by his London friend and bookseller 'Hum. Robinson'. One of these was dated, like Robert Beake's correspondence, 28 March 1657, which was the midpoint in the six-day period between Parliament's vote in favour of kingship and the formal offer of the crown to Cromwell. The letter was sent to Williamson in Paris and in it Robinson relates how:

> This week Parliament has finished the great work. There were 120 for a King and but 60 in the negative, yet our sections believe he will not accept it. I hear we have a crown made with a cross, which we thought would not be endured, and this being finished it is thought they will not [stay] much longer. . . . There is likely to have been a match between the Earl of Warwick's grandchild and the Protector's daughter, but this new dignity has altered it. It is reported that a match may be found in your parts.

The remark relating to the Protector's daughter is suggestive of a matter that in its extraordinariness easily matches the offer of the crown to a one-time East Anglian squire. Negotiations concerning a marriage between the Protector's youngest daughter, Frances, and Robert Rich, grandson and heir of the Earl of Warwick, were currently in progress but a final settlement was proving difficult owing to intransigence on the part of Cromwell. Now, in the middle of negotiations concerning another matter, the offer of the crown to Cromwell, a not unconnected potential further obstacle to the union between the Earl of Warwick's grandson and Frances Cromwell had presented itself. 'It is reported that a match may be found in your parts', Robinson had written to Williamson. The match referred to was the proposed union between the eighteen-year-old Frances Cromwell and Charles II.[15]

The only detailed account of this extraordinary affair comes from that Royalist-cum-Cromwellian Lord Broghill, or rather from two versions of Broghill's account penned by others – Thomas Morrice, his lordship's chaplain, and Gilbert Burnet, historian and Bishop of Salisbury, to whom the story was related by Broghill himself. The composite gist of the two narratives is that Broghill received instructions from Charles II to promote the idea of a match between the exiled King and Frances Cromwell. This had undoubtedly been prompted by the offer of the crown to Cromwell, concerning which many people, so it has been asserted, 'began openly to say, if we must have a King in consequence of so much law, as was alleged, why should we not rather have that King to whom the law certainly pointed than any other?' – to wit, Charles Stuart. Broghill carried out his scheme by first informing the Protectress and Frances and then spreading the rumour around London to the effect that the Protector was 'in treaty with the King who was to be restored and marry his daughter'. And this is how Cromwell was supposed to have heard about the 'design', as a rumour circulating in London and conveyed to him as such by the very man who had spread the rumour in the first place, Roger Boyle, Baron Broghill.[16]

To Broghill's surprise Cromwell expressed no indignation at the rumour regarding himself and Charles II but, 'with a merry countenance', asked his lordship 'And what do the fools think of it?' To which Broghill replied: 'All liked it and thought it the wisest thing he could do if he could accomplish it.' He explained how he saw Cromwell's own position as precarious in the extreme and the Protector 'could not expect to transmit his greatness to the next heir and perhaps would hardly be able to preserve it during his own life'. On the other hand Charles would be ready to listen to any proposition rather than continue in exile. Cromwell could therefore make his own terms with the King and be General of all the forces during the remainder of his life. 'The loyal party would readily join with him in the work. And if his daughter had children by the King (which was likely enough) he would thereby be endeared to King and country and would have such interest in the crown that nobody could ever attempt anything against him, having a King his son-in-law, an heir apparent to the crown his grandson and the whole power of the nation in his own hands. By all which his greatness would be for ever established.'[17]

Having pondered at some length over these points Cromwell is said to have answered: 'The King cannot and will not forgive the death of his father.' Broghill, 'who durst not tell him he had already dealt with his Majesty in that affair', offered to mediate for Cromwell on the matter of Charles I's execution. But the Protector was adamant that Charles II never would forgive him. To Broghill's counter that the Protector was one of many concerned in the death of Charles I but would be alone in the merit of restoring his son, Cromwell retorted: 'He [Charles II] is so damnably debauched he would undo us all; and so turned to another discourse without emotion.' From this Broghill concluded that the Protector had frequently considered the expedient of restoring the Stuarts. His lordship withdrew and meeting the Protectress and Frances they enquired of him how he had fared. Having given them an account of what had occurred he told them they must now try to interest the Protector in the scheme. 'But none could prevail. Guilt lay so heavy upon him that he thought there could be no reconciliation and so that business broke off.'[18]

A further, remarkably similar, story concerning Cromwell and the restoration of Charles Stuart involved another peer, William Seymour, Marquess of Hertford.

The marquess was one of Charles I's closest advisers but had lived quietly in retirement since the King's execution. During the kingship debate Cromwell invited Hertford to dinner, after which he is alleged to have confided to his guest that 'I am not able to bear the weight of business that is upon me; I am weary of it, and you, my lord, are a great and a wise man, and of great experience, and have been much versed in the business of government. Pray advise me what I shall do.' At first the startled nobleman was reluctant to give his advice. But after being pressed by Cromwell and given assurances that nothing he said would be in the least prejudicial to him Hertford felt he could not avoid venturing an opinion: 'Sir, upon this assurance you have given me I will declare to your Highness my thoughts by which you may continue to be great and establish your name and family for ever. Our young master that is abroad – that is, my master and the master of us all – restore him to his crowns, and by doing this you may have what you please.' To this an unperturbed Cromwell replied that Charles Stuart could not forgive and declined Hertford's offer to intercede with the exiled monarch in this respect. 'Thus they parted and the marquess received no prejudice thereby so long as Cromwell lived.'[19]

The Hertford story seems fanciful in the extreme but it is the sort of thing that would have gone down well at the Restoration, as indeed would Broghill's account. One difference between the two stories is that in Broghill's case, although in the detail the veracity of the account may be a little doubtful, the basic facts have been verified. Confirmation of these comes from someone for whom there would have been very little point in substantiating them had they been anything but true, while at the same time his credentials as a person privy to inside information are impeccable. The corroborator in question was one of the Protectoral court chaplains, Dr Jeremiah White. In a conversation White had with Samuel Pepys in 1664 'Cromwell's chaplain that was' told the diarist 'for certain that offers had been made to the old man [Cromwell] of marriage between the King and his daughter' but the Protector would not have it. Pepys goes on to relate how White 'thinks (with me) that it never was in his [Cromwell's] power to bring in the King with the consent of any of his officers about him. And that he scorned to bring him in as Monck did, to secure himself and deliver everybody else.'[20]

Coincidental with the proposition that Frances Cromwell should marry Charles II were negotiations concerning the marriage of the Protector's second youngest daughter, Mary. The prospective bridegroom was Thomas Belasyse, second Viscount Fauconberg, a young widower and owner of 'a very fair estate in Yorkshire', all of whose relatives, with the notable exceptions of Lord Fairfax and his son Sir Thomas Fairfax, had sided with the King in the Civil War. Fauconberg's Roman Catholic uncle, Lord John Belasyse, was even a founder member of the Sealed Knot, the faction-ridden and largely ineffectual Royalist secret society instituted early in the Protectorate with the aim of engineering an insurrection against the existing government in order to bring about a restoration of the Stuarts. Fauconberg was himself too young to have taken any part in the Civil War 'but, perceiving that the monarchy was dissolved and no prospect of restoration', to quote Mark Noble, 'he cast his eyes upon that quarter where power only could be obtained. This was his ruling passion, ambition. The death of his first lady paved the way for his attaining the height of his wishes in becoming son-in-law to the chief magistrate of the kingdom.' If Noble was correct in his assessment of Fauconberg, which mirrors that of Clarendon, then this particular nobleman would by no means have been alone in responding to the gravitational pull exercised by the source of national power and potential preferment. In the event the young viscount was as much sought after himself, Cromwell having already singled him out as a suitable husband for his second youngest daughter. To this end he was subjected to scrutiny by the regime. At the end of 1656, following the death of his first wife, Fauconberg had travelled to the Continent. In March 1657 the Protector's ambassador to France was ascertaining the viscount's whereabouts, the upshot of which was an interview in Paris between Fauconberg and the ambassador, Sir William Lockhart.[21]

Sir William Lockhart was another of those characters of the period whose existence exemplifies that allegiances were not necessarily as consistent as some people would like to think they were. The Lockharts were 'an ancient and knightly family in Scotland' and had 'much distinguished themselves by their attachment to their country and its sovereigns'. Sir William had been knighted by Charles I and in 1648 was in the Scottish army which came to the aid of the King after his escape to the Isle of Wight and was hammered by Cromwell at the Battle of Preston. Following a slight passed upon him by Charles II just before the Battle of Worcester Lockhart threw in his lot with the Commonwealth and when Cromwell became Lord Protector 'resolved to be as obedient a subject to him as he had been to the Charles's', sitting for his native county of Lanark in the first Protectorate Parliament. 'In July 1654, before that Parliament was chosen', Gardiner tells us, 'he sealed his devotion to the Protector by marrying his widowed niece, Robina Sewster.' Lockhart would seal his devotion to the Protector still further by naming his first born son of this union Cromwell. He became ambassador to the court of Louis XIV in the spring of 1656. Interestingly relations between Lockhart and the ex-Royalist turned zealous Cromwellian agent in Paris, Colonel Joseph Bampfield, were apparently far from cordial.[22]

Now Sir William Lockhart was to confirm the suitability of a candidate for marriage into the House of Cromwell. Generally speaking Lockhart's ambassadorial reports were addressed to Secretary of State John Thurloe but his account of the interview with Viscount Fauconberg was addressed to the Protector personally. Sir William writes:

> I have had the opportunity of seeing my Lord Fauconberg, who in my humble opinion is a person of extraordinary parts and hath (appearingly) all those qualities in a high measure that can fit one for his Highness and his country's service, for both which he owns a particular zeal. . . . He is of opinion that the intended settlement [Cromwell as King] will be very acceptable to all the nobility and gentry of his country, save a few, who may be biased by the interests of their relations.[23]

Fauconberg must have had good reason for believing that the 'intended settlement' would have such wide acceptance amongst the nobility and gentry. It seems unlikely he would have risked jeopardising his credibility by inventing such a thing merely to ingratiate himself with the Protectoral regime.

Obviously Fauconberg's political credentials matched all expectations. When it came to pressing his suit for Mary Cromwell's hand, however, things were to prove rather less straightforward. In early June 1657, three months after the viscount's first interview with Lockhart, the ambassador was compelled to approach Fauconberg again, this time concerning his apparent dilatoriness in his approach to the role of suitor. 'He professed much zeal in the business', Lockhart reported, 'but said he expected a clearer invitation and asked my authority for encouraging him.' Lockhart replied that he had already gone further than propriety would normally allow in assuring him he would be welcome and 'left the rest to his own merit and application'. It was arranged that the ambassador would receive Fauconberg's decision on the matter either that same day or the next. 'Do not attribute his not answering at once in an affair of that importance to a want of readiness for the thing', assured Lockhart.[24] One possible interpretation of this initial lack of responsiveness is that it was directly connected to the kingship debate. Before pressing his suit Thomas Belasyse, second Viscount Fauconberg, was waiting to see whether his prospective father-in-law would remain Protector Oliver or become King Oliver the First.

CHAPTER 7

Monarchy Asserted

One who was quite sanguine about the prospect of Oliver accepting the crown, even though others might think otherwise, was Member of Parliament for Coventry, and supporter of Cromwellian kingship, Robert Beake. In referring to the forthcoming formal offer of kingship to the Protector in the Banqueting House on 31 March 1657 he opined: 'I question not but it will within few days after be accepted of. However, many and great wagers are laid that he will not accept of it.' Parliament and the Protector duly met at the appointed time and place, the Speaker of the House of Commons, Sir Thomas Widdrington, making a speech on behalf of the whole House commending the title and office of King, after which the Humble Petition and Advice was read out and a copy 'engrossed in vellum' presented to his Highness. Cromwell answered by addressing Mr Speaker, referring to the new constitution as 'this frame of government that it hath pleased the Parliament by your hand to offer me'. He was only too aware that this was something of 'high and great importance . . . the welfare, the peace, the settlement of three nations, and all that rich treasure of the best people in the world being involved therein'. It was, he believed, a thing of weight, 'the greatest weight of anything that was ever laid on a man'. He asked therefore to be given time 'to deliberate and consider what particular answer I may return to so great a business as this', closing with 'I shall think myself bound to give as speedy an answer to these things as I can'.[1]

For the next two days Cromwell was incapacitated by 'some infirmity of the body' but on 3 April he requested a meeting with a parliamentary delegation in order to give his answer. His reply was, seeing that 'I cannot accept the things offered unless I accept all, I have not been able to find it my duty to God and you to undertake this charge under that title'. What Cromwell was referring to was the condition imposed by Parliament that the new constitution must be accepted by him in its entirety, including the kingly title, or not at all. This was intended to obviate the settlement favoured by the army, which was for Oliver to reject the royal title but accept everything else in the Humble Petition and Advice. So there was a sticking point – the title of King. 'And if the Parliament be so resolved, "for the whole paper or none of it",' Cromwell told the delegation, 'it will not be fit for me to use any inducement to you to alter their resolution.'[2]

This response was taken back to Parliament, which after some debate voted to renew the offer to Cromwell. And so on 8 April Protector and Parliament met again in the Banqueting House for the re-presentation of the Humble Petition and Advice. In so doing Speaker Widdrington told Oliver that Parliament had not yet received a satisfactory answer to their original offer. He went on to remind the Protector that the new constitution had been 'agreed upon by the Great Council and representative of the three nations' (i.e. Parliament) and the matters contained therein were, in their judgement, 'most conducing to the good of the people thereof, both in spiritual and civil government. They have therefore thought fit to adhere to this Advice and to put your Highness in mind of the great obligation which rests upon you in respect of this Advice, and again to desire you to give your assent thereunto.' In his reply Cromwell described the offer of kingship as 'a burden upon a man that is conscious of his own infirmities and disabilities'. He was mindful that this was the will of Parliament and, as he himself put it, 'no man can put a greater value than I hope I do, and shall do, upon the desires and advices of the Parliament'. But that was not enough. It was a matter of conscience. Would such an undertaking meet with divine approval? When considering where his duty lay he kept arriving at contrary conclusions. Like Hamlet, Prince of Denmark, here was a man who simply could not make up his mind. To assist him in his deliberations he asked Parliament to grant him the liberty 'to vent my own doubts and mine own fears and mine own scruples. . . . There are many things in this "Instrument of" Government, besides that one of the name and title, that deserve very much to be elucidated as to my judgement. It is you, and none but you, that can capacitate me to receive satisfaction in them.' But this must not be grounded in just his own good, or even Parliament's for that matter, but wholly in the good of the nation.[3]

A grand committee of close on a hundred members of Parliament was convened with 'power to receive from his Highness his doubts and scruples touching any of the particulars contained in the Humble Petition and Advice formerly presented' and in answering these to the Protector's satisfaction give reasons for the maintenance of Parliament's resolutions. Any particulars that his Highness could not be made satisfied with were to be reported to Parliament. Its terms of reference having been defined the grand committee delegated ten of their number to hear Cromwell's objections and put Parliament's case to the Lord Protector. The ten included some of the highest ranking law officers in the land – two Lords Chief Justice and the Master of the Rolls – as well as Protectoral Privy Councillors and Lord Broghill who, following the failure of the Charles II restoration plan, had obviously returned to his previous position of principal proponent of the proposal that Cromwell should be King. This committee first met the Protector on 11 April 1657 and would continue to do so at intervals over the next ten days. The burden of the committee's argument put by them to Cromwell on Parliament's behalf was that the maintenance of the nation's peace and safety and the rights and liberties, both spiritual and civil, of the people rested on Cromwell becoming King. The current settlement, with Oliver as Lord Protector under the Instrument of Government, would not possess the same inherent and very necessary stability were it to continue.[4] It transpired that for his part Cromwell had no objection in principle to Parliament considering a new settlement if that is what was seen fit. And it becomes plain through his often meandering responses that the 'doubts and scruples' the Protector was entertaining only involved the *title* of King, not the actual office. He was, of course, already de facto King but the nub of Oliver's argument was why could he not rule as King in the legal sense with the same title he had now?

The committee's assertion was that the title of Protector, being a new one for a sovereign, was not known by the law whereas that of King 'is known by the law of England . . . and more conformable to the laws of the nation'. Indeed, 'it carries more in it of weight than a mere title', it 'runs through the whole life and veins of the law'. There was, therefore, 'more of certainty and stability, and, of the supreme authority, civil sanction upon that title than upon the other'. So much so that changes, of whatever sort and for whatever reason, to the title with which sovereign princes had ruled the nation since time immemorial were perceived of as being inherently dangerous. Cromwell was reminded of the problems arising from James I's desire to be known as King of Great Britain instead of England and Scotland. This was 'a very slender change' in recognition of the union of the English and Scottish crowns but it was nevertheless subject to much debate in Parliament. Those opposed to it claimed that such a change in the monarch's title was without precedent and would result in the invalidation of all legal processes. In the event the new title was granted but with restricted use.[5]

The title King of Great Britain had replaced one even more favoured by James I in recognition of his enlarged dominions, that of Emperor, which would have been a much more radical change. Although it was never formally adopted, on a medal struck to commemorate the Scottish King's accession to the English throne James is nevertheless described as 'Emperor of the whole island of Britain and King of France and Ireland'. Furthermore, on his coronation medal James is described grandiosely as 'Caesar Augustus of Britain, Caesar the heir of the Caesars', a title arguably more appropriate to Cromwell than to his Stuart predecessor. From very early on in his rule Emperor had been persistently speculated upon as the alternative title to King should Oliver accept the crown. As we know, there was even a rumour to the effect that the first Protectorate Parliament had given Cromwell the title 'Oliver, the first Emperor of Great Britain, and the Isles thereunto belonging, always Caesar'. Now the crown was being formally urged on Cromwell it entailed the acceptance of the one title deemed to be 'interwoven with the fundamental laws of the nation', that of King. In Parliament's view, with this title and no other could Oliver legitimately exercise sovereign authority. This, therefore, precluded the designation Emperor and, more significantly, most certainly Protector. Lord Commissioner of the Great Seal Nathaniel Fiennes, one of those delegated to put Parliament's case to Cromwell, said of the latter title: 'Everyone knows it does not relate to him that hath the chief magistracy but to he who is tutor or guardian of another. That is the legal notion or use of the name Protector in this land and the holding unto of this name doth hold forth a gap of apprehension and expectation that there may be a change.' It was a change that was in any event necessary because, declared the Master of the Rolls, 'It's doubted, yea conceived not possible to annex the laws and the title Protector together'.[6]

Another delegate bluntly informed Cromwell: 'The law knows not a Protector and requires no obedience from the people to him. The Parliament desires a settlement whereby the people may know your duty to them and they their duty to you. The Parliament find the minds of the people of these nations much set upon this office and title [of King]. God hath by his providence put a general desire of it in the nation.' Furthermore, in this particular spokesman's opinion, when it came to things which were not unlawful and which were for their own good, the nation felt that their desires should be taken heed of and acted upon by those sent by them to sit in Parliament. Equally as forthrightly expressed to Cromwell was this same spokesman's view that because the Protector is not possessed of the name and office which 'hath for a thousand years been in this nation' those involved in attempts against his person received great encouragement from the fact that 'the law did not take notice of you as chief magistrate and that juries were generally backward to find any guilty of treason for attempting against you. The Parliament cannot think it fit to have their chief magistrate in such a condition.' It therefore behoved Cromwell to accept the name of King and this was expressed in a plea by this same forceful delegate to the Protector, again in no uncertain terms: 'I beseech your Highness consider, if you should refuse this title the Parliament present you with, you do not only deny yourself the honour they put upon you but you deny the nation, you deny the people their honour which by right they ought to have. 'Tis this honour and their birthright to have a supreme magistrate with the title of a King. I know Sir, though you can deny yourself yet you will not deny the nation their due when their representatives challenge it from you.' The delegate in question was the baronet Sir Charles Wolseley, of Royalist stock but a fervent Cromwellian and Protectoral Privy Councillor. He was also married to the daughter of the Puritan peer and Parliamentarian commander Lord Saye and Sele.[7]

Over the ten days of the debate the delegates continuously enlarged on and refined the points of their argument. The office, and with it the title, of King had not only 'been exercised in this nation from the time it hath been a nation' it was also 'approved of by the Word of God, that's plain'. The King's prerogative, being known to the law, was 'bounded as well as any acre of the land'. A Protector's prerogative, being not known by the law, was subject to no such legal constraints. It followed, therefore, that unlike a King, a Protector could do as he liked with impunity. These were the views of one of the Lords Chief Justice. Especially interesting in the light of his supposed involvement in the plan to restore Charles II was the contribution of Lord Broghill. His lordship averred that if the office of supreme magistrate were to be reconstituted with the office and title of King 'all those who reverence the old laws will obediently and cheerfully accept of him' in whom it is vested. 'If the title and office of King be vested in your Highness, and that thereby the people enjoy their rights and peace, it would be little less than madness for any of them to cast off those blessings only in order to obtain the same under another person.' At the same time a period would be put to any claim Charles II had to occupy the throne: 'There is at present but a divorce between the pretending King and imperial crown of these nations and we know that persons divorced may marry again but if the person be married to another it cuts off all hope.' And so it would go on with more legal, constitutional and historical precedents, not to mention the addition of Biblical allusions, being deployed to bolster the argument that Cromwell should defer to Parliament's, and therefore the nation's, will be accepting not just the office but also the title of King.[8]

Cromwell began his reply to the arguments presented to him by declaring his abiding respect for the will of Parliament: 'I confess I shall never be willing to deny or defer those things that come from the Parliament . . . if they come in the bare and naked authority of such an assembly as known by that name and are really the representation as a Parliament of so many people as a Parliament of England, Scotland and Ireland is. I say it ought to have its weight, and it hath so, and ever will with me.' He went on to say to the parliamentary delegation that 'here hath been divers things spoken by you today with a great deal of judgement and ability and knowledge'. Beset by so much erudition in so many Cromwell naturally felt apprehensive at having to put his own case: 'I think I have a very hard task upon my head, though it be but to give an account of myself.' In giving an account of himself the Protector revealed that he was still not entirely convinced of the absolute necessity of accepting the title King in order to occupy the office. His own words were in effect, why should the person in whom the supreme authority resides be any less a King simply because his title is spelled P-r-o-t-e-c-t-o-r? 'Signification goes to the thing, certainly it does, and not to the name.' Surely, Cromwell argued, as the office in question was being offered to him by Parliament it was therefore Parliament's to dispose of. Consequently Parliament had a perfect right to change the name of the kingly dignity to anything it wished without changing the nature of the office, which was all he was asking for, and this alone was sufficient to make it conformable to the law. That said, the Protector told the parliamentary committee bluntly that 'I hope it will be no offence to you to say as the case now stands . . . there is nothing of necessity in your argument'. He also believed that the nation was very much of his mind.[9]

Cromwell then cited two occasions when the name of the supreme authority had been exercised under a name other than that of King and had been complied with: the Keepers of the Liberties of England under the pre-Protectorate Commonwealth and Lord Protector under himself. 'And truly I may say that almost universal obedience hath been given by all ranks and sorts of men to both.' Oliver conceded that at the first of these 'alterations' the judges were 'somewhat startled' and initially demurred a little but after they had received satisfaction justice carried on as before. Indeed, he argued, since then the law had enjoyed more free exercise and been less interrupted by any hand of power, and the judges less solicited by letters or private interposition, either his own or other men's, than in double the same number of years during the 'halcyon days of peace in Elizabeth, King James and King Charles's time'. To Cromwell this was proof enough that it was not necessary for the supreme magistrate to have the title King for 'the law to have its free passage and do its office without interruption' and if Parliament 'determine that another name shall run through the laws I believe it may run with just as free a passage, which is all that I have to say upon that head'.[10]

Eventually, in a discursive exposition in which he went right back to the first battle of the Civil War, Cromwell got round to explaining the precise reasons why he did not wish to take the title of King. He was mindful of the men who, like himself, had taken up arms against the King. Such men as these, 'honest men and faithful men, and true to the great things of government, to wit, liberty of the people', would find it difficult to swallow a political settlement which had in it the title of King. It was a matter of duty and conscience that he should put their case and their case must be taken into consideration. These were, after all, men who had 'bled all along in this cause' and would not stomach anything in a settlement that was contrary to 'civil and gospel liberties'. There was something else besides. The Stuarts had lost the mandate of heaven and so had their kingly title. 'God hath seemed providential not only to strike at the family but at the name. . . . It is blotted out. It is a thing cast out by act of Parliament.' The title of King, providentially 'laid aside' by God and abolished by Parliament, 'and this not by sudden humour or passion but it had been the issue of ten or twelve years' civil war, wherein much blood was shed', was, in the Protector's view, now defiled. Did Parliament, acting on behalf of the nation, really wish him to accept a tainted title? There Cromwell rested his case. 'This is that poor account I am able to give of myself in this thing' were his closing words. This was after he had assured those present that 'I would rather I were in my grave than hinder you in anything that may be for settlement of the nation, for the nation needs and never needed it more. Therefore I am forever bound to do whatever becomes of me. . . . I shall pray to God Almighty that he would direct you to do what is according to his will.'[11]

At this point the proceedings were held up because Cromwell was ill. When he met the committee again three days later the Protector was obviously still far from well. 'He came out of his chamber half unready in his gown and [a] black scarf about his neck and made his apology for the loss of their former labour.' The committee's reply to Oliver's speech was an attempt at lancing the boil of his opposition to the proposed title with incisive counter reasoning and further refinements to their original arguments. This, apparently, was how God Almighty had directed them. The rights and liberties of the people were inextricably linked to kingly government. True, the supreme authority had been exercised under a different name, the Keepers of the Liberties of England and 'the title your Highness now bears', during which time 'we did enjoy our laws and justice was freely administered'. But that was because of God's beneficence and the nation's good fortune in the commendable nature of these regimes. As for the title of King being providentially laid aside by God and abolished by Parliament, it was neither the name nor office that was laid aside 'but that family which oppressed us'. Having 'thrown out that tyrant that oppressed in our spiritual and civil rights we can by our ancient laws graft another in that may be a fit instrument to preserve both'. And so the debate continued until 21 April.[12]

On that day the proceedings ended with another of Cromwell's discursive discourses, from which the Protector's intentions could still not be positively divined. 'Another long speech, as dark almost as before', was the assessment of the parliamentary diarist, Thomas Burton. Bulstrode Whitelocke, however, believed that 'the Protector was satisfied in his private judgement that it was fit for him to take upon him the title of King'. Thurloe, on the other hand, was a little more circumspect. In one of his regular missives to Henry Cromwell in Ireland he wrote: 'The truth of the matter is his [the Protector's] carriage in this debate was such that it gave great hopes to some that he would at last comply with the Parliament, but time must show. For the present we can but guess. It is certain the body of this nation doth desire it.' Royalist Stephen Charlton, in a letter to Sir Richard Leveson, gives us some idea of the general view prevailing at this time. 'The opinion of most men is that he will take it upon him.' In another letter he throws a little more light on the matter. 'The Protector has given the House some proposals whereby he may be capacitated to take the crown upon him. What the proposals are I cannot certainly relate, only I hear that he requires the laws to be regulated and some of the twelve articles moderated and that they must add £600,000 more per annum to the £1,300,000 which they have formerly allotted to him for maintenance, then he will maintain the war with Spain out of that revenue. . . . It is reported that these proposals have given the House so much work to do that it will take them up to a month.' Another Royalist, Richard Symonds, made special mention of the nigh on £2m per annum to be settled on Cromwell for the support of his government when 'the King never had above £700,000 a year revenue'.[13]

While Parliament busied itself on Cromwell's proposals Bordeaux, the French ambassador, was reporting on the pressures that the Protector was being subjected to in a bid to force his hand. Bordeaux believed that Cromwell would finally accept the crown 'even though several army officers were unable to agree to it in a conference they had these last few days with some Members of Parliament. They are at present deliberating and all the putting off appears to have been designed to win over the most obstinate in the meantime and to persuade the others that the Lord Protector is obliged by necessity to follow the actions of Parliament.' So confident was Sir Francis Russell that Cromwell would soon be King that when writing to his son-in-law, Henry Cromwell, from Whitehall on 27 April 1657, he ventured to say that his next letter was likely to be addressed to the Duke of York, the title traditionally given to the monarch's second son. There was, therefore, the interesting prospect of the existence of two Dukes of York, the exiled James, second son of King Charles I, who already held the title, and Henry, second son of King Oliver. Sir Francis, who had earlier doubted that Cromwell would ever accept the crown, went on to tell Henry that 'your father begins to come out of the clouds, and it appears to us that he will take the kingly power upon him. That great noise which was made about this business not long since is almost over and I cannot think there will be the least combustion about it. This day I have had some discourse with your father about this great business. He is very cheerful and his troubled thoughts seem to be over.' In fact it would appear that the crown was not the thing uppermost in Cromwell's mind at this time. 'Here hath been some troubles about the business of Mr Rich and my Lady Frances', Russell went on, 'they seem to me yet to continue and to trouble the minds both of your father and mother more than anything else.' Sir Francis returns to the subject of Cromwell and the crown in a marginal postscript: 'I was told the other day by Colonel Pride that I was for a King because I hoped that the next would [be] Henry's turn.'[14]

Dealing with Cromwell's proposals did not take up to a month as predicted. It took only a week. By 1 May Parliament had complied with all of the Protector's demands. 'Being weary of rolling from one thing to another and having an entire confidence in his Highness, they were willing to come to anything that is reasonable and may be judged secure for the good cause so long fought for.' This was the judgement of Secretary of State John Thurloe. There was now no reasonable impediment to the Protector accepting the crown. For his part Cromwell's response to Parliament's compliance with his demands was to say that 'he would take the particulars of this answer into consideration and as soon as might be he would return his answer'. Bulstrode Whitelocke relates how at this time the Protector consulted a group of advisers 'about this and other great businesses'. The group included Whitelocke himself, Lord Broghill and John Thurloe 'and they would be shut up three or four hours together in private discourse and none were admitted to come into him. He [Cromwell] would sometimes be very cheerful with them and, laying aside his greatness, he would be exceeding familiar with them, and by way of diversion would make verses with them and everyone must try his fancy. He commonly called for tobacco, pipes and a candle and would now and then take tobacco himself. Then he would fall again to his serious and great business and advise with them in those serious affairs. And this he did often with them and their counsel was accepted and followed by him in most of his greatest affairs.'[15]

But the promised announcement by Cromwell concerning the crown was a long time coming. By 5 May it was being reported that 'we are still expecting what will be the Protector's resolution. . . . He still puts the House off with further delays to take better consideration and to seek God in so weighty a business.' At this juncture even Thurloe did not know for sure what the outcome might be. 'On Thursday he [Cromwell] intends to give his final answer to the Parliament; what this answer will be God in his own heart knows.' But by the following day, 6 May, not only God but Thurloe and several Members of Parliament also knew what Cromwell's answer would be because he had told them privately that he intended accepting the Humble Petition and Advice and with it the title of King. The Protector duly sent word that he would meet Parliament in the Painted Chamber of the Palace of Westminster at 11 a.m. on Thursday, 7 May, to assent, so it was almost universally believed, to the crown being bestowed upon him. At the last minute, however, Cromwell cancelled the meeting and requested that the parliamentary committee dealing with the matter should meet him at five o'clock the same evening. The following day, Friday, 8 May, Parliament was informed that the Protector was now ready to meet them, this time in the Banqueting House. Cromwell's speech to the assembled company was short and to the point. 'Because I have been the unhappy occasion of the expense of so much time', he began, 'I shall spend little of it now.' He went on to praise the proposed political settlement under the Humble Petition and Advice as a government that sought to settle the nation on a good footing in respect of civil rights and liberties which, he believed, were the right of the nation. He hoped never to be found among those who would rob the nation of those rights but be one who served the nation in securing them. In what for Cromwell was a remarkably short time he arrived at the crux of the matter. 'I could have wished I had given it sooner but truly this is my answer. I think the government doth consist of very excellent parts in all but in that one thing, the title as to me. . . . I cannot undertake this government with the title of King, and that is mine answer to this great and weighty business.'[16]

Nineteenth-century dramatic representation of Cromwell refusing the crown, formally offered to him by Parliament on 31 March 1657. It was, however, only the title *of King to which the Protector had objected, not the office.*

Clearly something had happened to change Cromwell's mind, and at short notice too. But what was it? On 6 May, having finally resolved to accept the crown, the Protector was taking the air in one of the ex-royal parks put at his disposal, St James's, when he met his brother-in-law and Protectoral Privy Councillor, Colonel John Desborough. Desborough and Cromwell's son-in-law, General Charles Fleetwood, Lord Deputy in Ireland and also a Privy Councillor, were two Cromwellians who were not supporters of the move to make Oliver King. They did 'oppose . . . with all earnestness . . . this title but think the other things in the Petition and Advice very honest'. These two military grandees had advised the Protector against accepting the kingly title 'for they assured him that there was more in this matter than he perceived; that those who put him upon it were no enemies to Charles Stuart and that if he accepted of it he would infallibly draw ruin on himself and his friends'. Now, at their meeting in St James's Park, Oliver was to tell Desborough that he intended accepting the title. This caused Desborough to reply that he gave both the cause and the Cromwell family up for lost, adding that although he was resolved never to act against his brother-in-law he would no longer act for him either.[17]

In this resolve Desborough would be joined by Fleetwood and John Lambert, the 'three great men' together declaring that immediately after Cromwell's formal acceptance of the kingly title 'they must withdraw from all public employment, and so they believed would several other officers of quality that had been engaged all along in this war'. Hence the putting off of the meeting with Parliament in the Painted Chamber on the morning of 7 May and the hurried summoning of the parliamentary committee to a meeting that evening, which was not, as the French ambassador thought at the time, vacillation born of 'mere affectation'. By the time Cromwell arrived at the Banqueting House the next day for the rescheduled meeting with Parliament there had been further dramatic developments. That very morning while the House of Commons waited expectantly to be summoned to hear the Protector's formal acceptance of the crown they were presented with a petition. It was signed by two Colonels, seven Lieutenant-Colonels, eight Majors and sixteen Captains 'who, with such officers in the House as were of the same opinion, made up the majority of those relating to that part of the army which was then quartered about the town'. In the petition the officers stated that 'they had hazarded their lives against monarchy and were still ready so to do in defence of the nation'. They had 'observed in some men great endeavours to bring the nation again under their old servitude by pressing their General to take upon him the title and government of a King in order to destroy him and weaken the hands of those who were faithful to the Commonwealth. They therefore humbly desired that they [Parliament] would discountenance all such persons and endeavours and continue steadfast to the old cause, for the preservation of which they for their parts were most ready to lay down their lives.'[18]

Cromwell having been made aware of these developments word was sent to the House of Commons that the petition should not be debated until after the Protector had delivered his address. 'So the members came to Whitehall and Cromwell, with great ostentation of his self denial', says the unreconstructed republican Edmund Ludlow with characteristic disdain, 'refused the crown.' Cromwell had all along said that he would not accept the crown without the consent of the army. At the end of the kingship debate Thurloe believed that this consent would be forthcoming, notwithstanding the known opposition of Desborough, Fleetwood and Lambert. 'Many of the soldiers are not only content', the Secretary of State told Henry Cromwell, 'but are very well satisfied with this change. Some indeed grumble but that's the most for all I can perceive. And surely whatever resolutions his Highness takes they will be his own, there being nothing from without that should be any constraint upon him either to take or refuse it.' The most important thing was the advice of Parliament, 'which indeed hath weight in it'. Thurloe could not have been more wrong. When it came to it the soldiers were not well satisfied with the change. Whatever else, other than the army's opposition, might be hypothesised as the reason why Cromwell turned down the title of King, the author of the Preface to *Monarchy Asserted*, attributed to one of the major players in the drama, Bulstrode Whitelocke, seems to harbour no doubt concerning Oliver's refusal to accept the royal nomenclature: 'The Protector seemed very reluctant to accept the name and title even though he enjoyed the place and power because Lambert and some leading officers would not consent.' Thus, it would seem, Cromwell had indeed deferred to men who had bled all along in the cause and hazarded their lives against monarchy.[19]

Had Cromwell taken the crown he intended beginning his kingship with a 'grand design' which would have set the seal on him as the champion of Protestantism throughout Europe and beyond and the defender of all Protestants persecuted for their faith. This was a role grandiloquently exemplified by Edmund Waller in his *Panegyric To My Lord Protector*:

> Hither the oppressed shall henceforth resort,
> Justice to crave, and succour, at your court;
> And then your Highness, not for ours alone,
> But for the world's protector shall be known.

The grand design was to take the form of a Council for the Protestant Religion in opposition to the Congregation or College of the Propaganda set up by Rome in 1622 to propagate the Catholic faith throughout the world. Members of the council were to be drawn from Protestant communities in Europe as well as Turkey and the East and West Indies. Chelsea College, then an 'old decayed building', was to be refurbished for the council's use. This, at any rate, is what Jean Baptiste Stoupe, a Swiss agent in Cromwell's pay, allegedly told Bishop Gilbert Burnet. 'I thought it was not fit to let such a project as this be quite lost', Burnet concluded. 'It was certainly a noble one. But how far he would have pursued it must be left to conjecture.'[20]

Another Cromwellian enterprise which did not reach fruition (at least not until the nineteenth century) was a new educational establishment of the north at Durham. A charter was, however, granted on 15 May 1657 composed in the customary regal style of the Lord Protector: 'Know ye . . . that we, of our special grace . . . have thought fit to erect and found . . . a college of our said City of Durham . . . to be and continue a college from time to time hereafter for ever.' As we have seen from the experience of Westminster School educational establishments flourished under Cromwell's rule. The Protector directed his personal largesse at the university of which he was Chancellor, Oxford, bestowing on the library there a gift of twenty-four ancient manuscripts 'upon his own charge'. He also ordered that a hitherto private readership in divinity at Oxford should be paid for out of public funds. But a Protectoral scheme for 'the erecting and endowing of a college' for 'poor Protestant ministers, being foreigners and strangers born', using disused St Mary's Hall, Oxford, would share the fate of Durham College.[21]

CHAPTER 8

Protector Royal

You saw the ceremony?
That I did.
How was it?
Well worth the seeing.
Henry VIII, IV.i

Parliament's answer to Cromwell's refusal to accept the crown was a proposal eleven days later 'that Lord Protector shall be the title inserted into the Humble Petition and Advice and that it be referred to a committee to consider how that title may be bounded, limited and circumstantiated'. The title of King was therefore duly replaced with that of Lord Protector. Otherwise Cromwell would 'govern according to the Humble Petition and Advice in all things therein contained'. On 25 May 1657, seventeen days after he had effectively turned down the original document, Cromwell formally assented to the new constitution 'with the alteration made therein'. Certain doubts and questions that had arisen were clarified in an Additional and Explanatory Petition and Advice. Among other things this augmentation required 'that your Highness will be pleased, according to the usage of former chief magistrates [i.e. Kings] in these nations, and for the better satisfaction of the people thereof, to take an oath in the form ensuing':

> I do in the presence, and by the name, of God Almighty promise and swear that to the uttermost of my power I will uphold and maintain the true Reformed Protestant Christian Religion, in the purity thereof as it is contained in the Holy Scripture of the Old and New Testament, to the uttermost of my power and understanding, and encourage the profession and professors of the same; and that to the uttermost of my power I will endeavour, as chief magistrate of these three nations, the maintenance and preservation of the peace and safety, and of the just rights and privileges, of the people thereof. And shall in all things, according to my best knowledge and power, govern the people of these nations according to the law.

It was further required 'that your Highness's successors do, before they take upon them the government of these nations, take an oath in the form aforesaid'. Oliver's own successor would now be appointed and declared by him personally in his own lifetime. Privy Councillors too were to take an oath. Theirs was to be 'true and faithful to his Highness the Lord Protector' and 'not contrive, design or attempt anything against the person or lawful authority of his said Highness'. (One existing Privy Councillor, General John Lambert, would refuse to take such an oath.) Members of the Privy Council could not, however, be appointed or removed without the consent of Parliament.[1]

On 25 May 1657, the very day on which Cromwell gave his formal assent to the revised Humble Petition and Advice, Sir Francis Russell was again writing to his son-in-law, Henry Cromwell, in Ireland. This time the tone of his letter was very different and smacked somewhat of putting the record straight for posterity. He confessed that he had allowed himself to get carried away by his own optimism over the Protector's acceptance of the crown, although he claimed it was not entirely his own fault. 'At that time when I writ unto your lordship I had pretty good reason to be sanguine, for the little Secretary [Thurloe] was so and he 'twas that infected so many of us. But I hope I have pretty well recovered that infection, although it hath almost killed divers others.' He commended his son-in-law for his level-headedness in the matter. 'I am glad your lordship is so steady minded as not to be concerned with outward glory, for indeed he who is inwardly truly great cares not for shadows, which are only the chiefest happiness of all weak men and minds.' Sir Francis then went on to say that 'the truth is your father hath of late made more wise men fools than ever. He laughs and is merry but they hang down their heads and are pityingly out of countenance. All the lawyers are turned Quakers who before boasted they would make penknives of the soldiers' swords.'[2]

Oliver had every right to be happy because he had got what it seems he originally wanted, to occupy the office of King but with the title of Protector. This in spite of the fact that one of the original conditions had been that the Protector was obliged to accept the new constitution in its entirety, including the title of King, or not at all. The process of bounding, limiting and circumstantiating the replacement title by a parliamentary committee must therefore be interpreted as making the office of Protector conformable to the kingly dignity. Certainly the requirement that the Protector should take an oath 'according to the usage of former chief magistrates' must be interpreted thus because this was in effect a form of the oath taken by Kings at their coronation and not so very different in some of its fundamentals from the present day coronation oath. The agent of diplomat and merchant Richard Bradshaw for one believed that the Protectorship had been assimilated to the office of King. Writing, as usual from London, to his master in Copenhagen three days before Cromwell's acceptance of the revised Humble Petition and Advice Bradshaw's factor observed: 'Here is little save that of his Highness. The Parliament hath voted him Royal Protector and given him all the immunities and chosen a committee that he shall surrender all to the people due to them under the Kings and Queens of England.' Bradshaw's agent seems to have been voicing the generally held view of the revised constitution because Lady Elizabeth Conway gives a similar interpretation. Parliament had, she opined in a letter to France, 'settled the government which they proffered under the style of kingship to one as absolutely regal and hereditary, only altering the name to Protector'. And a letter written to John Percivall in Ireland from William Fitzgerald of Covent Garden a few days after Cromwell's formal acceptance of the revised constitution draws the same conclusion from 'the grand deliberation which has kept the whole Christian world in suspense until Monday ten o'clock, when the Parliament met his Highness . . . and made good their first offer to him with [the] name of King [but] under the style of Protector, which he accepted'.[3]

Those tidy-minded constitutionalists delegated to put Parliament's case to Cromwell in the kingship debate had maintained that to make the office of Protector conformable to the kingly dignity was not only undesirable but also well-nigh impossible. The office of King 'cannot be transmitted to another name without much labour and great hazard, if it may be at all', it was argued. Such a process would involve the identification and codification of all the individual duties and powers automatically possessed of a King by law as well as the people's legal obligations to the monarch, 'a work of so great labour that it would require months, yea years, if not ages'. But under the revised constitution the office of King *had* been transmitted to another name and with apparent ease. As Henry Cromwell had said of his father's proposed acceptance of the kingly title: 'For my own part I cannot apprehend the necessity of it, notwithstanding many wise men allege great reason on its behalf from the nature of several laws wherein I am not so well versed as to confute them. But notwithstanding all those arguments, I could never be yet convinced that all those excellent proposals of the Parliament are so inseparably affix'd to the name of King that all should stand or fall together as the adhering vote of Parliament seems to import.' All that was required now was a formal ceremony of public recognition of Cromwell's new dignity under the revised constitution. The form that this ceremony should take was the subject of a debate in Parliament, during which one member at least was in no doubt as to its precise purpose: 'You are making his Highness a great Prince, a King indeed, so far as he is Protector. Ceremonies signify much of the substance in such cases, as a shell preserves the kernel or a casket a jewel.'[4]

At the same time that plans for Oliver's second investiture were being made a new coinage began to be minted. 'On 1 June 1657', reported the Brandenburg agent in England, 'were issued the first coins with the Protector's bust and name, the coats of arms of the three countries and the Cromwell crest of a lion.' The original order for the new coinage had been issued as far back as August 1656 and it is thought that the first minting should have taken place in February or March 1657. There had been a similar sort of delay over the institution of the Protectoral Great Seal in 1655 pending a decision on whether or not Cromwell's title should be changed to King or Emperor. It seems possible, therefore, that the same situation may have occurred in the case of the Cromwellian coinage. In August 1656 the possibility of Cromwell becoming King was again under consideration and in February and March 1657 the kingship debate was in full flood following the formal offer of the crown to Cromwell. By June 1657 the kingship issue had been settled by assimilating the Protectorship to the royal dignity with Cromwell's title therefore remaining what it had been. Thus the minting of the new coinage, from the Spanish bullion seized in September 1656, could now proceed, although the date on the coins would be 1656 and not 1657.[5]

Above: *Coinage of the pre-Protectorate Commonwealth.*

Below: *Regal coinage of the Protectorate depicting on the obverse Cromwell wearing a laurel crown and on the reverse the Protectoral arms surmounted by the imperial crown of England, 'nearly exactly resembling the one used by King Charles I'.*

Like the Protectoral Great Seal the Cromwellian coinage was as regal as that which went before was republican. The obverse of pre-Protectorate Commonwealth coins displayed simply the cross of St George in a shield surrounded by a laurel wreath and the circumscription THE COMMONWEALTH OF ENGLAND. On the reverse were the arms of the Commonwealth – two shields side by side, one containing the cross of St George and the other an Irish harp – together with the denomination and a circumscription giving the date and the motto of the Commonwealth, GOD WITH US. Reverting to traditional royal practice the obverse of the new coins displayed a portrait of the ruler, Protector Oliver. He is imperially depicted wearing a laurel crown, a classical mark of distinction. Cromwell was the first British ruler to be portrayed crowned in this way and it set a trend that was followed for every succeeding male British monarch from Charles II (except for a few hammered silver coins early in the reign) to George IV who died in 1830. The circumscription on the obverse of the Cromwellian coinage also represents a reversion to traditional royal practice as it gives the ruler's title in Latin. As on the Great Seal it translates as Oliver, by the Grace of God, of the Commonwealth of England, Scotland and Ireland, and the Dominions and Territories thereunto belonging, Protector. The reverse depicts the Protectoral arms surmounted by the imperial crown of England, 'nearly exactly resembling the one used by King Charles I'. This crown is described as being 'formed of six arches springing from a jewelled circlet and meeting over the centre of the crown, surmounted by a mound and cross. The circlet is heightened by four crosses patée and four fleurs de lys placed alternately.' The circumscription is the motto of the Protectorate, PAX QUAERITUR BELLO (Peace is Sought Through War), accompanied by the date.[6]

The regal nature of the Cromwellian coinage was not the only thing to distinguish it from its republican predecessor. Previously all coins had been of the flat, relatively crude hammered type. But for the new coinage the Cromwellian regime employed the services of Peter Blondeau, a Frenchman who had invented a process for producing very fine coins. These milled coins had a sufficiently raised edge to accommodate an inscription, thus preventing clipping. The inscription on the edge of the 1656 Cromwellian half-crown was HAS NISI PERITURUS MIHI ADIMAT NEMO, which translates as 'These let no man spoil unless he wishes to perish'. (The spoiling of coins by clipping was regarded as treason and punishable by death.) The result of Blondeau's work, using dies engraved by medal maker to his Highness and chief engraver to the Mint, the unrivalled Thomas Simon, was coins of unparalleled beauty and fineness. Simon's portrait of Cromwell is particularly noteworthy as it is regarded as the truest of likenesses. It was, to Samuel Pepys's mind, certainly truer than the likeness on Charles II's coinage. Pepys also records that in 1663 Cromwell crowns (five shilling pieces) were being sold for five and six times their face value. This was because Cromwell coins never entered general circulation, which made them valuable collector's pieces. That apart, their sheer quality could be said to have been a reflection of the power of the nation under the Protectorate. And they were sufficiently regal to illustrate Cromwell's new dignity under the revised constitution, that of Protector Royal.[7]

Of Cromwell's first investiture as Lord Protector in December 1653 one twentieth-century historian wrote: 'The formal inauguration of the Protectorate went off with the rather drab propriety that tends to characterise ceremonies unwarmed by traditional sentiment and panache.'[8] This is not, however, a description that could be applied to the second investiture three-and-a-half years later because this was to all intents and purposes a king-making ceremony, transforming Cromwell from a de facto into a *de jure* King while retaining the title Lord Protector.

The ceremony would again take place in intensely historic Westminster Hall and the date set for it was Friday, 26 June 1657.[9] 'On the day appointed', relates Clarendon, 'Westminster Hall was prepared and adorned as sumptuously as it could be for a day of coronation.' It was an accurate observation. A raised platform was installed at the upper end of the hall, in the middle of which, below the great window, 'a prince-like canopy of state' had been set up. Underneath this there was a chair of state 'placed upon an ascent of two degrees covered with carpets'. In front of the chair of state stood a table covered with pink Genoa velvet fringed with gold. On the table had been placed traditional royal 'emblems of government and authority'. There was 'a robe of purple velvet, lined with ermine, being the habit anciently used at the solemn investiture of princes', next to that a large Bible 'richly gilt and bossed', then a 'rich and costly' sword and lastly a sceptre of solid gold weighing 168 ounces 20 grains and costing £650 13s. 6d.[10] It is not known if this was made of captured Spanish gold like the royal sceptre Edmund Waller had poetically advocated for Cromwell. Beside the table there was a chair. This would be occupied by the officiator at this ceremony, the Speaker of the House of Commons, Sir Thomas Widdrington, for the reconstituted Protectorate was to be a parliamentary monarchy in accordance with the Humble Petition and Advice of the knights, citizens and burgesses now assembled in the Parliament of this Commonwealth. 'The occasion of this great convention and intercourse', the Speaker was to tell Oliver, 'is to give an investiture to your Highness in that eminent place of Lord Protector, a name you had before but it is now settled by the full and unanimous consent of the people of these three nations assembled in Parliament.' On each side of the dais were banks of seating 'decently covered' to accommodate the members of that same Parliament, the judiciary and civic dignitaries.

This then was the setting for that most remarkable of ceremonies, the second investiture of Oliver Cromwell as Lord Protector. And it was a ceremony made the more remarkable by the fact that the chair of state on this occasion was the Coronation Chair, sometimes called St Edward's Chair, in which English and British sovereigns had been enthroned since Edward II in 1308 and would continue to be so until the present day. The chair was made for Edward I to accommodate, under the seat, the Stone of Scone, a 336 lb slab of sandstone on which Scottish Kings had been crowned. Edward, the 'Hammer of the Scots', had removed the Stone from Scone, near Perth, in 1296 after his conquest of Scotland. The Stone of Destiny, as it is also known, had, according to tradition, also been used at coronations of the High Kings of Ireland before its removal to Scotland. Legend has it that even further back in time the stone was the one used by Jacob for a pillow when he dreamt of angels ascending and descending a ladder reaching up to heaven. Over this immemorially ancient and mystically imbued lump of rock Protector Oliver would be installed 'as a successor of Fergus and Kenneth [ancient Scottish Kings], of Edward I and James I',[11] for which purpose the Coronation Chair had been removed from Westminster Abbey for the one and only time in its history. (The Stone of Scone would be returned to Scotland in 1996.)

The proceedings began at around two o'clock in the afternoon with the arrival of Cromwell at Westminster in princely state by Protectoral barge. Disembarking at Parliament steps he made his way to the House of Lords in the Palace of Westminster. Attended by his Council, officers of state and judges, Cromwell then met the Speaker of the House of Commons and Members of Parliament assembled in the adjacent Painted Chamber. Here he gave his assent to

Parliament's Additional and Explanatory Petition and Advice 'and all such other bills as were then presented to him'. The Speaker and Members of Parliament then left to take their places in Westminster Hall, the Speaker to his chair next to the table on which had been placed the princely raiment, Bible, sword and sceptre. The Protectoral procession into Westminster Hall comprised the customary court, state and civic dignitaries and functionaries, together with officers of the College of Arms, including Norroy King of Arms and Garter, Principal King of Arms. The sword of state, which had previously been borne before the Lord Protector by Major-General John Lambert, was carried by the Earl of Warwick. This was a return to royal tradition which dictated that the sword should be carried by a noble. On the Earl of Warwick's left walked, 'by his Highness's special favour', the Lord Mayor of London bearing the City sword. Cromwell himself was attended 'by his Council, the principal Secretary of State, divers of the nobility and other persons of great quality'. Among these were those nominated to sit in the Cromwellian Other House constituted under the Humble Petition and Advice (see Chapter 10). Also present at the ceremony, although with neither seats in the Other House nor places in the Protectoral procession, were 'no small number of Scotch and Irish nobles'.

Cromwell took his place under the canopy of state for the bestowal of the symbols of regality by the Speaker of the House of Commons, who used language not too dissimilar to that of the Archbishop of Canterbury when performing the same rite at a coronation. First the Speaker lifted the princely robe from the table saying 'this is an emblem of magistracy and imports righteousness and justice. . . . This robe is of mixed colour to show the mixture of justice and mercy. Indeed, a magistrate must have two hands, to cherish and to punish.' Then, assisted by the Earl of Warwick (so that 'this promotion might not be without any vote from the nobility'), state functionary Bulstrode Whitelocke 'and others', the Speaker vested the Lord Protector with it. Next the Bible was presented to Oliver with the words 'it is a book of books and doth contain both precepts and examples for good government'. After this Mr Speaker girded his Highness with the sword, 'not a military but a civil sword' the Protector was advised. 'It is a sword rather of defence than offence; not to defend yourself only but your people also.' Finally Oliver was presented with the last item on the richly trimmed velvet-covered table, the solid gold sceptre: 'not unlike a staff for you to be a staff to the weak and poor', counselled the Speaker. 'It is of ancient use in this kind. . . . Homer, the Greek poet, calls Kings and Princes sceptre-bearers.' At which Speaker Widdrington enthused: 'What a comely and glorious sight it is to behold a Lord Protector in a purple robe with a sceptre in his hand, a sword of justice girt about him and his eyes fixt upon the Bible! Long may you prosperously enjoy them all, to your own comfort and the comfort of the people of these three nations.'

The next step in the proceedings was the administration by Mr Speaker of an oath 'according to the usage of former chief magistrates', that is to say, a monarch's traditional coronation oath, 'engrossed in a roll of vellum'. The oath having been administered, with 'his Highness standing thus adorned in princely state according to his merit and dignity', one of the Protectoral court

Protector Royal. A twentieth-century representation of Cromwell's second investiture on 26 June 1657 at which Oliver was transformed from a de facto into a de jure *King while retaining the title Lord Protector.*

chaplains, Thomas Manton, 'by prayer, recommended his Highness, the Parliament, the Council, his Highness's forces by sea and land, the whole government and people of these three nations to the blessing and protection of God Almighty'. After this equivalent of the Archbishop of Canterbury's coronation benediction, 'the people giving several great shouts and the trumpets sounding', his Highness sat down in the Coronation Chair holding the sceptre in his hand.[*]

Immediately to the right of the throne sat the ambassador extraordinary of France and immediately to the left the ambassador extraordinary of the States General of the United Provinces (the ultimate recognition by these two major European powers – one Catholic and one Protestant). Also on the right of the throne stood the Earl of Warwick bearing the sword of state and on the left the Lord Mayor of London with the City sword. This was the first citizen of London exercising that same ancient right to stand with the great officers of state and in the immediate vicinity of the throne at a sovereign's coronation as he had at Cromwell's original investiture. Also exercising their prerogative to be in close proximity to the throne was Richard Cromwell and two of the Protector's sons-in-law, Lord Deputy in Ireland Charles Fleetwood and Master of his Highness's Horse John Claypole, together with his Highness's Council and officers of state. Standing 'upon the lower descent' near the Earl of Warwick were Privy Councillors Viscount Lisle and Admiral Edward Montague and on the other side Bulstrode Whitelocke, each bearing a drawn sword. These three swords, described in the esoteric language of coronation ceremonial as symbolising Justice to the Spirituality, Justice to Temporality, and Mercy, were always present at the crowning of a sovereign, being borne, like the sword of state, by great lords of the realm.

With his Highness sitting in state on the ancient seat of Kings a herald gave the signal for a trumpet fanfare to be sounded three times after which, by authority of Parliament, he proclaimed his Highness 'Lord Protector of the Commonwealth of England, Scotland and Ireland, and the Dominions and Territories thereunto belonging, requiring all persons to yield him due obedience'. The trumpets were again sounded 'and the people made several great acclamations with loud shouts: "God save the Lord Protector"'. Oliver was proclaimed a second time by another herald from a different part of the hall, after which the ancient stones again echoed to the cry 'God save the Lord Protector'. (An alternative version gives this as a thrice-acclaimed 'Long live his Highness' followed by three huzzas.) There followed a short pause, then the Lord Protector rose from his throne, saluted the ambassadors and other dignitaries present, and made his way through the hall, the train of his 'princely habit' being borne, as coronation tradition dictated, by 'several noble persons' – the Earl of Warwick's grandson, Robert Rich,

---

[*]According to legend the Stone of Scone, over which Cromwell had been enthroned, was supposed to groan if the sitter was royal and stay silent if he was a pretender. There is no record of how the stone responded on this occasion.

*The Coronation Chair in which English and British monarchs have been enthroned since 1308.
The chair was removed from Westminster Abbey for the one and only time in its history for the
king-making ceremony in Westminster Hall that was Cromwell's second investiture.*

prospective bridegroom of Cromwell's youngest daughter, Frances; the eldest son of the Parliamentarian commander Baron Robartes of Truro;* and the Irish peer Baron Sherard of Leitram, whom in true journalist fashion the official news-sheet reporting the investiture described incorrectly as Lord Sherwood. Once outside Westminster Hall his Highness entered his state coach, still in his regal robes. Accompanying him were his son Richard and, with the drawn swords they had borne at the investiture, the Earl of Warwick, Bulstrode Whitelocke, Viscount Lisle and Edward Montague. The coach was attended by the Protectoral Life Guard, the Yeomen of the Guard and officers of the College of Arms on horseback. Immediately behind the coach rode Master of the Horse John Claypole leading 'the horse of honour in rich comparisons'. Following on behind Claypole on the journey back to Whitehall were the coaches of the judiciary and state and civic dignitaries, 'the whole being managed with state and magnificence suitable to so high and happy a solemnity'. That evening 'were great proclaimings of joy and gladness, both in London, Westminster and the surrounding towns, villages and hamlets'.

Thus ended the coronation without a crown that was the second investiture of Oliver Cromwell as Lord Protector. Not only was there no crown but those 'worst dregs of popery and feudalism' of which the coronation was compounded, to use the words of the editor of the *Times* writing in 1831 at the time of William IV's coronation, were also dispensed with.[13] But then 'all coronations have differences in detail as they reflect the wishes of the monarch at the time' even though 'the essentials of the coronation ceremony do not change and date from the time of Edgar who was crowned as the first King of all England in 973'.[14] And it was the retention of the already seven centuries old essentials of the coronation ceremony at his second investiture that made Cromwell truly a King in all but name. There was the bestowal of the traditional regal 'emblems of government and authority', the princely habit, kingly sword and royal sceptre. (Interestingly, the presentation of the Bible was not a permanent feature of the coronation ritual but would become so with the crowning of William and Mary in 1689.) Cromwell had also taken the required coronation oath. Then there were those other requisite processes called election and recognition embracing the idea that while a King may indeed be appointed by God he must also be his subjects' elected choice, hereditary right notwithstanding, and formally recognised as such. The election involved the eve-of-coronation elevation or 'secular' enthronement of the monarch by bishops and nobles in Westminster Hall. As Cromwell's entire investiture was held in Westminster Hall, and was almost completely secular anyhow, then the election elevation, in the presence of nobles, as custom dictated, and puritan divines instead of bishops, could be deemed to have taken place at the same time as his enthronement in the

---

*Illustrative of the web of complex interrelationships which characterises the nobility, Baron Robartes's first wife had been the Earl of Warwick's daughter and his second and current wife was the earl's niece.[12]

A contemporary representation of Cromwell's second investiture. The figures at the outer edges of the picture are his Highness's Yeomen of the Guard. They are dressed in the Protector's own 'sumptuous' livery and armed, like their royal counterparts, with halberts.

Coronation Chair, another essential element in a king-making ceremony which normally occurred during the coronation proper across the way in Westminster Abbey. As for the recognition, this takes place at the beginning of a coronation when the monarch is presented to the assembled company as their undoubted sovereign, to whom is owed their homage and service, and this is followed by repeated acclamations. Cromwell's recognition could be said to have been at the end of the ceremony after his enthronement when all persons were required to yield him due obedience and those present gave their assent by repeated cries of 'God save the Lord Protector'. This approximates to the point in a coronation ceremony when the monarch is crowned, after which there are repeated cries of 'God save the King'.

Clarendon said of this second investiture of Cromwell as Lord Protector that there was 'nothing wanting to a perfect formal coronation but a crown and an archbishop', which is perfectly true. Cromwell was, however, made a King nonetheless. The crown is not actually that significant even though the crowning of a monarch marks the climax of the coronation ceremony. Indeed, in medieval coronations it was the sceptre rather than the crown which was regarded as the ultimate symbol of royal power as it seems to have been at Cromwell's investiture. Certainly his ten pounds in weight solid gold sceptre was a pretty substantial emblem of regality. And that is all the crown and sceptre really are, simply outward displays of the royal dignity, the trappings of sovereignty, along with the other insignia of office like the princely robe and sword. What makes a King is the process of election and recognition and the taking of the oath, which was something that was obviously well understood by those who had devised Cromwell's second investiture.

As for the want of an archbishop, in the context of a Protestant coronation the ministrations of the Archbishop of Canterbury were not strictly necessary. (Episcopacy had in any case been abolished by Parliament in 1646 and this was reconfirmed in article twelve of the Humble Petition and Advice.) As well as investing sovereigns with the symbols of regality, including the crown, the Primate of all England also anointed them with holy oil, a rite which was supposed to signify divine approbation. But the first Protestant Archbishop of Canterbury, Thomas Cranmer, took the view that these observances were a means whereby the papacy had sought to exercise control over monarchs by encroaching on their sovereignty and possessed no validity whatsoever. As he advised Edward VI (who was the archbishop's godson) at the time of the nine-year-old King's coronation in 1547: 'The Bishops of Canterbury for the most part have crowned your predecessors and anointed them Kings of this land, yet it is not in their power to receive or reject them, neither did it give them authority to prescribe them conditions to take or leave their crowns.' Cranmer, who was martyred nine years later under the Catholic Queen, Mary Tudor, went on to opine that 'King's be God's anointed, not in respect of the oil which the bishop useth but in consideration of their power, which is ordained, of their sword, which is authorised, of their persons, which are elected by God and imbued with the gifts of the spirit for the better ruling and guiding of his people. The oil, if added, is but a ceremony; if it be wanting that King is yet a perfect monarch notwithstanding and God's anointed as well as if he was inoiled.'[15]

Edward VI was, of course, of the blood royal which was generally regarded as an essential prerequisite to kingship, even for usurpers. This did not apply to Cromwell, although the Royalist antiquary Anthony à Wood claimed that 'when Oliver gaped after the Protectorship it was given out by those of his party that he was descended of the royal blood and had right to the crown of England'. The basis of this claim was supposed to have been the fact that Oliver's mother's maiden name was Steward, of which Stuart is a variation.[16] There were, however, lawyers who believed that a King's title rested as much on accomplished fact, which presumably announced God's choice, as on blood and descent. In 1652, when Cromwell was allegedly sounding out Bulstrode Whitelocke on the possibility of a restoration of the monarchy with himself as King, the then Lord General of the Army was supposed to have told Whitelocke that 'I have heard some of your profession observe that he who is actually King, whether by election or by descent, being once a King, all acts done by him as King are lawful and justifiable, as by any King who hath the crown by inheritance from his forefathers'.[17] Certainly blood and descent did not enter into the equation when the crown was eventually offered to Cromwell. Rather, it was because 'God who puts down and sets up another, and gives the kingdoms of the world to whomsoever he pleaseth', had 'by a series of Providence[s] raised you [Cromwell] to be a deliverer to these nations and made you more able to govern us in peace and prosperity than any other whatsoever'.[18] So to his supporters Oliver already possessed sufficient God-given attributes required of a King. Not least there was military prowess, which is supposed to imply spiritual strength. For this reason Cromwellians would have subscribed fully to the sentiments expressed in Voltaire's tragedy, *Mérope*, nearly a century later:

> The first King was a soldier, blest by Fate.
> Who serves his country well, needs no high ancestors.[19]

So Cromwell could be regarded as a perfect monarch, notwithstanding the absence of royal blood and the sacerdotal ingredients of a traditional coronation. 'I did always believe this Parliament would make him King before they parted', Sir Henry Vane had written in February 1657. And there were those on both sides of the political divide who perceived that this was precisely what had happened. 'His Highness was sworn Royal Protector . . . and had all the formalities as all the Kings had but a crown', ran one pro-Cromwellian description of Oliver's second investiture. While a Royalist account of the event similarly concluded that Cromwell had indeed been made 'Protector Royal'.[20]

In the days following his second investiture Cromwell was proclaimed, to the ringing of church bells, Lord Protector once again 'throughout the three kingdoms of England, Scotland and Ireland', only this time under the revised constitution and with increased grandeur as befitted his new status as *de jure* King. The proclamation, on July 1, at the points in the capital where new sovereigns were traditionally proclaimed must have made a brave sight, the size of the company taking part in the ceremony being as large as it was colourful. The assemblage moving out of the Palace of Whitehall on that July morning comprised, in order of each element's position in the procession, messengers of the Protector's Privy Council, trumpeters, his Highness's Life Guard, trumpeters again, the Protectoral version of the royal Gentlemen of the Privy Chamber, more trumpeters, 'divers officers of the army, gallantly mounted', yet more trumpeters, then Sergeants-at-Arms carrying their maces. Next came his Highness's heralds in their richly emblazoned tabards with Norroy King of Arms and, between two gentlemen ushers, Garter, Principal King of Arms, and finally his Highness's Privy Council and the principal Secretary of State in their coaches. The numbers were swelled and the colour greatly increased when the procession reached Temple Bar. Here it was joined by the Lord Mayor of London on horseback, in his crimson velvet gown and collar of Ss. Accompanying him was the Recorder and aldermen in their scarlet robes, also on horseback, the City mace-bearer, the City sword-bearer, wearing his cap of maintenance (the large fur head-dress still worn today), and another complement of trumpeters. The procession moved on into the City flowing through the narrow, medieval streets like a glistening multi-hued river. It paused at the designated places to proclaim Oliver anew in the time-honoured way and heard the people's thrice-uttered acclamation in reply: 'Long live the Lord Protector'. Obviously this splendour could not be matched by other cities and towns. But some in their own way came close to it. Gloucester's proclamation ceremony, which took place on 11 July, was particularly impressive. Afterwards, to musical accompaniment, cakes were distributed and French wine flowed in abundance.

Demonstrably royal letters patent for one of the Cromwellian hereditary peerages which the Protector began creating soon after his king-making second investiture.

That night there were bonfires and the ringing of bells throughout the city. Commenting upon this moment in Cromwell's rule Clarendon said of the Lord Protector that 'his greatness seemed to be very much established both at home and abroad as if it could never be shaken'.[21]

Within a month of his king-making second investiture Cromwell would demonstrate the true nature of his new status by exercising a prerogative only available to those occupying the office of King – the creation of hereditary peers. On 20 July the one-time Royalist and ex-Captain of his Highness's Life Guard, Charles Howard, was made Viscount Morpeth and Baron Gilsland. The richly ornamented letters patent for a Cromwellian hereditary peerage depict Oliver as what he is, a King. He is wearing royal robes and holds a sceptre in his right hand. Addressed 'To all and singular dukes, marquesses, earls, viscounts, barons, knights, provosts, freemen, and all our officers, ministers and subjects whatsoever to whom these letters shall come greeting', this manifestly regal document solemnly declares that 'Amongst other of the prerogatives which adorn the imperial crown of these nations none is of greater excellency or doth more amplify our favours than to be the fountain of honour'.[22] The use of terms such as 'our . . . subjects' and 'the imperial crown of these nations' says it all. Because of its close proximity to Cromwell's investiture one could stretch a point and describe Howard's ennoblement as a coronation peerage, a continuation of the practice, going back to the fourteenth century, by which monarch's marked their investiture with a special creation of peerages.

Although Charles Howard was the first to be elevated to the hereditary peerage by Cromwell, another kind of hereditary honour, that of baronet, had already begun to be conferred by the Lord Protector. Originally instituted by James I in 1611 to be granted to those who contributed to the expense of the Plantation of Ulster and later to the Plantation of Nova Scotia, the dignity of baronet constitutes the lowest hereditary titled order and ranks next below that of baron. Unlike barons though baronets are commoners and not peers of the realm. And like knights, over whose orders they take precedence, except that of the Garter, they bear the title Sir. The first Cromwellian baronetcy was conferred on 25 June 1657, the day before the king-making ceremony of the second investiture, which means that this, like Howard's hereditary peerage, could be described as a coronation honour. Ironically the recipient of the first Cromwellian baronetcy was John Read of Brocket Hall in Hertfordshire. A one-time Royalist, Read had been created a baronet by Charles I in 1642 but as this had not been recognised by Parliament or the Commonwealth Oliver gave him a new patent. The irony lies in the fact that Cromwell, as Lord Protector, was using the royal prerogative to confirm an honour originally bestowed by his royal predecessor contrary to what had been the consideration of both Parliament and the republic. And Read was not the only recipient of a disallowed Carolean baronetcy to be 'indulged with a new patent by Oliver'.[23]

Others honoured with a baronetcy by the Protector, which numbered in all about a dozen, included John Claypole, who received his baronetcy on 20 July 1657. Because of its close proximity to Oliver's investiture this too could be regarded as a coronation honour. Soon, from November 1657, there would be other honours. These were knighthoods conferred by Cromwell's son, Henry, after he had officially become Lord Deputy in Ireland. This was once again the restoration of a traditional practice under the monarchy, the royal prerogative of dubbing Knights Bachelor being inherent in the office of Lord Deputy as the representative of the sovereign in Ireland. Henry, very much the Viceroy (he had his own court, including a yeoman of the guard-style personal bodyguard), created fourteen knights in all during his tenure of office, usually at Dublin Castle. Oliver created about forty knights, of which Henry himself was one.[24]

In the same month of July 1657 yet more regal splendour was added to that which had already been attached to the kingly office of Lord Protector. The Privy Council gave its approval for new coats to be issued to the twenty-seven watermen who rowed the Protectoral barge and for the bargemaster and his assistant to wear his Highness's livery. The watermen and bargemasters' badges, portraying the original and decidedly republican arms of the Commonwealth,

Design for the badge to be worn by Cromwell's bargemasters and watermen in intentionally direct imitation of previous royal insignia following the assimilation of the office of Protector to the kingly dignity. This badge would also be worn by the Protectoral court lacqueys and Yeomen of the Guard, making them distinguishable from their royal counterparts only by the colour of their livery.

were exchanged for new ones representing the demonstrably royal arms of the Protectorate. These were to be worn on the front and the back of the watermen's and bargemasters' coats with the added embellishment of the letters O and P in gilt, one on either side of the top section of the badge in intentionally direct imitation of the insignia worn by previous royal watermen and bargemasters. In the reign of Charles I the letters displayed with the royal arms would, of course, have been C and R. In itself this single example, among so many, of more royal magnificence surrounding the Protector is of no great matter. But its timing, immediately after Cromwell's second investiture, does point up the complete assimilation of the Protectorship to the royal dignity.[25]

CHAPTER 9

Much Mirth With Frolics

Along with the complete assimilation of the Protectorship to the royal dignity life
at the Protectoral court now began to resemble even more closely life at previous
royal courts. This is no more exemplified than by two events which took place in
November 1657. These were the marriages of Cromwell's two youngest
daughters, Mary and Frances, 'gentlewomen of good virtue and modesty' one
influential Royalist was prepared to concede.[1] As befitted the daughters of a King
their weddings were to be even grander affairs than the splendid Whitehall Palace
nuptials of Cromwell's niece, Lavinia Whetstone, early in the previous year. Not
surprisingly perhaps the Protector's daughters were referred to as princesses.
This was particularly apt in Frances's case because, with her proposed marriage
to Charles II, she had already been viewed as a potential sacrifice on the altar of
dynastic expediency, the fate of many a royal princess.

Frances, now nineteen and the younger of the two by about a year, was the first
to be married. She was finally allowed to wed Robert Rich, the twenty-three year
old grandson, namesake and heir of Robert Rich, second Earl of Warwick.

Cromwell's second youngest daughter, Mary.
In November 1657 she and her younger sister,
Frances, married into the old nobility. The
nuptials of these two Protectoral princesses
were effectively royal weddings and celebrated
as such.

Warwick was, to quote Clarendon, a man of 'great estate and thoroughly engaged in the war from the beginning'. As a young man he had been a royal courtier and although amply endowed with the necessary wit and refinement for such a role he would nevertheless abandon court life for more energetic pursuits – colonial expansion and development combined with a successful career as a privateer. Puritan by background and personal inclination with leanings towards Presbyterianism, he became a prominent opponent of Charles I's religious and fiscal policies, giving succour to the Puritan cause and engaging in forthright opposition to the King's schemes for raising revenue without parliamentary consent. Naturally, in the Civil War he was a staunch supporter of Parliament, in whose name he seized the King's navy, becoming its Lord High Admiral. Warwick was no supporter of Charles's execution though or the abolition of the House of Lords and soon after the establishment of the republic, which executed his brother, the Earl of Holland, for treason in March 1649, he retired into private life. The earl became, however, an enthusiastic upholder of the Protectorate and admirer of Cromwell, who was also his friend. He played a highly significant role in Oliver's coronation without the crown. As well as carrying the sword of state before the Protector he assisted in vesting Cromwell with 'a robe of purple velvet, lined with ermine, being the habit anciently used at the solemn investiture of princes', so that 'this promotion might not be without any vote from the nobility'.

This calls to mind, although there is no direct parallel, that other period of internecine strife, the Wars of the Roses, two centuries before. Then another Earl of Warwick, Richard Neville the 'Kingmaker', raised up and deposed rival Yorkist and Lancastrian claimants to the throne at will. One of the offspring of this Earl of Warwick, a daughter, too married into the ruling House, becoming the consort of Richard III. But there exists a far less oblique link with the past than this fourteenth-century 'proud setter up and puller down of Kings'. In the 1530s Richard Rich, the great-great-great-grandfather of Frances Cromwell's bridegroom and the founder of his family's fortune, had ridden to influence on the back of Oliver's great-great-great-uncle, Thomas Cromwell, and then advanced himself still further by giving evidence against his former patron when Thomas fell out of favour with the King, Henry VIII, in 1540. Now, a century later, the Cromwell and Rich families were to be formally and agreeably entwined by the forthcoming nuptials.

This happy union, however, had not been without its obstacles. The relationship between Frances Cromwell and Robert Rich can be dated to at least late January/early February 1657 at the time of John Ashe's formal tentative proposal that the Protector should take the crown. This is known because in his communiqué conveying this intelligence the French ambassador also reported that 'his [Cromwell's] eldest son, to make himself agreeable to the Presbyterians, attends their chapel, and it is rumoured that one of his daughters is to marry the grandson of the Earl of Warwick, one of the leaders of the sect'. Problems over the match were such that even at the height of the kingship debate the matter reportedly exercised the minds of the Protector and Protectress more than anything else. And in June 1657 Mary Cromwell was writing to her brother in Ireland about 'this business of my sister Frances and Mr Rich', over which, Mary

Robert Rich, second Earl of Warwick, who was a prime mover in forging an alliance between his family and the ruling House of Cromwell through the marriage of his grandson to Frances Cromwell.

confided, 'for these three months I think our family, and myself in particular, have been [in] the greatest confusion and trouble as ever [a] poor family can be'. The Protector's intransigence concerning his youngest daughter's marriage was at the heart of this 'confusion and trouble'. It seems that as far as Cromwell was concerned the amount of money to be settled on Robert Rich by his grandfather, the Earl of Warwick, when Rich married Frances was insufficient. Consequently negotiations over the 'business' of the marriage were broken off. Mary Cromwell suspected that the financial obstacles which her father had erected were only a pretext. The real reason for the obstructionism was connected to reports that Cromwell had received portraying Robert Rich as a young man given to dissipation. This had been one of the reasons that the Protector was supposed to have given for his objection to the marriage of Frances to Charles II. Even after the reports about Rich had proved to be false Cromwell continued to quibble over the sum to be settled on the hopeful bridegroom in spite of the Earl of Warwick's attempts to be accommodating. 'I fear my Lord Protector does not mean you shall have his daughter, his demands are so high. . . . I assure you nothing could have made me come to half that I have offered but seeing your great affection to my Lady Frances and her good respect to you', wrote the Earl of Warwick to what must have been a very disappointed grandson.[2]

But Frances Cromwell was to prove as resolute in love as her father had been in battle. 'I must tell you privately', Mary confided to her brother Henry on the matter of her sister and Robert Rich's problematic marriage plans, 'that they are so far engaged as the match cannot be broken off. She [Frances] acquainted none of her friends with her resolution when she did it. . . . I think I ought to beg of God to pardon her in her doing of this thing.' Frances had apparently attempted to force the issue by anticipating her wedding night, something which Mary conceded her sister was driven to by the unsatisfactory state of affairs. Not that the couple were without the odd powerful ally. Robert Rich's maternal grandmother, who had been kept abreast of the progress of events by the Earl of Warwick, lent moral support. In a letter to her grandson, in which Frances Cromwell is described as 'the most excellent and principal person to whom all your devotions are addressed', she writes: 'I am extremely glad to hear that you find yourself better in your health. I beseech you for these few days neglect nothing that may improve it. Though you slight a cold yet others look upon it with trouble. Care of yourself will now be more considerable than ever that this romance may receive a happy close.' And therein lies the probable true reason for Cromwell's objection to the marriage between Frances and the grandson of his firm friend and great admirer, the Earl of Warwick. Robert Rich's health was indeed a problem. In fact he was suffering from the potentially fatal disease of scrofula, or the 'King's Evil'. Rich's solicitous maternal grandmother, who addressed him as 'Sweet Robin', was the Dowager Countess of Devonshire, that same Dowager Countess of Devonshire whose son had been killed by Cromwell's regiment in the Civil War and who somehow managed to combine zeal for Charles II's cause with a willingness to be of service to the Protectoral regime.[3]

In spite of the dowager countess's optimism the business would rumble on unresolved for some time to come. Major hiccups along the way came with the offer of the crown to Cromwell and the proposed marriage of Frances to Charles II, as illustrated by that piece of private correspondence sent from London to Paris in late March 1657: 'There was likely to have been a match between the Earl of Warwick's grandchild and the Protector's daughter, but this new dignity [kingship] has altered it. It is reported that a match may be found in your parts.' A settlement which allowed Frances Cromwell to marry the man of her choice was, however, finally agreed to in August 1657, the arrangements being concluded with the Earl of Warwick by Secretary of State John Thurloe and two Protectoral Privy Councillors. Royal marriages, which this effectively was, are of necessity more than simply affairs of the heart, they are also matters of state. Hence the involvement of a state functionary and two state dignitaries.[4]

As with most significant events in the lives of the Protector and his family the wedding was dished up for public consumption in all its essential detail by the press. *Mercurius Politicus* for 11 November 1657 reported that 'this day the most illustrious lady, the Lady Frances Cromwell, youngest daughter of his Highness the Lord Protector, was married to the most noble gentleman, Mr Robert Rich, son of Lord Rich, grandchild of the Earl of Warwick and the Countess Dowager of Devonshire, in the presence of their Highnesses and his grandfather and father and the said countess, with many other persons of high honour and quality. The solemnities of the happy nuptials were continued and ended with much honour.'[5]

The most detailed account of Frances Cromwell's wedding was penned by the Royalist and anti-Cromwellian William Dugdale: 'On Wednesday last was my Lord Protector's daughter married to the Earl of Warwick's grandson. Mr Scobell, as Justice of the Peace, tied the knot after a godly prayer made by one of his Highness's divines. And on Thursday was the wedding feast kept at Whitehall where they had 48 violins and 50 trumpets and much mirth with frolics besides mixed dancing (a thing heretofore accounted profane) 'till 5 of the clock yesterday morning. Amongst the dancers there was the Earl of Newport who danced with her Highness. There was at this great solemnity the Countess of Devonshire (grandmother to the bridegroom) who presented the bride with £2,000 worth of plate.'[6] The '48 violins' was a general term for an orchestra comprising that number of string instruments. The one performing at the court of Protector Oliver had a half-size counterpart at the court of Louis XIV. This was known as the King's Twenty-Four Violins, which the exiled Charles II was so taken with that he instituted a similar orchestra of his own after the Restoration. Similarly '50 trumpets' was a general term for a wind band which included oboes, drums and other instruments.[7]

One oft-quoted Royalist anecdote of this glittering affair tells of Cromwell's alleged boorishness: 'The Protector threw about sack posset [a drink made of hot milk and white wine] among all the ladies to soil their rich clothes, which they took as a favour . . . and daubed all the stools where they were to sit with sweetmeats.' He also pulled off the bridegroom's wig 'and would have thrown it into the fire but he did not, yet he sat upon it.' If this were true then it could be interpreted as yet more evidence of the re-establishment of traditions associated with royalty – having to endure a monarch's unreasonable behaviour without giving the impression that you may not be enjoying it as much as he is.[8]

Once more the ex-royal Palace of Whitehall echoed to the sound of princely celebrations attended by the essential high-born guests, high-born guests which were now related to the ruling House of Cromwell. This even extended to her Highness the Protectress's dancing partner, the Earl of Newport. The eldest of three illegitimate sons of the Dowager Countess of Devonshire's father-in-law, the first Earl of Devonshire, Newport was also the Earl of Warwick's half-brother (they shared the same mother). Something of an oddity, Mountjoy Blount, first Earl of Newport, displayed such capriciousness in the Civil War that it is difficult to tell precisely whose side he was supposed to be on. By 1655, however, he was said to have been one of the chief correspondents in England of Edward Hyde, later the Earl of Clarendon, principal adviser of the exiled Charles II. Newport's go-between was probably his countess who was in the habit of travelling from England to the Continent on passes issued by the Protectorate government, even attending the royal court in exile. This led to the one-time Royalist turned Cromwellian agent, Colonel Joseph Bampfield, recommending that the countess be apprehended and examined. Newport had himself fallen foul of the Protectoral regime. In 1655 he was committed to the Tower for a time on suspicion of treason.[9] None of this seems to have stood in the way of the Earl of Newport providing aristocratic adornment to the wedding of Cromwell's youngest daughter.

Like the guest list the father of the bride was sartorially more than equal to the occasion. For what was to all intents and purposes a royal wedding the Lord Protector was resplendently attired in a shirt of fine linen trimmed with a richly laced neckband and cuffs, a costly doublet and breeches 'of the Spanish fashion' made of uncut grey velvet, a pair of silk stockings with shoestrings and gold-laced garters to match and gold-buttoned shoes of black Spanish leather.[10] This image is somewhat removed from the impression gained by the Royalist Sir Philip Warwick of Cromwell as a relatively obscure Member of Parliament for Cambridge: 'The first time that I ever took notice of him was in the very beginning of the Parliament held in November 1640 when I vainly thought myself a courtly young gentleman (for we courtiers valued ourselves much upon our good clothes). I came one morning into the House well clad and perceived a gentleman speaking (whom I knew not) very ordinarily apparelled, for it was a plain cloth suit which seemed to have been made by an ill [i.e. unskilful] country tailor. His linen was plain and not very clean, and I remember a speck or two of blood upon his little band which was not much larger than his collar. His hat was without a hat-band.'[11] Similarly, when he forcibly dissolved the Rump of that same Parliament in April 1653 the, by then, Lord General Cromwell 'came into the House clad in plain black clothes with grey worsted stockings'.[12]

Cromwell may well have 'preferred the little ornaments of the soul before those of the body', as his hagiographer Samuel Carrington seemed to think, but as Lord Protector he could ill afford to act on these sentiments. 'I lived to see this very gentleman', Sir Philip Warwick further relates, 'by multiplied good successes and by real (but usurped) power, having a better tailor and more converse among good company . . . appear of a great and majestic deportment and comely presence.' Sir Philip had witnessed this 'in my own eye when for six weeks together I was a prisoner in his [the Protector's] sergeant's hands and daily waited at Whitehall'. It was his Royalism which had led to Sir Philip's brief detention in 1655 by the Cromwellian regime. But although he enjoyed the trust of Royalist leaders this Carolean courtier never overtly involved himself in plots against the Protector's government, hence his release after only six weeks. During that time he had witnessed the comings and goings at the very centre of Protectoral power and been allowed to see for himself the changes wrought on Oliver by his elevated status.[13]

It was because of Cromwell's elevated status that the ex-royal Palace of Whitehall echoed once more to the sound of princely celebrations. Any doubts that this was not to all intents and purposes a royal wedding are laid by the following newsletter dated 17 November 1657. 'The solemnities of the nuptials Wednesday and Thursday last were kept with much privacy and honour, several of the nobility being then entertained according to their quality, and as that occasion required their joy being answered by the City's ringing of bells and by the firing [of] great guns from the Tower.' The key phrase is 'as the occasion required', the ringing of the City's bells and the discharge of ordnance from the Tower of London being the precise manner in which such royal occasions had previously been marked. The last of these would have been the marriage of Charles I to Henrietta Maria in 1625.[14]

Like most royal weddings Frances Cromwell's marriage and the forthcoming nuptials of her older sister were very much *the* current events. This is borne out by private correspondence of the time. In one letter, dated 14 November 1657, the writer states tersely: 'Little news, only the great wedding at court on Wednesday last, and continues yet; the Lord Fauconberg with the Lady Mary will be next, all things being concluded.' Another piece of correspondence, this time dated 17 November, informs us that 'the discourse of the town has been much filled up with the great marriage at Whitehall, which was solemnised there three or four days last week with music, dancing and great feasting, and now begins for two or three days at the Earl of Warwick's. The marriage of the other sister to Lord Fauconberg they say is concluded.' The writer signs off with an afterthought in which he divulges some titbits concerning Frances Cromwell's recent nuptials: 'I forgot to tell you that amongst other lesser presents to the bride the Lady Devonshire gave some pieces of chamber plate all of gold with one they call the *pièce royal*: 'tis such as I have seen used for the waiter to carry a glass upon. The Lady Claypole's was two sconces of £100 apiece, they say; and somebody I heard presented a good quantity of Barbary wine.'[15]

Negotiations concerning Mary's marriage had been almost as prolonged as her sister's, having begun with that Paris meeting between Fauconberg and Ambassador Lockhart in March 1657. And like Frances, in the months between the inception and completion of Mary's marriage arrangements there was speculation involving other possibilities. In Mary's case though there were two alternative, rather surprising, 'suitors'. Both were Royalists – the Duke of Buckingham and the Earl of Chesterfield. This is particularly interesting in the light of the complaint that Royalists 'very much confined their marriages and alliances within their own party'. At least that was supposed to have been the situation in 1655. But much had happened since then. George Villiers, second Duke of Buckingham, had, in the spring of 1657, removed himself from the court of Charles II after he had incurred the King's displeasure 'because of some slight suspicion of loyalty'. He then asked permission to return to England to make his peace with Cromwell. The request was granted, together with a promise that should an accommodation not be made the duke could return to the Continent. This was to the 'general astonishment' according to the Venetian envoy. Also according to the Venetian envoy 'they even talk of a marriage between the duke and a daughter of his Highness', who is regarded as being Mary. All of which is corroborated in correspondence between Clarendon and Charles II's secretary, Sir Edward Nicholas: 'The Duke of Buckingham is, I believe, in London. A petition has been delivered in his name to Cromwell and graciously received. And it is said he shall have one of the young princesses.' In the event the Duke of Buckingham married another Mary, the only child of Cromwell's old Commander-in-Chief in the New Model Army, Sir Thomas Fairfax. In the reign of Charles II Buckingham became a notable wit, literary figure, politician and, even by Restoration standards, notorious rake. As Mary Fairfax was to discover, marriage to the Duke of Buckingham would have been as gruesome for Mary Cromwell as a union with Charles II would have been for Frances Cromwell had the Protector agreed to such a match. Mary Fairfax was originally betrothed to Philip Stanhope, second Earl of Chesterfield, that other Royalist nobleman with whom Mary Cromwell's name had been linked. Chesterfield claimed that the Protector had offered him a command in the army and the hand of one of his daughters, again taken to be Mary, which he refused.[16]

Mary may not have married the Duke of Buckingham or the Earl of Chesterfield but, like her sister Frances, she would nevertheless form a creditable enough alliance by marrying into the old nobility. Arrangements for the marriage were eventually concluded to everyone's satisfaction, enabling Thurloe to write to Henry Cromwell in Ireland on 3 November 1657 to the effect that: 'I suppose I need not acquaint you that my Lord Fauconberg is a servant of my Lady Mary. He is a person of very good abilities and seems very sober. His estate is £5,000 per annum. I believe it will be a match.' The wedding took place at Hampton Court on 18 November and was a rather more muted, but in its own way no less regal, affair than the Whitehall nuptials of Frances a week earlier. It too received press coverage: 'Yesterday afternoon', reported *Mercurius Politicus* for 19 November, 'his Highness went to Hampton Court and this day the most illustrious lady, the Lady Mary Cromwell, third daughter of his Highness the Lord Protector, was there married to the most noble lord, the Lord Fauconberg, in the presence of their Highnesses and many noble persons.'[17]

The wedding featured an entertainment written by the unofficial Protectoral poet laureate, Andrew Marvell, whose long sought-after post of Latin secretary in the Cromwellian civil service had recently been confirmed. Marvell's wedding entertainment took the form of *Two Songs at the Marriage of the Lord Fauconberg and the Lady Mary Cromwell*. In the first of these, a two-character musical dialogue with chorus, the bride appeared as Cynthia, the moon goddess, and the bridegroom as Endymion, the handsome and perpetually youthful shepherd with whom, in Greek mythology, the moon goddess falls in love. When it came to initiative in love, however, the roles were reversed: 'poetic convention, as well as Marvell's admiration for the Protector demanded that the suitor's humility and the boldness of his suit should be exaggerated'. The final chorus begins:

> Joy to Endymion
> For he has Cynthia's favour won.
> And Jove himself approves
> With his serenest influence their Loves.

Cromwell himself is thought to have played the non-vocal role of the approving Jove, father and king of the gods in Roman mythology. The next two lines, 'For he did never love to pair/His Progeny above the Air', are regarded as a possible allusion to the proposed marriage between Mary Cromwell's younger sister Frances and Charles II. A more direct, and rather risqué, reference to Frances appears in the second chorus:

> Anchises was a Shepherd too;
> Yet is her younger Sister laid
> Sporting with him in Ida's shade.

Anchises, whose beauty captivated Aphrodite, the Greek goddess of beauty and sensual love, resulting in her bearing him Aeneas, the Trojan hero, is obviously meant to be Robert Rich. While 'Yet is her younger Sister laid/Sporting with him in Ida's shade' (Ida was a mountain in the vicinity of Troy) alludes to Frances Cromwell taking 'the boldest step' in order to make her marriage to Robert Rich 'necessary' by anticipating her wedding night. Now that Frances was safely married her precipitous action could presumably be treated with amused indulgence.[18]

Marvell's second offering is in similar vein to the first. Its single chorus begins and ends on a note of unalloyed optimism with:

> Joy to that happy Pair,
> Whose Hopes united banish our Despair

The choruses of Marvell's *Two Songs* would most probably have been sung by the vocalists among the Gentlemen of his Highness's Musique, together with the two boys in training, under the direction of Master of the Music John Hingston. The music itself and the name of the composer are both lost to posterity.[19] Andrew Marvell's *Two Songs at the Marriage of the Lord Fauconberg and the Lady Mary Cromwell* are seen as belonging 'to the same revival of interest in the drama as Davenant's *Entertainment at Rutland House* (May 1656): it is also an attempt, though on a much smaller scale, to reconcile Puritanism and the stage, on lines laid down by *Comus*, with music as an excuse for acting'.[20] *Comus* was a masque written by John Milton and performed at Ludlow Castle in 1634. Unlike traditional masques, however, it relied little on spectacle and was more in the

Andrew Marvell, Cromwellian civil servant and unofficial Protectoral poet laureate. The entertainments he wrote for Mary Cromwell's wedding represented a revival, albeit in shadowy form, of royal court masques.

nature of a pastoral drama, which is also a fair description of Marvell's *Two Songs*. Thus it could be said that 'Protector Oliver's court witnessed the revival, albeit in extremely shadowy form, of those magnificent masques which had helped to make the courts of the first two Stuarts among the most extravagant in Europe'.[21] Sir William Davenant, too, invoked the Muse to mark Viscount Fauconberg and Mary Cromwell's union by writing an Epithalamium, a song or poem which flourished as a literary form during the Renaissance. This has been cited as another example of the pardoned Royalist's excessiveness in his attempts to curry favour with the Cromwellian regime.[22]

Although *Mercurius Politicus* had gone on to report that the Protector and Protectress, together with the newly married couple, returned to Whitehall from Hampton Court the day after the wedding, the celebrations obviously continued for several more days. 'This week hath in great part been taken up solemnising the marriage of my Lady Mary with my Lord Fauconberg. They were married at Hampton Court upon Thursday', wrote Thurloe to Henry Cromwell in Ireland four days after the nuptials. Thurloe goes on to express the opinion that the Protector's new son-in-law 'is a person of very great parts and sobriety and I hope his Highness and his family will have comfort in him'. The Secretary of State's conviction was justified and his hopes fulfilled. Not only did Thomas Bellasyse, second Viscount Fauconberg, prove a worthy consort to a daughter of the ruling House but, in the short time left to the regime, he was also a loyal functionary of the Cromwellian Protectorate, as he would be of the government of the restored Stuart King, Charles II. In the meantime Fauconberg would receive from his father-in-law, through a Protectoral court official, the sum of £15,000, this being 'the full marriage portion', or dowry, of Mary Cromwell.[23]

Both Protectoral princesses were married in accordance with the 1653 'Act touching Marriages and the Registring thereof'. This means that they were essentially civil ceremonies before two or more witnesses at which a Justice of the Peace, not a cleric, officiated. 'No other marriage whatsoever within the Commonwealth of England, after the 29th September, in the year one thousand six hundred and fifty-three', the act stipulated, 'shall be held or accompted a marriage according to the laws of England'. By secularising marriage in this way rites which were anathema to Puritans and which had been contained in the Book of Common Prayer, such as the use of the ring and the husband promising to worship his wife with his body, were eradicated leaving no possibility of ambiguity. Hence at Frances's wedding it was Clerk to the Protector's Privy Council Henry Scobell, in his capacity as a Justice of the Peace, who 'tied the knot, after a goodly prayer made by one of his Highness's divines'. But Clarendon, commenting upon the nuptials of the Protector's two daughters, which, he says, were celebrated 'with all imaginable pomp and lustre', states that 'it was observed that though the marriages were performed in public view according to the rites and ceremonies then in use, they were presently afterwards in private married by ministers ordained by bishops and according to the form in the Book of Common Prayer; and this with the privity of Cromwell who pretended to yield to it in compliance with the importunity and folly of his daughters'. In Mary's case this was supposed to have taken place at the little church of St Gregory by St Pauls which she and her older sister, Elizabeth Claypole, used privately to attend. The incumbent there, and probable officiant at Mary's second ceremony, was Dr John Hewett, an openly practising Anglican divine and overt Royalist who occasionally made collections in his church for the exiled King under the transparent disguise of urging the congregation 'to remember a distressed friend'.[24]

The 'royal' weddings of Mary and Frances Cromwell tell us a considerable amount about the Cromwellian regime. This is over and above the obvious fact that life at the Protectoral court was now beginning to resemble even more closely life at previous royal courts and that Cromwell's religious toleration, when it also involved paternal indulgence, knew no bounds. These nuptials demonstrate too that the likes of Mountjoy Blount, first Earl of Newport, and Christiana Cavendish, Dowager Countess of Devonshire, although they may have hankered after a return of the Stuarts, did not scruple to be seen at the court of Protector Oliver whose daughter had become the dowager countess's grandchild-in-law. Neither did the dowager countess stint herself in her generosity towards her 'dear Lady Frances' and 'Sweet Robin', whose union she herself had hoped for. It is difficult to believe that the motives of this Royalist noblewoman were entirely those of a doting grandmother at first anxious and then happy to see her ailing grandson achieve his hearts desire. The inference is that she may have begun positively to shift her allegiance, prompted by the possibility that, with the assimilation of the office of Protector to the royal dignity, Cromwell could yet make his position truly acceptable by taking the title King. The same might be said of the eccentric Earl of Newport, who, incidentally, would go on to compound his unconventionality by developing a belief in the wholly unfashionable creed of Quakerism.[25]

Other members of the old nobility clearly identified with the new order, a new order which now had all the appearance of the beginnings of a fresh royal dynasty. Amplification of the royal prerogative to create not just knights and baronets but also to confer hereditary peerages – new lions to join the old under a new throne – had already made Cromwell a reconstituted fount of honour and an upholder of the hereditary principle. At around the time of the 'royal' weddings of Mary and Frances Cromwell a new catalogue of Stuart honours, together with 'those made by his Highness', was selling in London 'at double the true worth of a book of that size'. Although the Protector may have courted the old nobility this was by no means a one-sided affair. While the second Viscount Fauconberg had indeed been 'reviewed by Cromwell as a possible husband for his third daughter Mary' the young viscount seems to have needed little persuasion to declare his unqualified, and fulsomely expressed, support both for the Protectoral regime and the offer of the crown to Oliver. And it is worth remembering that in the case of Frances Cromwell's match it was the Earl of Warwick who pressed for the marriage of his grandson to the youngest of the Protectoral princesses in the face of the Protector's concern regarding the young man's suitability. The earl's close association with the Protectoral regime and his admiration for Cromwell make it even less likely than it was in the case of the Dowager Countess of Devonshire that his motivation was solely the happiness of his grandson. A personal desire to see his family allied to the ruling House of Cromwell would almost certainly have been a consideration. 'Such pitiful slaves were the nobles of those days', was Lucy Hutchinson's comment, in hindsight, on the marriages of Cromwell's two youngest daughters. She was just as contemptuous of the honours bestowed by the Protector who 'wanted not many fools, both of the army and the gentry, to accept of, and strut in, his mock titles'. This is not to say that the old nobility, whether Royalist or Parliamentarian, beat a path to the Protectoral court in any great number. Like many another peer, the Earl of Manchester, one of Cromwell's Civil War Commanders-in-Chief, was 'a great stranger at Whitehall' during the Protectorate. Being much related to the Earl of Warwick – he had been married to Warwick's daughter and was currently married to his niece – clearly did not inspire Manchester to join his fellow Presbyterian in the role of Cromwellian courtier. He would, however, go on to take the Earl of Warwick's widow as the fourth of his five wives.[26]

CHAPTER 10

Tempest And Foul Weather

As far back as April 1653, eight months before the establishment of the Protectorate, one Royalist lady, Dorothy Osborne, had speculated about the opportunity lost in not marrying into the Cromwell family. Commenting upon the then General Cromwell's dissolution of the Rump by military force in a letter to her lover, also a Royalist, she wrote teasingly: 'If I had been so wise as to have taken hold of the offer made me by Henry Cromwell I might have been in a fair way of preferment, for sure they will be greater now than ever.'[1] The following month Henry married Elizabeth Russell whose family had fought on Parliament's side in the Civil War. At the time of writing it is unlikely that Dorothy Osborne could have had any idea just how great the Cromwells would become. As Oliver himself is alleged to have said: 'None climbs so high as he who knows not whither he is going.'

The heights to which Cromwell had climbed was exemplified in November 1657 by yet another example of Oliver functioning as a King and involved a custom whose origins dated from the reign of Edward I. This was the Trial of the Pyx by which samples of newly minted gold and silver coins were periodically placed in a pyx (boxwood vessel) to be tested for quality by a jury of London goldsmiths. The process was, and still is, supposed to ensure that the weight and purity of the coinage were being maintained to the correct standard. The last such trial had taken place in November 1649 by order of the Council of State. But that was in the days of the pre-Protectorate Commonwealth. Now, with a reversion to monarchy, the warrant commanding a Trial of the Pyx once more emanated from the sovereign, Protector Oliver. The actual trial took place on 3 December 1657 and the warrant authorising it was regal to the utmost degree.[2]

Something else which could be said to have regal implications occurred roughly contemporaneously with Cromwell's royally authorised Pyx. The Privy Council moved that the Protector be advised to make his eldest son, Richard, a Privy Councillor. That was on 8 December 1657. On 31 December *Mercurius Politicus* reported that 'this day the most illustrious lord, the Lord Richard Cromwell, took the oath of Privy Councillor and sat a member of his Highness's most honourable Privy Council'. Three years before his accession James I's eldest son, Charles, Prince of Wales, was sworn in as a member of his father's Privy Council 'for his better experience in matters of state'. As it had been for the heir to the royal throne of King James so it was with him whose destiny it would be to succeed to the Protectoral throne of Oliver Cromwell.[3]

It is hardly surprising, fitting even, that there should be a rapid acceleration at this time in the Protector's assumption of the trappings of monarchy. 'And now he models his house that it might have some resemblance unto a court, and his liveries and lacqueys and Yeomen of the Guard are known whom they belong unto by their habit.' This appears immediately after a brief description of Cromwell's second investiture in *Memoirs of the Reign of King Charles I with a continuation to the Happy Restoration of King Charles II* by the historian and Stuart courtier Sir Philip Warwick.[4] But what precisely does it mean? It means that the court lacqueys and Yeomen of the Guard, in addition to their Protectoral livery of velvet collared coat of grey cloth welted with velvet and silver and black silk lace, now wore the same regal device for a badge as the Protector's bargemasters and watermen, making them distinguishable from their royal counterparts only by the colour of their livery.

Sir Philip is also drawing attention to the fact that in the late autumn and winter of 1657/8 the Protectoral household was remodelled on more regal lines: 'And now he models his house that it might have some resemblance unto a court' – more evidence, if any were needed, of a total assimilation of the Protectorship to the royal dignity following Cromwell's second investiture. The post of Lord Chamberlain, the most senior royal court official who exercised overall control in the household, was reconstituted in December 1657. Sir Gilbert Pickering 'being so finical, spruce and like an old courtier, is made Lord Chamberlain of the Protector's household or court'. This is how one anti-government pamphlet, printed in what it describes as 'the fifth year of England's slavery under its new monarchy', reported Pickering's appointment. Sir Gilbert was formally presented with the traditional symbols of his office in February 1658. These were a key and a white wand which was customarily broken in half on the death of the sovereign. The lord chamberlainship had already been very briefly revived in 1655 amid intense speculation that Cromwell was about to accept the crown and its abandonment was, significantly, coincident with the kingship issue coming to nothing.[5]

Not all the posts found in a royal household were revived under the Cromwellian regime but then the Protectoral household never did achieve the scale and complexity of its immediate royal predecessors, nor was it as expensive to maintain. Two other senior posts that were reconstituted after Cromwell's second investiture were those of Comptroller and Cofferer of the Household. These were two of the officers who, in a royal court, ran the household below stairs. Traditionally the Comptroller and Cofferer had been members of the committee which scrutinised the expenditure of the household and arranged the purchase of supplies. This was known as the Board of Greencloth, the name being derived from the covering originally used on the table at which the committee conducted its business. The Board of Greencloth too was revived in both name and function after Cromwell's second investiture, with the Comptroller and

Privy Councillor Colonel Philip Jones who became Comptroller of the Household following the remodelling of the Protectoral household on more regal lines in the autumn and winter of 1657/8.

Cofferer of the Protectoral household taking their places on the board in direct imitation of their counterparts in previous royal households. Even the room in the Palace of Whitehall where the royal Board of Greencloth had previously met was cleared so that the Protectoral Board of Greencloth could meet in the same place.[6]

One important deviation from royal practice involved the status of high office holders in the Cromwellian household. Generally speaking in the past very senior court posts had been held by peers of the realm. Royal Lords Chamberlain, for instance, were usually earls. These posts also conferred on their holders ex officio membership of the Privy Council, giving them high positions in the administration. None of Cromwell's senior household officers had hereditary peerages and none was given one even though the Protector conferred such honours on others. Not even Lord Chamberlain of the Household Sir Gilbert Pickering's baronetcy (of Nova Scotia) was Cromwellian but a royal creation dating back to before the Civil War. He was, though, already a Privy Councillor, as, indeed, were Protector Oliver's Comptroller of the Household, Colonel Philip Jones, and Captain of the Yeomen of the Guard, Walter Strickland, although his particular post did not normally carry with it ex officio membership of the Privy Council. So under the Cromwellian Protectorate the system worked in reverse. Instead of being an elevator to high positions in the administration senior Protectoral court posts were conferred on men who were already politically powerful as a means of bestowing further dignity. The odd man out was the Master of the Horse, John Claypole. Like the captaincy of the Yeomen of the Guard this office, the third most senior post in a royal household, was established early on in Cromwell's rule. Again it was traditionally held by a peer of the realm, Charles I's Masters of the Horse being, respectively, the Dukes of Buckingham and Hamilton. But Claypole was not a member of the Privy Council and therefore not a Protectoral grandee. He was, however, Cromwell's son-in-law. Although the Protectoral senior court officials were not hereditary peers, as their royal counterparts had been, they would nevertheless sit as 'life' peers in the second chamber, or 'Other House', of the Protectorate Parliament on the very same benches as royal senior court officials had done as hereditary members of the House of Lords.[7]

The Cromwellian Other House convened for the first time on 20 January 1658. This was the day on which the second Protectorate Parliament reassembled as the Parliament of the Protectorate royal, having been adjourned since Oliver's coronation without the crown on 26 June 1657. Appropriately the procedure for the opening of this new session of Parliament followed more recent royal precedent to the letter. Cromwell addressed what was now both Houses of Parliament from the throne of the House of Lords as all sovereigns had done since 1536, and still do to this day, the Usher of the Black Rod having been sent to summon the House of Commons to the bar of the upper chamber. And the Protector began his speech in near old regal style with: 'My Lords, and Gentlemen of the House of Commons.' The newly constituted second chamber was intended as 'a screen or balance betwixt the Protector and Commons as the former Lords had been betwixt the King and them'. Cromwell had been long mindful of the merits of such an assembly, the House of Commons, by its actions, standing 'in need of a check or balancing power, meaning a House of Lords or a House so constituted'. The Protector voiced this in a speech to army officers at the beginning of the 1657 kingship debate. To support his argument he cited the case of James Naylor, a Quaker subjected to horrendous punishments in 1656 for blasphemy by a House of Commons which did not share Cromwell's views on toleration and which had acted unconstitutionally without a second chamber to rein it in. 'The case of James Naylor might happen to be your case', the military men were told.[8]

Membership of the Other House was fixed at no less than forty and no more than seventy. It comprised 'life' peers (a species resurrected in 1958), the one Cromwellian hereditary peer created so far, and selected members of the old nobility. All were nominated by the Protector personally. Between them they represented a cross-section of what has been described as the most important interests upon which the government of the Protector depended – territorial magnates, the landed gentry, naval and military commanders, the legal profession and the official and commercial classes, together with a clutch of Cromwell's relatives. There was even a small number of members whose origins were distinctly plebeian.[9] In certain respects this cross-sectional nature of the Cromwellian second chamber puts it way ahead of its time.

Writs had been issued to those nominated to sit in the Other House in the manner and style of a King summoning peers to Parliament. Originally the judiciary had maintained that 'until his Highness did accept of the title of King no legal writs could be made nor House of Peers constituted'. Writs were nonetheless eventually issued by a Protector who presumably felt that he was acting within his rights in accordance with the revised constitution. In the event out of the seven English hereditary peers summoned to sit in the Other House only three obeyed the writ and one of these, Charles Howard, Viscount Morpeth, was a Cromwellian creation. The only Scottish hereditary peer nominated to sit also refused to take his place.[10] Such conspicuous absenteeism was not entirely borne of hostility to the Cromwellian regime. One of the absentees was, after all, the Earl of Warwick. There were other considerations, not least the fact that the Protectoral second chamber was not conceived of as being a properly constituted House of Lords. Membership was at the ruler's pleasure and not by hereditary right. Acceptance of this new arrangement would mean accepting the abolition of the principle on which the old House of Lords had stood and with it the freedom of the nobility to be, as Viscount Saye and Sele had written to fellow peer, Lord Wharton, 'the beam keeping both scales, King and people, in an even posture without encroachments one upon the other to the hurt and damage of both'. But the absence of these Puritan magnates – the Earls of Warwick, Manchester, Mulgrave and Cassillis, Viscount Saye and Sele and Lord Wharton – was crucial. C.H. Firth believed that it deprived the Cromwellian Other House of reputation and weight. 'They were men whose political ability and experience would have been of great value to the government.'[11]

What the new session of Parliament would have though was a House of Commons containing those upwards of one hundred malcontents who had previously been excluded. They were there because free elections with no interference from the executive had been enshrined in the revised constitution, although both Houses of Parliament were required to swear fealty to the Lord Protector.[12] Almost from the start the republican-led opposition in the House of Commons engaged themselves in a disputation over the second chamber. Was it to be called the Other House, as it had been termed in the Humble Petition and Advice, or the House of Lords, which was how Cromwell had addressed it at the opening of Parliament? If it was to be the House of Lords then this would invest the new second chamber with the same powers as the old House of Lords, including the authority to sanction or negate legislation passed by the House of Commons, an arrangement wholly unacceptable to republicans. The disputation continued until on 4 February, only ten days after he had opened this session of Parliament, Cromwell entered the Palace of Westminster at short notice and told those assembled there: 'I think it high time that an end be put to your sitting. And I do dissolve this Parliament. And let God be judge between you and me!'[13]

'I had very comfortable expectation that God would make the meeting of this Parliament a blessing', expounded Cromwell in his dissolution speech. 'The blessing which I mean, and which we ever climbed at, was mercy, truth, righteousness and peace, which I desire may be improved.' But all Parliament had done, the Protector maintained, was to wrangle over the constitutional settlement. What was worse, this constitutional settlement, framed, to use Cromwell's own words, 'in reference to the ancient constitution' (i.e. King, House of Lords and House Commons), had been instituted by Parliament itself, 'by you especially of the House of Commons'. Such wrangling was endangering the state by giving encouragement to Royalist and other plotters against the regime, which was the reason Cromwell gave for the premature dissolution. But the assembly that had instituted the new constitution was not a 'free' Parliament as over one fifth of the returned members of the House of Commons had been excluded. Now those excluded members were back and Cromwell had an infinitely less manageable House of Commons to contend with, more especially since about forty of his supporters had been translated from the Commons to the Other House.[14]

All of which could be seen as rather ironic because there was widespread speculation to the effect that this particular session of the second Protectorate Parliament was to have formalised completely the Protector's already regal status by giving him the title of King. Writing on 9 December 1657, more than six weeks before Parliament re-assembled, William Dobbins expressed the opinion to his cousin, John Percivall, in Ireland that: 'I fear land will be cheaper hereafter in Ireland than 'tis now and the times not so settled. Moreover, we may still fear new combustions. But if his Highness be King the next session (as there is very much likelihood he will be and some forerunning signs of it) we hope it will be the hopefullest way of settlement.' Two more pieces of correspondence, one Royalist and the other Cromwellian, convey the same intelligence. Both are dated the middle of January 1658, just days before Parliament re-assembled. 'The news from England', Charles II's secretary, Sir Edward Nicholas, was informed by Thomas Mompesson, 'is that Cromwell has summoned the members that are to sit in the new conventicle, which are not called Lords as yet but only the Other House. They may not take their new honours till Cromwell has assumed the title of King, which is believed in England will be soon done.' The author of the Cromwellian correspondence was no less a personage than Marchamont Nedham, editor of *Mercurius Politicus* and the official mouthpiece *Public Intelligencer*. In a letter from Whitehall to William Swift, secretary to Sir William Lockhart, Cromwell's ambassador in France, Nedham relates how 'all our talk is concerning the Other House, as 20 January is approaching, and what name shall be given it, as also what will be the issue of this next meeting. Popular chat bespeaks a King, because they will have it so.'[15]

According to yet another piece of contemporary correspondence the very dissolution of this session of Parliament was seen as bidding fair to usher in that same constitutional change. 'You will have a Parliament called in a short time of real Lords and Commons, according to the will of the nation', Richard Bradshaw was advised by James Waynwright two weeks after Cromwell had dissolved the second Protectorate Parliament. Waynwright believed that this new Parliament, 'constituted according to the ancient rights of the nation in the late King's time', would meet on 1 September 1658 but from what he had heard others seemed to think that it might be as early as 1 May.[16] So in spite of everything Fortune still seemed to decree that the by now seriously ailing Cromwell should not simply occupy the office of King as Protector Royal but be King in name as well.

But 'Fortune is glass; just as it becomes bright it is broken.' By early 1658 the glass if not broken was most certainly beginning to crack. 'After all this lustre and glory in which the Protector seemed to flourish', says Clarendon, 'the season of the year threatened some tempest and foul weather.' On 16 February Cromwell's niece, Lavinia Whetstone, died almost exactly two years after her grandly staged marriage in the Palace of Whitehall to Major Richard Beke, soon to be made Captain of the Protectoral Life Guard. The same night Frances Cromwell's twenty-three-year-old bridegroom succumbed to scrofula, just three months after the couple's lavish and joyous 'royal' wedding. The body was removed from Whitehall to the Earl of Warwick's residence in Holborn where it was 'set up in great state'. The Protectoral court responded to young Robert Rich's demise in the same way that previous courts had responded to the death of a member of the royal family: 'His Highness mourned three days in purple (as is used by persons of his quality). The rest of the family is in close mourning for his lordship.' Purple, the colour of the Protector's mourning, is associated with royal majesty and regarded as a sign of imperial power, having been worn by Roman and Byzantine emperors. It became (and still is) the royal colour of mourning but only for sovereign princes, that is 'persons of his [Cromwell's] quality'. No one else, no matter how exalted, may wear this mourning hue. Thus we have Samuel Pepys recording in his diary in September 1660, just after the Restoration, that he saw Charles II at Whitehall in purple mourning for his brother, the Duke of Gloucester, who had died of smallpox.[17]

The Earl of Warwick was completely broken by the demise of his only grandson and the consequent probable extinction of the direct male line. Nevertheless, in a letter to Cromwell acknowledging the Protector's condolences the one-time jovial buccaneer's admiration for his friend still shines through. The letter, addressed to 'My Lord' and signed 'Your Lordship's most affectionate

Princess in mourning. Frances Cromwell as a young widow. Her husband died within three months of their 'royal' wedding and the Protectoral court responded in the same way that previous courts would have done on the death of a member of the royal family, the Protector wearing the purple mourning reserved exclusively for sovereign princes.

servant, WARWICK', while expressing the grief he feels at his own great loss also praises Cromwell's stewardship as ruler and declares that: 'Other's goodness is their own; yours is a whole country's, yea three kingdoms'.' Within two months of his grandson's death the seventy-year-old earl was himself dead. According to Clarendon, Cromwell 'seemed to be much afflicted at the death of his friend, the Earl of Warwick, with whom he had a fast friendship, though neither their humours nor their natures were [a]like'. Misfortunes never come singly. There were to be more – but not just yet. Meanwhile the Protector continued to exercise his peculiarly royal prerogative of creating hereditary peerages by making his cousin, Edmund Dunch, Baron Burnell of East Wittenham by letters patent dated 26 April 1658. Dunch had served in both of Cromwell's Parliaments and 'was much beloved and trusted by that sovereign'.[18]

Another patent was issued on 1 May for the appointment of John Maynard as his Highness's Sergeant. This was the Protectoral version of King's Sergeant, an honour awarded by the sovereign to the more distinguished of those senior barristers, Sergeants-at-Law. Maynard was not the only person to be so honoured by Cromwell but his appointment is certainly the most interesting. A Presbyterian and member of the Long Parliament Maynard had supported the Parliamentarian side in the Civil War but being essentially a monarchist he wished only to curtail the prerogative of the crown not abolish the monarchy altogether. On the establishment of the Protectorate he swore allegiance to the new regime and became one of the first barristers to be appointed a Cromwellian Sergeant-at-Law. He then went on to distinguish himself as a defender of those who had come into conflict with the Protectoral regime when, along with two other barristers, he acted on behalf of the defendant in the celebrated Cony case of 1655.[19]

George Cony, a City merchant, had been arrested for non-payment of duty on some silk he had imported. Maynard and his colleagues maintained that the duty had been levied without the consent of Parliament and both Cony's detention and the imposition of the duty were illegal because they had been laid without any lawful authority. As the Protectoral government had seen itself as acting within its rights then what Cony's counsel were saying cast doubt on the sovereign authority vested in the office of Lord Protector and by extension called into question the validity of the written constitution which was the basis of that sovereign authority. For their flagrant presumption Maynard and the two other barristers involved in Cony's defence were sent to the Tower until they apologised, which they duly did. Committal to the Tower had, of course, been a long-established practice of English monarchs when dealing with those who had

John Maynard, one of the first Cromwellian Sergeants-at-Law (since superseded by King's or Queen's Counsel), which had formerly been a crown appointment. In May 1658 Maynard became his Highness's Sergeant, the Protectoral version of King's Sergeant, which was an honour awarded by the sovereign to distinguished Sergeants-at-Law.

incurred their displeasure. The judiciary was also apparently brought to book, Chief Justice Henry Rolle being summoned to appear before the Protector's Council on the same day that he allowed Cony's counsel to make their highly contentious speeches without interruption.[20]

Clarendon opens out this aspect of the case but what he says, although much quoted, has more than a whiff of fancy about it. According to Clarendon, when what he refers to as the 'judges' were sent for and severely reprehended for allowing Maynard and the other members of Cony's defence counsel 'to question and make doubt of' the Protector's authority, 'they, with all humility, mentioned the law and Magna Carta'. In reply to this 'Cromwell told them their Magna Farta should not control his actions, which he knew were for the safety of the Commonwealth. . . . Thus he subdued a spirit that had been often troublesome to the most sovereign power.' Magna Carta was, significantly, 'the first great instance of general dissatisfaction with the King's government provoking resistance and the setting down, in writing, of limitations on royal power'. Clarendon does, however, go on to say that 'in all other matters which did not concern the life of his jurisdiction he seemed to have a great reverence for the law and rarely interposed between party and party'.[21] Dr George Bate, another, in his case opportunely reconstructed, anti-Cromwellian reluctantly concurs with Clarendon: 'To give the devil [Cromwell] his due, he restored justice . . . almost to its ancient dignity and splendour, the judges without covetousness discharging their duties according to law and equity and the laws (unless some few that particularly concerned Cromwell) having full and free course in all courts without hindrance or delay.' Interestingly Bate's otherwise generally vituperative denunciation of Cromwell is said to have been written with Clarendon's assistance.[22]

Two years after the Cony case when Parliament called upon Cromwell to accept the title of King, Maynard, 'a lover of monarchy', was among those strongly urging acceptance. Maynard referred by implication to the circumstances leading to his incarceration in the Tower when he argued that 'the title of King, with defined prerogatives, was more favourable to liberty than that of Protector, who was often driven to do arbitrary acts from the novelty of his dominion'. Cromwell refused the title of King but nevertheless went on to rule with the 'defined prerogatives' of the kingly dignity and to honour the man he had once imprisoned by appointing him Lord Protector's Sergeant. The bestowal of this Cromwellian distinction did not militate against Maynard at the Restoration. Both he and the other Lord Protector's Sergeant, Lord Chief Justice John Glynne, would be made King's Sergeants by Charles II.[23]

CHAPTER 11

Moses My Servant Is Dead

The spring and summer of 1658 brought widespread rumour that the Protector would finally grasp the nettle and adopt the title of King. A Royalist writing from London on 27 April relates how Cromwell appeared to be 'strengthening himself for reception of kingship, when the seasonable time comes, by Parliament or otherwise'. Then, on 15 May, came the strongest of intimations regarding Cromwell and the crown when it was reported that 'the two caps of crimson and purple velvet, worn only by princes and now making up by order of the Master of the Wardrobe, make the people talk largely of kingship'. The headgear referred to are caps of estate which were worn by Kings as badges of rank in place of a crown. Also in May there was an instruction from the Privy Council concerning a sword once belonging to the late King that had been purchased for his Highness's use. Although the connotation is regal, in point of fact this was a ceremonial sword ordered to be delivered up to the sword bearer of the High Court of Justice. The court had been established to try suspects in the latest Royalist conspiracy, one of whom was Dr John Hewett the probable officiate at Mary Cromwell's Anglican marriage ceremony six months before.[1]

Confirmation of the rumour concerning the Lord Protector and the kingly title is provided by George Fox, founder of the Society of Friends. In his journal he recorded that 'there was also talk about this time of making Cromwell King, whereupon I was moved to go to him. I met him in the park and told him that they that would put him on a crown would take away his life. And he asked me what I did say. And I said again, they that sought to put him on a crown would take away his life; and I bid him mind the crown that was immortal. He thanked me and bid me go to his house. Afterwards I was moved to write to him more fully concerning that matter.' This entry in Fox's journal does more than confirm that there was at this time speculation about changing Cromwell's title, something that would apparently have put the Lord Protector's immortal soul in jeopardy. It illustrates Cromwell's remarkable forbearance, the more so considering that Quakers had a reputation for being socially and politically disruptive. They were regarded, except by Cromwell himself, as a potential threat to the stability of the Protectoral regime and were generally disliked. It also illustrates the extraordinary degree to which this prince, at whose very name foreign rulers trembled, was so readily accessible. In so doing, it and a later example refute Clarendon's description of Cromwell at this point in his rule as a man so beset by paranoia that it was difficult to get near him.[2]

Something that could possibly have facilitated Cromwell's acceptance of the kingly title occurred in late June. The Flanders town of Dunkirk was seized from the Spaniards by military force and ceded to the Commonwealth. This was a national triumph whose heady effects are clearly evident in the following report from this latest addition to the increasing number of territories which Cromwell now ruled: 'When the oath of allegiance to his Highness was propounded here the townsmen took it with very much cheerfulness and resolution. But the soldiers deserve high commendation, who echoed forth their fidelity with most affectionate acclamations "Long live the Protector" and showed that this garrison is not to be wrested out of our hands by any enemy at an easy rate.'[3]

This was indeed the highest of times, something which the nineteenth-century writer of *The Life of John Milton*, David Masson, managed, from his Victorian standpoint, to encapsulate perfectly: 'O how stable and grand seemed the Protectorate in the month of July 1658! Rebellion at home in all its varieties quashed once more, and now, as it might seem, for ever; the threatened invasion of the Spaniards and Charles Stuart dissipated into ridicule; a footing acquired on the Continent and 6000 Englishmen stationed there in arms; foreign powers, with Louis XIV at their head, obeisant to the very ground whenever they turned their gaze towards the British Islands and dreading the next bolt from the Protector's hands; those hands evidently toying with several new bolts and poising them towards the parts of Europe for which they were intended; great schemes, besides, for England, Scotland, Ireland and the colonies in that inventive brain!'[4]

But for every high there is a low, a truism testified to by Samuel Carrington who, in another example of his characteristic lyricism, linked the Dunkirk triumph with a corresponding, albeit unrelated, disaster. 'The laurels of victory against the Spaniards, and of the taking of the town of Dunkirk, were soon withered and the joys abated by the interposing of the cypress tree [a symbol of mourning] which death planted on the tomb of the illustrious and most generous Lady Claypole.' Betty Claypole, Cromwell's second eldest, and favourite, daughter, wife of the Protectoral Master of the Horse, John Claypole, died at Hampton Court Palace in the early hours of the morning of 6 August 1658. Death had come at the age of twenty-nine after a painful and protracted illness. Carrington described her as 'this most illustrious daughter, the true representative and lively image of her father, the joy of his heart, the delight of his eyes and the dispenser of his clemency and benignity' who 'died in the flower of her age . . . despising the pomps of the Earth'. Betty Claypole may have despised earthly pomp and although this was reflected in the manner of her funeral her corpse would nevertheless not be denied the sort of princely burial that befitted a daughter of the nation's ruling House. As the words engraved on the silver plate of her coffin affirmed in the customary Latin 'the most illustrious lady, the Lady Elizabeth' had been the wife of 'the most honoured Lord John Claypole, Master of the Horse' and also the second daughter of 'the most serene and eminent

Prince Oliver, by the Grace of God of England, Scotland and Ireland &c. Protector'. And even as Betty Claypole was enduring her death agony rumours persisted that the most serene and eminent Prince Oliver's title was about to change. On 3 August, three days before Betty died, Rachel Newport was writing from London, which she described as oppressively hot, dysenteric and 'extreme empty', to the effect that 'his Highness, with his family, is settled at Hampton Court, Lady Claypole being still very ill and the physicians much fearing [for] her. There is a hot report now of a coronation which shall be shortly, but it is not believed until it is seen done.'[5]

Betty Claypole's funeral took place at night, which had been the custom since early in the century, four days after her demise. The body was conveyed from Hampton Court by water 'being accompanied by a great number of barges filled with persons of honour and quality'. It was about an hour before midnight when the flotilla reached Westminster Stairs. From here the corpse was carried into the Palace of Westminster. In the palace's Painted Chamber, where Cromwell had addressed his first Parliament four years before, and which was now 'nobly adorned with mourning', a 'stately hearse' or catafalque had been prepared to receive the mortal remains of the Lord Protector's beloved daughter. The body remained there a while before being carried across to Westminster Abbey at between midnight and one o'clock in the morning, 'attended by the same persons of honour', and interred in Henry VII's Chapel 'in a vault made on purpose' close to the tomb of the chapel's founder, Henry VII. Here Betty Claypole joined six of her father's royal predecessors, Henry VII himself, of course, Edward VI, Mary Queen of Scots, Mary Tudor, Elizabeth and James I. She also joined Parliamentarian, Commonwealth and Protectoral dignitaries, whom it had been seen fit to inter in the Chapel of the Kings, together with other recently deceased members of the Cromwell family, including the Protector's mother, also named Elizabeth, who had died a nonagenarian at Whitehall in 1654. But then, as the report of Betty Claypole's obsequies in *Mercurius Politicus* concluded: 'The whole ceremony, though managed without funeral pomp, was nevertheless in all respects such as became the quality of so illustrious and meritorious a lady.' Because of their singular poignancy and stark grandeur Elizabeth Claypole's obsequies have exercised an extraordinarily powerful influence on the imaginations of historical writers, resulting in such rhapsodical interpretations as: 'the story of her funeral reads like a page of an old romance' or 'the ceremony itself had a strange Arthurian quality about it'.[6]

Samuel Carrington's juxtapositioning of the taking of Dunkirk (which Charles II would sell to the King of France four years later) with the death of Betty Claypole could not have shown in higher relief the contrast between the obvious success of one aspect at least of Oliver's policies as ruler and the rather different personal fortunes of the Protectoral House of Cromwell at this time. And the veritable iliad of woes with which the year 1658 had been punctuated so far was set to continue. The cracking glass was now about to splinter. Even as the red-coated soldiery were affirming their loyalty in Dunkirk with cries of 'Long live the Protector', which occurred in early August after the newly-acquired dominion's formal cessation, Cromwell was about to lose his grip on life. Already beginning to ail

Posthumous portrait of Cromwell's second eldest daughter, Elizabeth, wife of Protectoral Master of the Horse John Claypole. She is depicted as Minerva, daughter of Jupiter, father and king of the gods in Roman mythology, a clear reference to her father's power.

himself the Protector had ministered to his dying daughter personally. Andrew Marvell would devote a substantial portion of his *Poem on the Death of O.C.* to these ministrations, including their effects and 'Eliza's' ultimate demise on Cromwell's own precarious health, effects from which he was destined never to recover.[7]

Cromwell was too stricken to attend his daughter's funeral. Thurloe gave 'gout and other distempers contracted by the long sickness of my Lady Elizabeth' as the cause of the Protector's condition. During this time little in the way of official business could be carried out so that on 17 August Thurloe was bemoaning 'the sad condition of the public affairs' over the past fourteen days. Bordeaux provides confirmation of this suspension of official business in a missive dated 12 August. 'There does not appear presently to be anything of great import going on internally nor has anything been brought up except the convening of Parliament.' At the same time the ambassador corroborates the current reports of Cromwell still becoming King and the irresoluteness surrounding the design. 'Kingship is also mentioned from time to time but with so little certainty that it cannot be said it is a well established resolution.' This lack of resolution, he explains, was not so much because the people did not desire it, the territory acquired in Flanders having won the Lord Protector their affection, but because even with regard to that it was no less dangerous a step to take than in the past. Bordeaux relates too an example of deft diplomatic sidestepping by the Protector over the seizure of Dunkirk, made necessary by having allied himself with one Catholic power, France, to humble another Catholic power, Spain: 'He gave thanks to God throughout England for this conquest . . . without giving us grounds for complaint. Instead of promising that this conquest will be of great advantage to the Protestant religion there is now only talk of the Christian religion.'[8]

By 17 August Cromwell had recovered sufficiently to go riding for an hour, during which he was accosted by that indefatigable self-appointed keeper of his conscience, George Fox. Not only does Fox's journal entry provide us with another example of the Protector's accessibility but also, under the circumstances, his almost saint-like forbearance: 'I went to Kingston and thence to Hampton Court to speak with the Protector about the sufferings of Friends. I met him riding into Hampton Court Park and before I came to him as he rode at the head of his Life Guard I saw and felt a waft of death go forth against him; and when I came to him he looked a dead man. After I had laid the sufferings of Friends before him and had warned him, according as I was moved to speak to him, he bid me come to his house. So I returned to Kingston and the next day went to Hampton Court to speak further with him. But when I came he was very sick and Harvey [Charles Harvey, Groom of the Bedchamber to his Highness], who was one that waited on him, told me the doctors were not willing I should speak with him. So I passed away and never saw him more.'[9]

The day following the Protector's ride in Hampton Court Park London witnessed an event involving that ancient and regally established City institution, revived by Cromwell in 1656 with himself as 'royal' patron, the Artillery Company. Having just received a new set of rules and orders for its governance (believed to be the oldest regimental standing orders in existence), the Artillery

Company now resumed the tradition of holding an annual feast. 'The most distinguished of these, or at least that which seems to be most distinguished in the company's archives,' according to one authority writing in the early nineteenth century, 'is that of 18 August 1658.' It was held in Merchant Taylors' Hall with many eminent guests present, including the Lord Mayor and aldermen of London, a City link reinforced by the resumption in that year of the Artillery Company's attendance on the Lord Mayor as a sort of civic Yeomen of the Guard. This is a function still performed by the company when it attends the first citizen of London's coach at the annual Lord Mayor's Show. Prior to the feast the Artillery Company had had a general muster and field exercise before marching through the City to St Paul's Cathedral for divine service. The grandest of all the Artillery Company feasts, at least up to the early nineteenth century, would, however, also be the last under the patron who had brought about this institution's revival, Protector Oliver.[10]

George Fox's dismal prognosis of Cromwell's condition had been correct when he said of the Protector that he 'saw and felt a waft of death go forth against him'. Although Thurloe felt able to report on the Protector's outing in Hampton Court Park to the effect that 'he finds himself much refreshed by it so that this recovery of his Highness doth much allay the sorrow for my Lady Elizabeth's death', the Secretary of State's obvious relief at the apparent improvement in Oliver's condition would be short lived. That evening he suffered a relapse and after seventeen more days of relative improvement and further relapses, due to gout, a stone and malarial attacks, finally expired at about three o'clock in the afternoon of Friday, 3 September. It was the anniversary of the battles of Dunbar (1650) and Worcester (1651), Cromwell's two great victories as Commander-in-Chief of the Army of the English republic, a singular coincidence that one news-sheet managed to interpret in the most positive of lights: 'Thus it hath proved to him to be a day of triumph indeed, there being much Providence in it, that after so glorious crowns of victory placed on his head by God on this day, having neglected an earthly crown, he should now go to receive the crown of everlasting life.'[11]

Oliver's success in the field had put paid to attempts to reinstate the monarchy under Charles II. Ultimately Cromwell would himself become a monarch, despite 'having neglected an earthly crown', a fact no more exemplified than by his final acts as ruler, which included the use of that exclusively royal prerogative he had become accustomed to exercising. On 21 August he signed a bill for a patent to make Bulstrode Whitelocke a viscount, which the proposed recipient turned down because he 'did not think it convenient for him'. And on 28 August, just six days before he died, the Protector conferred the honour of baronet on a Somersetshire gentleman, William Wyndham of Orchard Wyndham, 'a person of very noble extraction, of much merit and of high esteem in his country'. On the Protector's death the machines, which had only just begun to mill the 1658 issue of those coins that were so illustrative of Cromwell's undoubted regality, ceased.[12]

As a King in all but name it was only fitting that Oliver should breath his last in the sumptuous surroundings of the royal Palace of Whitehall. Also only fitting were those other trappings associated with monarchy, from the liveried servants and Yeomen of the Guard, wearing the manifestly regal Protectoral arms for a badge, to the high officers of the household, such as the Lord Chamberlain and Master of the Horse. There was too a clutch of court physicians and chaplains who ministered to the dying ruler. On the Sunday following Oliver's demise one of these Protectoral court chaplains, Hugh Peter, delivered a sermon in the chapel at Whitehall, the text of which was taken from Joshua 1:2, 'Moses my servant is dead.' This not uncommon likening of the Protector to the liberator of the Israelites would subsequently undergo a slight adjustment in Oliver's favour when Henry Dawbeny came to pen his 'lively parallels' between Moses and Cromwell: 'Moses was permitted only to see the land of promise . . . yet suffered not to enter. But our sacred second Moses has not only entered but enjoyed for divers years his land of promise.' Perfect parallelism is, however, restored by Dawbeny's assertion that 'Moses . . . after he had satisfied himself with the fair prospect of the promised land, willingly steps into his much longed for tabernacle of repose. Just thus, and no otherwise, did our great Protector and gracious second Moses depart from us.'[13]

On the death of Oliver 'the Privy Council immediately assembled and being satisfied that the Lord Protector was dead, and upon sure and certain knowledge that his late Highness did in his life time according to the Humble Petition and Advice declare and appoint the most noble and illustrious lord the Lord Richard eldest son of his said Highness to succeed him, it was resolved at the Council with no dissension that his late Highness hath declared and appointed the said most noble and illustrious lord to succeed him in the government'. Thus did Richard Cromwell succeed his father to the kingly office of Lord Protector of the Commonwealth of England, Scotland and Ireland, and the Dominions and Territories thereunto belonging. The Council's resolution was conveyed to the chief officers of the army who 'unanimously concurred thereunto, being resolved to their utmost to maintain the succession according to law'.[14]

By its very nature the accession of Richard could be said to mark the consummation of the assimilation of the Cromwellian Protectorship to the office of King. He was proclaimed Protector at the usual places in London and Westminster on the morning following Oliver's demise and later throughout the length and breadth of the land. The London and Westminster proclaiming of his father in December 1653 had occurred three days after Oliver's first investiture and had to take account of the fact that the new ruler was not following a monarchical regime. Likewise, the splendidly theatrical proclaiming anew of Oliver throughout the capital in July 1657, which marked the inauguration of a new constitutional arrangement, took place five days after the Protector's second investiture. The proclaiming of Richard was different. His came immediately after his father's death and was therefore a precise replication of the traditional procedure followed when sovereign had succeeded sovereign.

Protector Richard's proclamation document too, unlike his father's, followed previous royal form, at least as far as circumstances allowed. Both in its content and presentation it was a modified version of Charles I's accession proclamation of 1625 and not too dissimilar to succeeding royal accession proclamations, down to and including that of Elizabeth II in 1952. The text of Protector Richard's

RICHARD Lord Protector of England Scotland &
Ireland, and the Dominions & Territoryes
therevnto belonging:

Following Protector Oliver's death on 3 September 1658 Richard Cromwell was acknowledged as the lawful successor to 'his royal father's throne'. One member of his Parliament would refer to him as Richard the Fourth.

proclamation opens with 'Whereas it hath pleased the most wise God, in his Providence, to take out of this world the most serene and renowned Oliver, late Lord Protector of this Commonwealth . . .', which is an appropriate echo of its royal model: 'Whereas it hath pleased Almighty God to call to his mercy our late sovereign lord, King James, of blessed memory.' The signatories to the Protectoral document then asserted that:

> We therefore of the Privy Council, together with the Lord Mayor, aldermen and citizens of London, the officers of the army and numbers of other principal gentlemen, do now hereby, with one full voice and consent of tongue and heart, publish and declare the said noble and illustrious Lord Richard to be rightfully Protector of this Commonwealth of England, Scotland and Ireland, and the Dominions and Territories thereunto belonging; to whom we do acknowledge all fidelity and constant obedience, according to law and the said Humble Petition and Advice, with all hearty and humble affections, beseeching the Lord by whom princes rule, to bless him with long life and these nations with peace and happiness under his government.

Similarly, those who signed Charles I's accession proclamation declared that:

> We therefore, the Lords Spiritual and Temporal of this realm, being here assisted with those of his late Majesty's Privy Council, with numbers of other principal gentlemen of quality, with the Lord Mayor, aldermen and citizens of London, do now hereby, with one full voice and consent of tongue and heart, publish and proclaim that the high and mighty Prince Charles is now, by the death of our late sovereign of happy memory, become our only lawful, lineal and rightful liege lord, Charles, by the Grace of God King of Great Britain, France and Ireland, Defender of the Faith, &c; to whom we do acknowledge all faith and constant obedience with all hearty and humble affections, beseeching God, by whom Kings do reign, to bless the royal King Charles with long and happy years to reign over us.

According to their respective successor proclamations Richard Cromwell owed his title 'to law and the Humble Petition and Advice' and King Charles to lineal descent, which for all practical purposes was also true of Protector Richard, the hereditary dynastic principle having obtained in his case as much as it had for Charles I.[15]

In strict accordance with royal precedent the first signature on Protector Richard's accession proclamation was that of the Lord Mayor of London, followed by those of his Highness's Privy Councillors. These included members of the Privy Council who had held court posts under Protector Oliver and would continue to do so under his successor: Lord Chamberlain of the Household Gilbert Pickering, Comptroller of the Household Philip Jones and Captain of the Yeoman of the Guard Walter Strickland. Among others who signed was Master of Ceremonies Oliver Fleming. The document ends with 'God Save His Highness Richard Lord Protector', paralleling the 'God Save King Charles' of its immediate royal predecessor. The accession proclamation of Charles I provides

Hereas it hath pleased the most wise God, in his Providence, to take out of this world the most Serene and Renowned, Oliver late Lord Protector of this Commonwealth; And His said Highness having in His life-time, according to the Humble Petition and Advice, declared, and appointed the most Noble, and Illustrious, the Lord RICHARD, Eldest Son of His said late Highness, to succeed Him in the Government of these Nations; We therefore of the Privy Council, together with the Lord Mayor, Aldermen, and Citizens of London, the Officers of the Army, and numbers of other principal Gentlemen, Do now hereby, with one full voice, and consent of tongue, and heart, publish, and declare the said Noble, and Illustrious Lord RICHARD to be rightfully Protector of this Commonwealth of England, Scotland and Ireland, and the Dominions and Territories thereto belonging; to whom we do acknowledge all Fidelity, and constant obedience, according to Law, and the said Humble Petition and Advice, with all hearty and humble affections; Beseeching the Lord, by whom Princes Rule, to bless Him with long life, and these Nations with Peace, and happiness, under His Government.

Richard Chiverton, *Mayor*.	Fauconberg.
He. Lawrence, *President*.	Edw. Whalley.
Nathaniel Fiennes, *C. S.*	W. Goffe.
John Lisle, *C. S.*	Tho. Cooper.
C. Fleetwood.	Oliver Flemming.
P. Lisle.	John Clerk.
Jo. Disbrowe.	Tho. Pride.
E. Montagu.	Edm. Prideaux.
Gil. Pickering.	Tobias Bridge.
Cha. Wolseley.	Ed. Salmon.
Philip Skippon.	J. Biscoe.
Wm. Sydenham.	Waldine Lagoe.
Wal. Strickland.	John Mill.
Phi. Jones.	E. Grosvenor, &c.
Jo. Thurloe.	

4)

God save His Highness RICHARD, Lord Protector.

London Printed by *Henry Hills* and *Iohn Field*, Printers to His Highness the Lord Protector, 1658.

Proclamation of Richard Cromwell as Lord Protector. This followed previous royal form, being a modified version of Charles I's accession proclamation of 1625.

yet another example of history's little ironies in that one of its signatories was Robert Rich, Earl of Warwick, the very same Robert Rich, Earl of Warwick, who was destined to become such a staunch supporter of the Cromwellian regime.[16]

On 4 September Richard's first proclamation as Protector was promulgated. This was 'a proclamation signifying his Highness's pleasure that all men being in office of the government at the decease of his most dear father, Oliver, late Lord Protector, shall continue till his Highness's further direction'. Again, this customary first, or near first, proclamation of the new ruler was a more perfect replication of the previous royal version than Oliver's had been. Indeed, Richard's was a perfect replication. Oliver had succeeded a republic whereas Richard had succeeded his 'most dear and beloved father . . . by whose decease the authority and power of the most part of the offices and places of jurisdiction and government within these nations did cease and fail, the sovereign person failing from whom the same was derived'. This is almost word for word what appeared in the proclamation by the King which signified 'his Majesty's pleasure that all men being in office of government at the decease of his most dear and most royal father, King James, shall so continue till his Majesty's further direction', promulgated by Charles I immediately after his succession in 1625.[17]

To celebrate the proclaiming of Richard church bells were rung, just as they had been for Oliver fifteen months before and all previous monarchs. The expenditure involved in the ringing of bells for Richard was, however, appreciably less than it had been for his father. The church of St Peter Mancroft in Norwich, for instance, spent 8s. 6d. to ring the bells for Oliver's proclamation but only 2s. 6d. for Richard's. Likewise the Westminster church of St Martin in the Fields expended 10s. and 3s. 6d. respectively on bell ringing to commemorate the proclaiming of Oliver and Richard. Edmund Ludlow had it that the bells which ushered in the new reign rang in more ears than they did hearts, the proclamation of Richard as Lord Protector being met 'with as few expressions of joy as had ever been observed on the like occasion'. This unreconstructed republican is fully entitled to his jaundiced view but what he says is belied by the widespread celebrations marking Richard's accession, which were the same as those usually associated with suchlike royal events. At Southampton a conduit was filled with claret for all to drink and there was a discharge of great ordnance. Likewise, at Kilkenny in Ireland Richard was proclaimed 'with beat of drum, sound of trumpet, peals of muskets and firing of cannon, wine and beer being also set at the market cross for the people to drink'. While at Exeter the civic authorities attended in their scarlet gowns crying out 'Amen, Amen. God preserve my Lord Richard, Lord Protector', with the sounding of trumpets, ringing of bells and making of bonfires.[18]

Then followed the customary loyal addresses, very much like those that would be sent to Charles II less than two years later. They came from every city, county and town in the land but those sent by Oxford and Beverley suffice as illustrations. The 'Mayor, Bailiffs and Commonalty of the City of Oxford' assured the new Protector that 'since the lamented death of his most renowned father (whose memory will be ever famous amongst them and their generations to come) they all know that he is now the person designed by God and man to reign over them, and that by the laws of the nation they owe all fealty and allegiance to his

Above: *Great Seal of 'Richard the Fourth'.*

Below: *Signature of Richard Cromwell as Lord Protector.*

person and government, and do rejoice that the disposer of all things had placed him on his royal father's throne'. Similarly, the civic authorities and inhabitants of Beverley declared and attested their loyalty to Protector Richard and 'with all humility bow down their heads unto his Highness as their lawful sovereign and Protector, and do say they present him with their hearts and hands to serve him'.[19] Others were infinitely more fulsome and this touched William Dugdale's Royalist nerve. Commenting upon these 'solemn congratulatory addresses', in which 'this youngster', Richard, was 'highly magnified for his wisdom, nobleness of mind and lovely composition of body', Dugdale relates scathingly how 'his father, Oliver, was compared to Moses, Zerubbabel, Joshua, Gideon, Elijah, to the Chariots and Horsemen of Israel, to David, Solomon and Hezekiah. Likewise to Constantine the Great and to whomsoever else that either the sacred scripture, or any other history, had celebrated for their piety and goodness.'[20]

So it was that Oliver was succeeded as Protector Royal, to quote what has become almost a cliché, as quietly as any King had ever been succeeded by any Prince of Wales. At the time this was seen as a disaster for the Stuart cause, as Clarendon testifies:

> The next morning after the death of Oliver, Richard, his son, was proclaimed his lawful successor. The army congratulate their new General and renew their vows of fidelity to him. The navy doth the like. The City appears more unanimous for his service than they were for his father['s] and most counties in England, by their addresses under their hands, testified their obedience to their new sovereign without any hesitation. The dead [Oliver] is interred in the sepulchre of the Kings and with the obsequies due to such. And his son inherits all his greatness and all his glory without that public hate that visibly attended the other. Foreign princes addressed their condolences to him and desired to renew their alliances. And nothing was heard in England but the voice of joy and large encomiums of their new Protector. So that the King's condition never appeared so hopeless, so desperate.[21]

From the very heart of the regime itself Thurloe was able to assure Henry Cromwell that: 'It hath pleased God hitherto to give his Highness, your brother, a very easy and peaceable entrance upon his government. There is not a dog that wags his tongue, so great a calm are we in. The Lord continue it and give him a just and understanding heart that he may know how to go out and in before this great people, whose peace and liberty he is entrusted with.' Thurloe's sanguinity is not, however, without reservation: 'I must needs acquaint your Excellency that there are some secret murmurings in the army, as if his Highness were not General of the Army as his father was and would look upon him and the army as divided, and as if the conduct of the army should be elsewhere and in other hands.'[22] A cloud no bigger than a man's hand had already formed in the dawn sky of the reign of the new Protector Royal who one Member of Parliament chose to call 'Richard the Fourth'.*[23]

---

*Richard was, incidentally, the only monarch of that name to die peacefully in his own bed.

CHAPTER 12

The Last Act Crowns The Play

My soul, sit though a patient looker-on;
Judge not the play before the play is done:
Her plot has many changes; every day
Speaks a new scene; the last act crowns the play.
Francis Quarles (1592–1644)

If the accession of 'that most noble and illustrious Prince', Richard, marked the consummation of the assimilation of the Cromwellian Protectorship to the kingly dignity, then his father's burial, 'with more than regal pomp in the sepulchre of our monarchs', most certainly represented the high-water mark in the ever rising tide of royal ritual, ceremony, pomp and pageantry which had been an essential part of that assimilation process. This same event could also be said to have betokened the highest point in the Protectorate itself. The last act did indeed crown the play.[1]

The funeral rites were, it was reported, 'to be performed with all honour and magnificence'. Some notion of what this would entail can be derived from what the Venetian envoy wrote in one of his reports: 'At Whitehall they are now preparing for the funeral of the late Protector . . . which will take place . . . with extraordinary pomp and magnificence. They are consulting ancient books to see what was done by the Kings on such occasions, and say that it will be more splendid than ever before. . . . It was decided to follow the forms observed at the burial of King James, but this will be much greater.' And that is exactly what happened. The obsequies of 'his most serene and renowned Highness Oliver, Lord Protector', who 'from the private condition of a gentleman advanced himself to the highest pitch of government and sovereign authority', were identical in almost every detail to those of King James, the last monarch to be afforded a state funeral, which 'was performed with great magnificence' some thirty years earlier. His executed son, Charles I, was buried without any public ceremony, the relatively meagre sum of £500 being allocated for that purpose.[2]

The records having been consulted it was decided that the Protector's lying in state should be in one of the ex-royal palaces, Somerset House,* situated in the Strand and three-quarters-of-a-mile downriver from Whitehall. Built by Edward Seymour, Duke of Somerset, who was Lord Protector during the minority of his nephew, Edward VI, Somerset House was the first large-scale classical building in England. It passed to the crown after the duke's execution in 1552. Subsequently it was used for the lying in state of Anne of Denmark, after whom the place was renamed Denmark House for a while, and then for that of her husband, King James I. Somerset House would now witness another royal lying in state, for which purpose it was furnished 'according to former times', no doubt giving some of those who attended both King James's and Protector Oliver's lying in state a distinct feeling that they were witnessing the same event.[3]

Before reaching the lying-in-state chamber it was necessary to pass through three large rooms. These were the former royal Presence Chamber, Privy Chamber and Withdrawing Chamber. All were furnished the same. They were hung completely with black velvet and had escutcheons (i.e. shields) of his Highness's arms, crowned with an imperial crown, 'very thick upon the walls'. Upon a dais at the end of each room there was a chair of state set under a rich canopy to the head of which had been fixed 'a large majesty escutcheon [i.e. a shield bearing an imperial crown] fairly painted and gilt upon taffety'. Having experienced the majestic solemnity conveyed by three royal throne rooms, hung throughout with mourning, adorned with glorious emblems of the dead ruler and guarded by the Yeomen of the Guard resplendent in their sumptuous Protectoral livery, those present would have been psychologically prepared to enter the fourth room. Here they would witness the awesome spectacle of the lying in state. What would not be on view, however, was an actual body. Royal custom decreed that the monarch's embalmed corpse should be enclosed in a lead coffin which was itself encased in a coffin made of wood. Thus after James I's death 'his royal corpse was forthwith embalmed with all due rites appertaining thereunto and being cered and wrapped in lead was put into a sumptuous coffin which was filled up with odours and spices within and covered without with purple velvet, the handles, nails and other ironwork about it being richly hatched with gold; and upon the King's breast was fixed an inscription on a plate of gold'. The inscribed plate, which was in Latin, listed the dead sovereign's style and titles, the length of his reign, the date of his demise and age at the time of death.[4]

This contemporary account has its almost perfect echo in the report of, and instructions for, the preparation of Protector Oliver's corpse for burial. The day after the Protector's demise, at the same age as James I, it was announced that 'this afternoon the physicians and surgeons, appointed by order of the Council to embowel and embalm the body of his Highness and fill the same with sweet odours, performed their duty'. Ten days later the new Protector's Privy Council commanded 'that his Highness's corpse being embalmed with all due rites

---

*Not the building currently occupying the same site, which dates from the mid-eighteenth century.

appertaining thereunto, and being wrapped in lead, there ought to be an inscription on a plate of gold to be fixed upon his breast before he be put into the coffin'. The plate, of copper, doubly gilded and bearing the arms of the Protectorate impaled with Cromwell's personal arms, fell into private hands after the disinterment of Cromwell's body in 1661. Its inscription, which like James I's is in Latin, reads: 'Olivarius Protector Republicae, Angliae, Scotiae, et Hiberniae Natus 25 Aprilis Anno 1599 Inauguratus 16 Decembris 1653 Mortuus 3 Septembris Anno 1658 hic situs est.' Cromwell's 'elegant' outer coffin 'of the choicest wood' was an exact replica of James I's, being 'filled with odours and spices within and covered without with purple velvet, the handles, nails and all other ironwork about it richly hatched with gold'.[5]

Royal custom also decreed that for the lying in state the coffin should be placed under a bed of state upon which lay a life-like effigy of the dead sovereign. And it was to and around this representation, rather than the body itself, that all the symbolism and ceremonial of the obsequies were attached and revolved. The first recorded instance of this was at the obsequies of Edward II in 1327 and it is thought that the last British ruler to have a funeral effigy was Oliver Cromwell. This fabricated likeness of a deceased monarch is an expression of the concept of the King's two bodies. Like all men a sovereign has a mortal body subject to death and decay, a body natural, now coffined and therefore hidden from view. He also has a social body, a body politic, which never dies because the office of King will continue after the physical death of an individual monarch. Normally invisible because in life it is combined with the sovereign's mortal body, the body politic was separated out for the state funeral and displayed in the form of a life-like effigy of the deceased monarch, accoutred with the symbols of sovereignty. In this way was continuity asserted. The kingly dignity will endure in spite of the physical demise of this particular monarch. In other words 'the King never dies'.[6]

In the spring of 1657 this very concept had been advanced as one of the reasons why it was necessary for Cromwell to accept the title of King. Then it was argued that in law only when the ruler has the title of King can the office survive an individual monarch's death. The concept of the King never dies was not transferable to any other title. Without the kingly title continuity would be replaced by a dangerous vacuum between regimes. If Cromwell were to take the title of King then when he died 'the necessary inconveniences and mischiefs that may arise to the people', as a consequence of such a vacuum, could be avoided. But with the assimilation of the Protectorship to the office of King the concept that the King never dies clearly had been transferred to another title. Hence the kingly dignity of Lord Protector continued uninterrupted after Oliver's death in his 'declared and undoubted successor', his eldest son.[7]

The original intention had been to transfer the Protector's body by barge from Whitehall to Somerset House for the lying in state, just as Elizabeth I's had been brought from Richmond to Whitehall for burial in Westminster Abbey. As this was to be accomplished at night illumination would be provided by torches. These were to be carried by the Yeomen of the Guard accompanying the body in the Protectoral barge and by guards and footmen in other barges following immediately behind. The effect would have been a spectre-like ribbon of flickering light flowing majestically down the River Thames, the silence broken only by the creaking of rowlocks and the splashing of oars. As it happened it was considered more convenient to convey the body of his late Highness by land rather than by water.[8]

On the night of 20 September 1658 Cromwell's body was removed to Somerset House for the lying in state 'in a private manner, being attended only by his servants'. These were members of the Protectoral household carrying out the precise duties of their royal counterparts when the body of James I was borne, also at night, to his lying in state. There was the Lord Chamberlain, the Comptroller of his Highness's Household, Gentlemen of the Bedchamber, the Protectoral version of the royal Gentlemen of the Privy Chamber, Gentlemen of the Life Guard acting in the role of royal Gentlemen Pensioners, Yeomen of the Guard 'and many other officers and servants of his Highness'. Two heralds went before the body, which like that of King James was conveyed in a hearse drawn by six horses to Somerset House. There it lay, as the Venetian envoy recorded, 'in extraordinary pomp'.[9]

But was this the body of Oliver Cromwell or simply an empty coffin? The story goes that the embalming of the Lord Protector's corpse proved unsuccessful. 'Though his [Cromwell's] bowels were taken out and his body filled with spices, wrapped in a fourfold cerecloth, put first into a coffin of lead and then into a wooden one' the matter from the putrefactive spleen 'purged and wrought through all, so that there was a necessity of interring it [the corpse] before the solemnity of the funeral.' The source is Dr George Bate, personal physician to both Charles I and Protector Oliver, attending the latter in his final illness and performing the autopsy. The probability is that he also embalmed the Protector's corpse. The story is contained in Bate's virulent condemnation of Cromwell, the original publication of which coincided with the return of Charles II in whose court the doctor managed to get himself restored to the post of royal physician. There was, however, no mention, official or otherwise, of such an occurrence at the time of Cromwell's death in 1658, not the botched embalming nor the consequent expedient burial. It is therefore possible, probable even, that Bate's version of events was more in the nature of a timely exercise in rehabilitation than a true account of what actually happened. 'The inference was that the result of Bate's incompetence was really the manifestation of some essential evil surrounding Cromwell. In an age when nothing could so readily instil awe into men's collective reasoning than implicit portentous speculation, Bate's "revelation" was bound to have an anathematising effect on the memory of Cromwell. What better means of disassociation from a master whom he had been only too pleased to serve, and of enhancing his esteem in the estimation of the restored Stuart dynasty, could there have been for Bate?'[10]

The story was certainly made good use of by later anathematisers of the Lord Protector, such as James Heath who gave it his own distinctive treatment in *Flagellum: or the Life and Death, Birth and Burial of O. Cromwell the Late Usurper*: 'His [Cromwell's] body being opened and embalmed his milt [spleen] was found full of corruption and filth which was so strong and stinking that after the corpse was embalmed and filled with aromatic odours and wrapped in cerecloth, six double, in an inner sheet of lead and a strong wooden coffin, the filth still broke through them all and raised such a noisome stink that they were forced to bury him out of hand; but his name and memory stinks worse.' In supplying this anathematising gem Bate, royal, Protectoral and then once again royal physician, could be said to have confirmed the truism that:

> I should fear those that dance before me now
> Would one day stamp upon me. 'T has been done.
> Men shut their doors against a setting sun.
> *Timon of Athens*, I.ii

Bate would go on to claim that he had actually poisoned Cromwell with the knowledge of Charles II. But this was a death-bed confession when Bate was in the terminal stage of syphilis, one of the symptoms of which is delusion. Rumours of poisonings were in any case rife in the seventeenth century. Hearsay had it that even James I died in this way. If only because of later reports which would seem to refute Bate's claim (see below), the probability is that it really was the body of the Protector and not just an empty coffin that was conveyed from Whitehall to Somerset House for the lying in state.[11]

In the lying-in-state chamber, reclining above Cromwell's coffin on a bed of state, 'as becomes the dignity and renown of so great a prince', was the customary representation of the dead sovereign. Oliver's effigy was 'curiously [i.e. with minute accuracy] made to the life according to the best skill of the artist in that employment'. Its wooden body, which like King James's would have had 'several joints in the arms, legs and body to be moved to several postures', was made by his Highness's master carver. While the face, moulded out of wax and with eyes of coloured glass which opened and closed, was the work of medal maker to his Highness, Thomas Simon. In all probability Simon based the likeness on a death mask, thought to have been the practice since the funeral of Henry VII in 1509. Royal effigies were sumptuously dressed, usually in clothes from the monarch's own wardrobe, over which would be draped the raiment of sovereignty. Oliver's effigy was likewise clothed in the elegant attire that the Protector had worn at his daughter Frances's wedding almost a year earlier – a fine linen shirt with richly laced neckband and cuffs, costly doublet and breeches 'of the Spanish fashion' made of uncut grey velvet, silk stockings with matching shoestrings and gold-laced garters, and gold-buttoned shoes of black Spanish leather. The next layer of attire was a surcoat, richly laced with gold, which came down to the knee. Over this was draped an ermine-lined royal robe of purple velvet four yards in length and finished with gold lace, rich cordings and purple and gold bosses. The figure was girded with a richly embroidered belt from which hung 'a fair sword richly gilt and hatched with gold'. The right hand held a golden sceptre 'representing government' and the left an orb 'representing principality'. On the head had been placed that substitute for the crown, a purple velvet cap of regality 'furred with ermine'. This was probably one of those made up for Cromwell earlier in the year, which had given rise to the rumour that the Lord Protector was about to adopt the title King and formalise completely his already regal status. This regal status was as graphically exemplified as it possibly could be by the existence of another symbol of royal power, an imperial crown set with stones which 'lay high that the people might behold it' upon a chair of state covered in gold cloth behind the head of Cromwell's effigy.[12]

The bed of state on which the regally accoutred effigy of the Lord Protector lay was covered with a large pall of black velvet under which was a sheet of fine linen. (Considerably more velvet and linen were used on Cromwell's bed of state than on that of James I.) At the feet of the effigy stood 'the royal crest of arms [a lion standing upon an imperial crown] as usual on all ancient monuments, and over all the following inscription':

OLIVER CROMWELL,
Lord Protector of England, Scotland, and Ireland.
Born at Huntingdon,
Of the name of Williams, of Glamorgan, and by
King Henry VIII changed into Cromwell;
Was educated in Cambridge, afterwards of Lincoln's Inn.
At the beginning of the Wars, Captain of a Troop of Horse
raised at his own charge;
And by the Parliament made Commander-in-Chief.
He reduced Ireland and South Wales;
Overthrew Duke Hamilton's Army, the Kirk's Army,
at Dunbar;
Reduced all Scotland;
Defeated Charles Stuart's Army at Worcester.
He had two Sons,
Lord Richard, Protector in his Father's room;
Lord Henry, now Lord Deputy in Ireland;
And four Daughters,
Lady Bridget, first married Lord Ireton, afterwards
Lieutenant-General Fleetwood;
Lady Elizabeth, married Lord Claypole;
Lady Mary, married Lord Viscount Fauconberg;
Lady Frances, married the Hon. Robert Rich,
Grand-child to the Rt. Hon. the Earl of Warwick.
He was declared Lord Protector of England,
Scotland, and Ireland, Dec. 16, 1653.
Died Sept. 3, 1658, after fourteen days sickness, of
an ague, with great assurance and serenity of mind,
peaceably in his bed.
Natus, Apr. 25, 1599.
Dunkirk, in Flanders, surrendered to him, June 20, 1658

By the sides of the bed had been placed a rich suit of complete armour representing Cromwell's generalship. The bed itself was 'ascended unto by two ascents' and surrounded by velvet-covered rails with a square pillar, also covered

Protector Oliver's lying in state. Cromwell's magnificent state funeral was modelled in almost every detail on that of James I thirty-three years earlier.

in velvet, at each corner. Each of these pillars was decorated with 'trophies of military honour, carved and gilt' surmounted by crowned beasts – supporters of the Protectoral arms, described now as 'the imperial arms' – the English lion and Welsh dragon holding streamers in their paws. The bases supporting the pillars were adorned with gilt shields and crowns 'which makes the whole work noble and complete'. Eight five-feet high silver candlesticks (to King James's six), holding three feet long candles of virgin wax, stood within the rails. Set upright in sockets next to the candlesticks were 'funeral ensigns of honour' – standards and banners emblazoned with the heraldic insignia and royal devices of the nations of the Commonwealth and the arms of Cromwell's own family – 'all of taffety, richly gilt and painted'. These would be borne in the funeral procession. As a final touch the bed of state had above it a black velvet and fringed canopy of state with a majesty escutcheon fixed to the head. In the room were court functionaries dressed in mourning, bareheaded and holding black wands. Some stood about the bed of state while others ushered people through the room.[13]

The lying in state lasted for seven weeks. Then, on 10 November, the effigy was removed to the hall of Somerset House and set up in a standing position on a dais under a canopy of state, following yet again the precedent of James I. 'The old Protector is now got upon his legs again in Somerset House', wrote Roger Burgoyne to Ralph Verney on 11 November, 'but when he shall be translated to the rest of the gods at Westminster I cannot tell. Pray, do you come and see.' Burgoyne's reference to the fact that he does not know when the Protector's funeral will be was because the event, originally scheduled for 9 November, had been put off five days before it was due to take place without any future date being designated. Had it taken place on 9 November this would still have been sixty-seven days since Cromwell's demise, an unusually long time span when set against James I's funeral which occurred forty-one days after the King's death. But as the Venetian envoy reported 'they cannot have everything ready earlier for the magnificent and pompous function which they intend to have'.[14]

The interment of the actual body finally took place, it would seem, on the same day the effigy was moved out of the lying-in-state chamber for the standing in state, Wednesday, 10 November. This is confirmed by two entirely separate accounts. These are the reports which would seem to refute Bate's claim implying that Cromwell's corpse had to be buried soon after he died. The first account, dated Saturday, 13 November, appears in the papers of Army Secretary William Clarke. In a matter-of-fact style it states that 'the corpse of his late Highness was on Wednesday last removed from Somerset House and passing through James's Park was carried to Westminster and there interred in the vault of Henry VII's Chapel'. The second account is in a piece of correspondence from Lady Hobart, thought to have been written on 11 November, which also makes reference to Cromwell's state funeral being postponed with no alternative date in prospect: 'My Lord Protector's body was buried last night at one o'clock very privately and 'tis thought that [there] will be [no] show at all.' Nevertheless a 'show' there would be. Cromwell's corpseless state funeral would eventually take place on 23 November, eighty-one days after the Protector's demise. In his report of this spectacle, dated 6 December, the Venetian envoy comments on Cromwell's 'actual body having been buried privately many weeks ago', which is an obvious reference to the November 10 interment recorded by William Clarke and Lady Hobart. To receive the body a vault had been prepared at the east end of Westminster Abbey's Henry VII's Chapel, its massive walls abutting immediately on the vault of Henry VII and constituting the only addition to the structure of the Abbey during the Commonwealth period.[15]

But why did Cromwell have a private burial prior to his state funeral? The answer is probably contained in an ordinance passed by Parliament in March 1645 which incorporated *A Directory for the Publique Worship of God*. In this it was ordained that 'when any person departeth this life let the dead body, upon the day of burial, be decently attended from the house to the place appointed for public burial and immediately interred without any ceremony'. Such customs as 'kneeling down and praying by, or towards, the dead corpse, and other such usages in the place where it lies before it be carried to burial' were regarded as superstitious. As for 'praying, reading and singing, both in going to and at the grave', these practices were seen as having 'been grossly abused, are in no way beneficial to the dead and have proved many ways hurtful to the living. Therefore let all such things be laid aside.' Instead it was judged fitting 'that the Christian friends which accompany the dead body to the place appointed for public burial do apply themselves to meditations and conferences suitable to the occasion, and that the minister, if he be present, may put them in remembrance of their duty'. With its insistence on few rites and no ceremony the *Directory* represented a codification of Puritan burial practices which were based on the belief that the body, when the soul has left it, is nothing more than so much decaying matter and as such is not to be revered. These precepts had obviously been followed at the obsequies of Cromwell's daughter, Elizabeth Claypole, because although her body was buried in the Chapel of the Kings in Westminster Abbey the ceremony itself was 'managed without funeral pomp'.[16]

There was, however, a codicil to the *Directory* containing a typically English compromise: 'This shall not extend to deny civil respects or differences at the burial suitable to the rank and condition of the party deceased while he was living.' In other words in spite of the general undesirability of ceremony an elaborately ritualistic funeral was perfectly acceptable but only when appropriate. This allowed Puritan grandees to have very magnificent, and on the face of it very un-Puritan, state funerals in Westminster Abbey, as did the Parliamentarian commander, the Earl of Essex, in 1646, Henry Ireton, Cromwell's son-in-law and Lord Deputy in Ireland under the pre-Protectorate Commonwealth, in 1652, and Protectoral Admiral, Robert Blake, in 1657. It would seem that Cromwell's obsequies combined one of these elaborate stage-managed state funerals in Westminster Abbey with the sort of non-ceremonial low-key Puritan interment set out in *A Directory for the Publique Worship of God*, also in Westminster Abbey – a private burial of the actual body on 10 November 1658 for the private Cromwell, in keeping with what he and his family would probably have most wished for, and a public funeral centred around a regally accoutred effigy for the public Cromwell. There is a recorded instance of this sort of combination dating back to 1624 when the body of the Duke of Richmond was buried quietly soon after his death but two months later he was given a sumptuous public funeral in Westminster Abbey centred around an effigy of the duke dressed in his Parliament robes.[17]

Meanwhile Cromwell's effigy continued to stand in state in the hall of Somerset House for the remainder of the protracted funeral preparations. Attended by bareheaded court functionaries in mourning carrying black wands, as had been the case for the lying in state, it stood in a railed-off area, both rails and the ground of the area being covered in crimson velvet. The effigy was still dressed in royal robes, girded with a kingly sword and held an orb and sceptre. But there was one difference and it was fundamental. Instead of the cap of regality worn for the lying in state the effigy was now crowned with the richly ornamented imperial crown that had been on prominent display in the lying-in-state chamber. Thus the crown Cromwell did not accept in life was now bestowed on him in death.[18]

Oliver's regally accoutred funeral effigy standing in state. The pamphlet in which this illustration appeared aptly described the late Lord Protector as his Royal Highness.

But there was also symbolism of another, rather more contentious, kind. This was the transference of the effigy from the subdued atmosphere of the lying-in-state chamber, in which 'the daylight was excluded and no other but that of wax tapers to be seen', to the hall of Somerset House where 'four or five hundred candles set in flat shining candlesticks were so placed round near the roof of the hall that the light they gave seemed like the rays of the sun, by all of which he [Cromwell] was represented to be now in a state of glory'. The process represented the passage of the soul from the sufferings of Purgatory, during which it is purged of sin, into the brightness of heaven. On the face of it this was a blatant manifestation of what most contemporary Englishmen would have called popery, the doctrine of Purgatory having been rejected by the Church of England and regarded with abhorrence by Puritans. Not surprisingly therefore the standing in state of Cromwell's effigy was seen by some as an affront. 'This folly and profusion', commented the Puritan republican Edmund Ludlow, 'so far provoked the people that they threw dirt in the night on the escutcheon that was placed over the great gate of Somerset House.' Ludlow even claimed that the Lord Protector's obsequies were based on those of that most Catholic of monarchs Philip II of Spain who had died sixty years earlier in 1598. Similarly the Quaker Edward Burrough saw the very existence of a representation of Oliver in effigy as an affront. It pained him 'that an idolatrous image and picture should be made of him when he is dead, decked and laid in a sumptuous manner, visited and then carried from place to place (as was usual in the time of popery) for multitudes of foolish people to gaze upon, wonder after, admire and praise'.[19]

Burrough interpreted this as signifying that the zeal against popery was now extinguished. He bemoaned what he saw as the dead Cromwell, who had himself fought against popish worship and practices, being made a fool of 'in a popish way and manner, for such practices are no other than foolery and foolishness, tending to the dishonour of a good man'. As was perhaps only to be expected the founder of the Society of Friends, George Fox, would add his voice to the chorus of Quaker, and by extension divine, disapproval: 'Now was there a great pother made about the image or effigy of Oliver Cromwell lying in state; men standing and sounding with trumpets over his image after he was dead. At this my spirit was greatly grieved and the Lord, I found, was highly offended.' The attitude of Ludlow, Burrough and Fox to Cromwell's obsequies was, of course, generated by their sincerely held religious beliefs, for which Burrough would die a prisoner in Newgate Prison in 1662. But in reality the Lord Protector's funeral was simply a classic example of the precedent-ridden English indulging their taste for forms and ceremonies carried over from the past, elements of which no longer have any meaning. Coronations, for example, would not cease to be compounded of the 'worst dregs of popery and feudalism' even when the nation was no longer Roman Catholic or feudal. Although these carried-over elements were missing in Cromwell's coronation without a crown there would be no deviation from precedent when it came to the Protector's state funeral. Cromwell was a monarch and therefore precedent dictated that his obsequies must be those of a monarch and arranged accordingly to the utmost degree. As with a King the Protector's crowned effigy, or 'idolatrous image and picture', as Edward Burrough chose to call it, would remain standing in glory, its eyes now open, until the day of the actual state funeral.[20]

In the interim the funeral arrangements had occasioned a dispute involving officials of Westminster Abbey. Whenever there was a coronation, an opening of Parliament or the funeral of a King, Queen, Prince or peer of the realm these officials had, by right and custom, been allowed to create viewing stands outside the Abbey for the general public. This was at their own expense but they could charge the public for access to the stands. The Abbey officials were now complaining that with the approach of the late Protector's funeral 'some particular persons' of the parish of St Margaret's Westminster, whose church was next to Westminster Abbey, had encroached upon their 'ancient rights and the accustomed dues'. What these encroachers had done was to farm out the ground on which the officials of Westminster Abbey had customarily erected their stands to fellow parishioners for the same purpose 'pretending that the profit arising thereby shall go to the use of the poor of the said parish' of St Margaret.[21] All of which clearly demonstrates that the exploitative possibilities traditionally presented by state events were no less seized upon for Cromwell's funeral than they would have been for the obsequies of any other monarch.

CHAPTER 13

A Great Show

I beheld a great multitude of people gathering together and thronging and pressing exceedingly. And the whole streets were filled, from one side to the other, upwards and downwards, so far as I could see, with abundance gazing forth at every window and upon the balconies and house tops, and the glass was pulled down for people to look out into the street. An exceeding number of people there was, all the streets so thronged that I thought it could not be possible that any more could throng in or pass by. There were guards of soldiers, both of horse and foot, and they stayed me and stopped my horse and said I might not pass that way. Neither indeed could I by reason of the throng of people. I stayed a little but presently passed back another way in a kind of wondering at this great stir I found in my way. I beheld all spirits of people were up in wonderment and admiration, gazing they were and hurrying as if some marvellous and great thing had happened to them or was to be seen by them. I felt the spirits of men, women and children were all on fire and they were in an admiring frame and in a condition not usual.

So runs Edward Burrough's highly evocative account of the bustle and excitement engendered by the Protector's state funeral on Tuesday, 23 November 1658.[1]

The proceedings began with the removal from Somerset House of the effigy, 'having been beheld by those persons of honour and quality which came to behold it'. It was borne with great solemnity by ten Gentlemen of his Highness's Household, with six others carrying a canopy of state 'very rich' over it, to a waiting hearse. Sitting on the hearse, one at the feet and the other at the head of the effigy, were two Gentlemen of his Highness's Bedchamber. The very large velvet and fine linen pall on which the effigy lay extended beyond each side of the hearse and was borne up by 'persons of honour appointed for that purpose'. In the performance of these duties the officers of the Protectoral household involved were acting out the precise roles of their royal counterparts at the funeral of James I. And like that of James I the hearse was adorned with plumes of feathers and escutcheons and drawn by six horses covered with black velvet and also adorned with plumes of feathers. It would travel the mile or so to Westminster Abbey along a railed-off route lined with soldiers to prevent spectators from crowding the funeral procession. New red coats with black buttons and facings had been issued to the soldiers for the occasion, 'given them by his Highness [Richard], which makes them not a little joyful in his favour', and their ensigns were wrapped in cypress as a symbol of mourning.[2]

The funeral procession was led, as royal custom dictated, by the Knight Marshal on horseback carrying a black truncheon tipped at both ends with gold, attended by his deputy, with a silver-tipped truncheon, and thirteen marshal's men also on horseback. The Knight Marshal and his men's day-to-day duties were to police the monarch's court and constituted a sort of internal royal security department. At a sovereign's state funeral their chief function was crowd control. In the description of King James's obsequies their orders were 'to ride to and fro . . . to make way and keep the street clear' and in Protector Oliver's 'to clear the way'. This was a much easier task in the latter case because Cromwell's funeral route was lined with soldiers from a large standing army, something that did not exist in James's day.[3]

Following the Knight Marshal were all those who by tradition walked in the sovereign's funeral procession, with the addition of military commanders, and in the positions demanded by royal precedent. Those at the head of the procession were furthest away from the cortège and therefore possessed the lowest status. Which is why what were described in the account of both Protector Oliver and James I's state funeral as 'poor men of Westminster', followed by another group of 'poor men', all in mourning gowns, came immediately after the Knight Marshal. The material for the gowns worn by the accustomed poverty personified vanguard of the funeral procession would have been issued through a special committee of Privy Councillors which sanctioned the distribution of mourning cloth to all those eligible. These included the three major poets employed by the Protectorate government as French and Latin Secretaries, John Milton, John Dryden and, unofficial Protectoral poet laureate, Andrew Marvell, who took their places in the funeral procession with other, similarly employed, state servants.[4]

In addition to mourning some of the principal mourners may have been wearing funeral medals suspended from the neck, possibly on a black ribbon. Such medals were certainly made for the occasion. The work of Thomas Simon, who also walked in the funeral procession, they are, as is to be expected, outstanding examples of the engraver's art. Quite small, oval in shape with a loop for suspension and struck in gold, the Protectoral funeral medal displays, on the obverse, a laurel crowned bust of Oliver, looking careworn, and a circumscription of the Protector's title. The reverse depicts two shepherds tending their flocks and the stump of a cut-down tree, next to which stands a flourishing olive. There is a circumscription in irregular Latin which reads NON DEFITIENT OLIVA (The olive will not be wanting). The date of Cromwell's death, 3 September 1658, is also given. The allegorical design of the reverse is based on a popular play on Cromwell's name, Protector Oliver being frequently compared to the olive tree, an emblem of peace. The old olive is dead, represented by the stump of the cut-down tree. But Olivers will not be wanting because the Protectoral line will continue in Cromwell's son, symbolised by the flourishing olive tree. Under his rule the nation, represented by the shepherds tending their flocks beneath the protection of the olive tree, will continue to enjoy a peaceful existence.[5]

The funeral procession of the old Protector was so long that it was seven hours before the effigy, which was close to the rear of the cortège, reached Westminster Abbey. It included a myriad other state servants and, together with their attendants where appropriate, ambassadors of friendly foreign powers, civic dignitaries, clerics, representatives of the government, army, navy, legal institutions and judiciary. There were also such individuals as Dr 'Richard Birchhard' Busby, headmaster of Westminster School. Westminster old boy John Dryden could have derived some satisfaction, had he been so minded, from knowing that his position in the funeral procession was superior to the one occupied by Busby, whose enthusiasm for flogging left an indelible impression on the poet's mind. Busby's pupils, among whom were the curiously retained King's Scholars and Bishop's Boys, had been assembled to witness the spectacle of Protector Oliver's state funeral just as they had been to pray for King Charles I as he mounted the scaffold ten years before. Then there were those other emblems of continuity, the Poor Knights of Windsor, one-time adjuncts of the Order of the Garter, and, in their tabards, Officers of the College of Arms – Kings of Arms, Heralds and Pursuivants – who had, as was the custom, organised the funeral. Yet another emblem of continuity, the ancient and newly revived City Artillery Company, had solicitously petitioned to take part in the funeral procession as the representative of London's own military forces, the militia, or trained bands, being regarded as too numerous for the purpose. It had also been the custom for members of the royal household and purveyors of goods and services to take part in a King's obsequies and so it was with Cromwell's state funeral. Palace fire lighters, porters and kitchen staff, falconer and huntsman, shoemaker, hatter and tailor, court musicians, surgeons and chaplains, chief officers of the household with their own minions, all these and many, many more 'servants of his Highness, inferior and superior', took their accustomed places in the cortège. The bargemasters and watermen, too, occupied their traditional positions, the manifestly regal device they wore as a badge hidden under mourning cloaks.[6]

'The whole of this grand assembly went along in divisions, each division being distinguished by drums, trumpets, standards, banners and horses, whereof there were twelve in all; four being covered with black cloth, seven in velvet and one state horse covered also in velvet and ornamented with spreading plumes of feathers.' And all the while the thunder of cannon boomed across the capital from the ramparts of the Tower of London. The standards and banners were the national ensigns normally carried on such occasions. They were the same in number as, and very similar to, those borne at the funeral of James I. Some of them were certainly as explicitly regal. The Protectoral 'standard of the lion of England', for instance, corresponded almost exactly to its royal equivalent, displaying as it did a lion of England royally crowned standing upon a crown imperial, 'all of gold, properly ornamented'. It also had, in regal style, the letters O and P for Oliver Protector decorating the vacant places. Likewise the Protectoral standard of Scotland displayed, as the royal 'standard of the lion of Scotland' would have done, the Scottish crown surmounted by a lion wearing 'a royal crown proper'. While what was described as the 'banner of the union of the two crosses of England and Scotland' carried in King James's funeral procession had its counterpart in the exceptionally grand 'great banner of the states, called the union' borne at Protector Oliver's obsequies. This had a single instance of the letters O and P in gold at the top left-hand and top right-hand corners respectively, between which was an 'imperial crown of gold proper beautified with lilies, roses and crosses pattée', and under this 'a royal mantle of estate, displayed, being of ermine and gold with tassels of gold'. Within the royal mantle of estate were the crosses of St George for England and St Andrew for Scotland. All these were explicitly royal devices for what was in effect the funeral of a King. Providing additional regal splendour was the suggestion in the official memoranda for the funeral that the ceremonial horses accompanying the standards and banners should each be attended by two equerries and a groom, together with fifes, drums and trumpets, and that the fifes, drummers and trumpeters 'must have long coats trimmed with ribbons'.[7]

Towards the end of the long cortège, and therefore relatively close to the hearse, came 'members of the Other House, that is, House of Lords', the train of their mourning cloaks borne by an attendant. At James's obsequies these had all been hereditary peers. Reflecting the composition of the Cromwellian Other House those in Oliver's funeral procession were a mixture of nominated hereditary members of the old nobility, including those who had refused to take their seats, and the new-style 'life' peers. The presence of the hearse itself was proclaimed by the chief horse of mourning going before it. Here, yet again, everything was almost exactly as it had been for the funeral of James I. Following behind the chief horse of mourning were officers of the College of Arms – the arcanely titled Lancaster, Somerset and York Heralds, and Clarenceux and Norroy Kings of Arms – bearing the chivalric emblems of helm and crest, spurs, gauntlet, shield and coat of arms. In his accustomed place immediately in front of the hearse walked the most senior court official, the Lord Chamberlain of the Household, carrying his wand of office, the train of his mourning cloak borne by an attendant. Accompanying the hearse were twelve bannerols, six on each side, their bearers 'twelve persons of honour' attended by footmen. These were banners, traditionally borne at the funerals of great men, depicting the deceased's family arms. These showed Cromwell impaled (i.e. joined) with Bourchier, the Protector's wife, Cromwell impaled with Steward, his mother, and so forth in the same way that James I's family connections were displayed. One of James's twelve bannerols had been carried by the late Protector's uncle, godfather and namesake, Sir Oliver Cromwell. Sir Oliver had several times entertained James at Hinchingbrooke House, the first time in 1603 when the then new sovereign, travelling down from Scotland to claim the English crown, was provided with 'the greatest feast that had been given to a King by a subject'. A deviation in the Protectoral funeral from that of King James was the presence, walking between the hearse and the bannerols, of 'honourable persons, officers of the army, eight in number', each one bearing a piece of the rich suit of armour that had lain beside the effigy at the lying in state as a symbol of Cromwell's generalship.[8]

Immediately behind the hearse walked the chief officer of the College of Arms, Garter, Principal King of Arms, accompanied by two gentlemen ushers. And behind Garter, Principal King of Arms came the chief mourner, Charles Lord Fleetwood. 'This procession being assimilated as much as possible to the ceremonials of royalty, the new Protector [Richard] could not mourn in public for his father and Henry Cromwell was still in Ireland. Thus the late Protector's

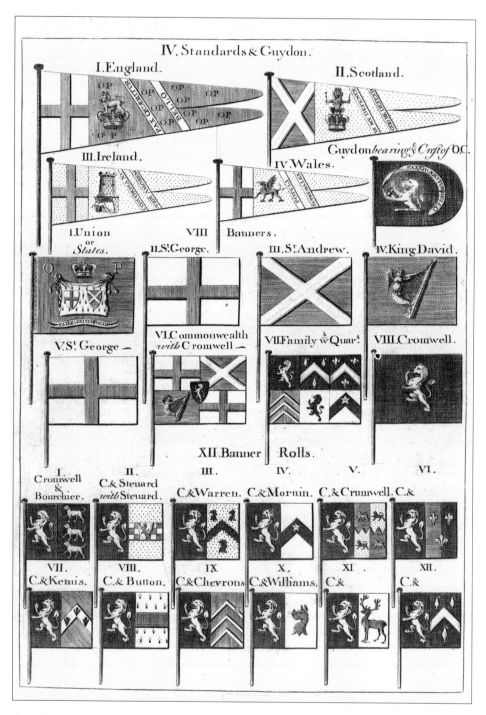

Standards and banners carried in Protector Oliver's funeral procession, some of which were practically identical to those borne at James I's obsequies being emblazoned with explicitly royal devices as befitted what was in effect the funeral of a King.

son-in-law became chief mourner.' Charles I, however, had been chief mourner at the funeral of his father, James I. As already intimated this was less consistent with accepted custom than the non-attendance at Oliver's of Protector Richard, whose absence is confirmed by the Venetian envoy. Anthropologist Ilse Hayden explains why: 'Despite the legal maxim that the new reign commences the instant that the old sovereign expires, the death of a British monarch is still followed by an interregnum – even if it is merely a ceremonial one. The King's successor remains socially invisible (and thus, in a sense, nonexistent) throughout the funeral period while the dead monarch is accorded sovereign honours. It is only at the end of the royal funeral that any ambiguity about who is the undoubted incumbent of the kingly office ceases.' In this respect at least Protector Oliver's state funeral was even more traditionally regal than the royal obsequies on which it was modelled.[9]

As chief mourner Fleetwood was attended by two 'supporters', one on each side of him. The official memoranda for the funeral had stipulated that they should be earls, which was the custom on such occasions. As it turned out these honours were performed by Viscount Lisle, heir to the earldom of Leicester, and Viscount Fauconberg, another of Cromwell's sons-in-law. The memoranda had also stipulated that the chief mourner's train should be borne by five peers and that a further group, the 'fourteen assistants to the chief mourner', should be earls or barons. This again followed established practice. Cromwell's friend and admirer the late Earl of Warwick had been one of the fourteen earls who had been assistants to the chief mourner at the funeral of King James. Fleetwood's five trainbearers, however, were not peers. They seem to have been close relatives of Protectoral grandees. The identity of the fourteen assistants is not known. Although they are described, along with the chief mourner's supporters, as 'lords and noble persons' in accounts of the funeral it is unlikely that they were all earls or barons. Obviously the memoranda was more in the nature of a notation of what had been done before than a definitive instruction of what must be.[10]

Conventionality was, however, restored by the presence, behind the assistants to the chief mourner, of the horse of honour, 'ornamented in very rich trappings embroidered on crimson velvet and adorned with white, red and yellow plumes of feathers', led on a long rein by the Master of the Horse. The tradition of a dead King's riderless horse following behind the hearse originated with the ancient, and pagan, custom of burying or burning a deceased's steed in order that it may transport its master's soul to the spirit world. Bringing up the rear of the procession were his Highness's Yeomen of the Guard, walking in twos with their halberts in all probability reversed as a token of truce for the burial, followed by gentlemen porters and warders of the Tower of London and, finally, a troop of horse. 'The whole ceremony', reported *Mercurius Politicus* with undisguised pride, 'was managed with very great state to Westminster, many thousands of people being spectators.'[11]

Someone who witnessed the event and recorded his impressions was John Evelyn. As well as describing the procession, emphasising its obvious magnificence, Evelyn also tells us that 'it was the joyfullest funeral I ever saw for there was none that cried but dogs, which the soldiers hooted away with a barbarous noise, drinking and taking tobacco in the streets as they went'. This account has often been cited by later generations as evidence of the existence of a lack of respect for the memory of the late Lord Protector. What is more likely, however, is that the soldiery were merely following custom and habit. At one time there was a tendency for historians to believe that the 1645 *Directory for the Publique Worship of God* codified practices which were an already established trend and had been for some time. But it now seems that the austere Puritan-style funerals laid down in the *Directory* were not as prevalent as was originally thought and that some of the more traditional rites and practices remained very much in vogue. This could include the consumption of large quantities of alcohol. It has also been suggested that as the Protector's body was known to have already been buried two weeks before, and the obsequies were centred around a fabricated likeness of the deceased and nothing else, the soldiers were behaving as they would have done at an ordinary state pageant. The same could be said of the behaviour of the Westminster schoolboy who snatched one of the imperially crowned escutcheons from the Protectoral hearse and escaped with it into the crowd, a schoolboy prank which is almost universally portrayed as an act of Royalist defiance provoked by the blatant display of such emblems of sovereignty.[12]

As a state pageant Cromwell's funeral 'must rank very high among those held in England at any age' was one modern observation of this remarkable event. This could probably be extended to include London's Lord Mayor's Shows, those spectacular City pageants which had been revived in the second year of Protector Oliver's rule, after which they would become a more or less permanent annual feature of London life. The 1658 Show took place in the middle of the preparations for Cromwell's state funeral. As is to be expected it was an appropriately muted affair with only two pageants.[13] One was a chariot emblazoned with, among other things, the arms of the Protector. From this a human representation of honour closed the pageantry with a speech to the Lord Mayor which opened with a poignant allusion to Cromwell's death:

> Though some dark clouds do interpose our joy,
> And seems her comely beauty to destroy:
> The argent's now by sables over-borne,
> And honour should in the same livery mourn;
> Yet that this day may not obscured be,
> We've set our confin'd heart at liberty.[14]

But the splendid state, indeed royal, pageant that was Cromwell's obsequies did not cease when the funeral procession reached the west door of Westminster Abbey. The effigy was removed from the hearse by those same ten Gentlemen of the Protectoral household who had carried it to the hearse from the standing in state at Somerset House, with the rich canopy of state borne over it as before. 'In this magnificent manner', *Mercurius Politicus* informs us, 'they carried it up to the east end of the Abbey and placed it [in Henry VII's Chapel] on that noble structure which was raised there on purpose to receive it, where it is to remain for some time exposed to public view' in accordance with royal tradition. This noble

The catafalque of James I designed by Inigo Jones on which Oliver's catafalque was modelled, only the Lord Protector's was 'much more stately and expensive'.

structure was in effect a catafalque 'built in the same form as one before had been on the like occasion for King James but much more stately and expensive'. As the catafalque for James's effigy, designed by Inigo Jones, was itself a most magnificent structure then Protector Oliver's, described by contemporaries as a monument, must have been amazing to behold. On a visit to London a young country gentleman, the Roman Catholic and staunchly Royalist baronet Sir Francis Throckmorton, 'could not resist a desire to go to Westminster Abbey to see the tombs and the Protector's monument, which cost him 2s. 6d.'. Such was the draw of Cromwell's sumptuous catafalque. 'This is the last ceremony of honour', was how *Mercurius Politicus* closed its description of Cromwell's extraordinary royal state funeral, 'and less could not be performed to the memory of him to whom posterity will pay (when envy is laid asleep by time) more honour than we are able to express.'[15]

Not everyone was appreciative of the honours given to the late Lord Protector. Edmund Ludlow had as much time for Cromwell's funeral as he did for the Protectorate, which was none at all. Having displayed his Puritan credentials by registering the disgust provoked by the 'folly and profusion' of the standing in state of the Protector's effigy in Somerset House, all he could bring himself to say was: 'I purposely omit the rest of the pageantry, the great number of persons that attended the body, the procession to Westminster, the vast expense in mourning, the state and magnificence of the monument erected for him, with many other things that I care not to remember.'[16] And it was the nature and scale of the obsequies that would likewise dismay Edward Burrough. To men such as Ludlow and Burrough Cromwell's state funeral was a blatant manifestation of those very evils against which the Civil War was supposed to have been waged and the Lord Protector himself had fought. Burrough, however, was rather more forthcoming in his condemnation than Ludlow as he reflected on what he had witnessed in the great multitude of people who had gathered to watch the procession:

All this abomination and sinful idolatry is about the funeral of the late Oliver Cromwell. . . . I knew the man when he was living and had the knowledge of his spirit and I was persuaded if it had been asked him in his lifetime if such work should be acted about him . . . I say I believe he would have denied it and said it shall not be thus with me when I am dead. . . . But upon another consideration, I said this is come to pass after this manner: though he was once zealous against popery yet he did too much forget that good cause, and too much sought the greatness and honour of the world and loved the praise of men and took flattering titles and vain respects of deceitful men.'[17]

The motivations behind Ludlow and Burrough's accounts of the Protectoral obsequies were clearly ideological and theological. But another description of the event, this time penned by the poet Abraham Cowley, was motivated, to say the least, by rather different considerations. Cowley was out on bail at the time of Cromwell's funeral. He had been sent into England as a spy in the exiled King's cause only to be netted, probably by mistake, in a round-up of suspects in 1655 following the discovery of the Royalist plot 'against his Highness and the present government'. He would, however, go on to display a grudging admiration for Cromwell and a disposition to acquiesce with the Protectoral regime. At the Restoration Cowley, like others of his countrymen with an eye to future royal preferment, attempted to rehabilitate himself by going into print. His *Ode, upon the Blessed Restoration and Return of his Sacred Majesty, Charles the Second* was published two days after the King had ridden into London. And the work in which his hostile and self-serving account of Cromwell's funeral appears, *A Vision, Concerning his late Pretended Highnesse Cromwell, the Wicked*, is generally considered to have been part of that rehabilitation process, even though for some unaccountable reason it was published anonymously.[18] This was in 1661 but Cowley claimed to have written it 'in the time of the late Protector Richard the Little':

> It was the funeral day of the late man who made himself to be called Protector, and though I bore but little affection, either to the memory of him or the trouble and folly of all public pageantry, yet I was forced by the importunity of my company to go along with them and be a spectator to that solemnity, the expectation of which had been so great that it was said to have brought some very curious persons from as far as St Michaels Mount in Cornwall and the Orkney Islands. I found there had been much more cost bestowed than either the dead man, or indeed death itself, could deserve. There was a mighty train of black-robed assistants, among which divers princes in the persons of their ambassadors were pleased to attend. The hearse was magnificent, the effigy crowned and (not to mention all other ceremonies which are practised at royal interments and therefore by no means to be omitted here) the vast multitude of spectators made up, as it used to do, no small part of the spectacle itself. But yet I know not how the whole was so managed that methought it somewhat represented the life of him for whom it was made; much noise, much tumult, much expense, much magnificence, much vainglory. Briefly, a great show, and yet after all this but an ill sight. At last (for it seemed long to me and, like his short reign, very tedious) the whole scene passed by and I retired back to my chamber, weary, and I think more melancholy than any of the mourners.[19]

The concerns that motivated these condemnatory accounts of Cromwell's obsequies may have been different but among the things most of them have in common is their mention of the cost involved, for which estimates vary widely between £28,000 and £100,000, with £60,000, 'more by one half than was used for royal funerals', as the median contender. Although the lowest of these figures is generally accepted as being nearer the mark this was still a considerable sum, especially for an already straitened regime, and over £19,000 for mourning cloth alone was still owing in August 1659, three months after the collapse of the Protectorate. Evelyn, Ludlow, Burrough and Cowley all point up the resultant splendour of this expense, the 'more than regal' state obsequies of a man described grandiloquently in a funeral elegy dedicated to him as 'the High and Mighty Prince, Oliver, Lord Protector of England, Scotland and Ireland, &c.'.[20]

CHAPTER 14

Farewell! A Long Farewell To All My Greatness!

Henry VIII, III.ii

Outwardly at least in the first month of Richard's rule the tenor of life continued as before. The new Protector seemed to be acquitting himself well enough, Bulstrode Whitelocke noting that at an audience given to the French ambassador 'Richard did carry himself discreetly and better than expected'. On 27 January 1659 Londoners witnessed Protector Richard being conveyed majestically from Whitehall to Westminster 'in a stately new-built galley' for the state opening of Parliament, which was effected with all the customary regal pomp and pageantry. Richard addressed Parliament in the House of Lords as his father had done a year earlier, 'standing on the ascent, railed on purpose in royal manner, under the cloth of state'. He told the assembled Lords and Commons that 'being by the Providence of God, and the disposition of the law, my father's successor, and bearing that place in the government that I do, I thought it for the public good to call a Parliament of the three nations, now united and conjoined together into one Commonwealth, under one government'. Richard closed his speech by commending everyone to use their utmost endeavours to make this 'a happy Parliament'.[1]

But this was to prove the most faction ridden of Parliaments and the Protector was forced into an early dissolution under pressure from senior military commanders led by Charles Fleetwood and John Desborough. This led to a call from among the more junior officers for a restoration of the Rump Parliament and precipitated the collapse of the Cromwellian Protectorate royal with Richard's abdication only eight months after his accession. That cloud no bigger than a man's hand in the dawn sky of the new Protector's reign had grown big with menace, breaking in calamity on Richard's head. 'A wonderful and sudden change in the face of the public. The new Protector Richard slighted, several pretenders and parties strive for the government. All anarchy and confusion. Lord have mercy upon us', was John Evelyn's striking entry in his diary for 25 May 1659. Eleven days later Evelyn was availing himself of what would become one of the enduring legacies of the Cromwellian regime, a night at the

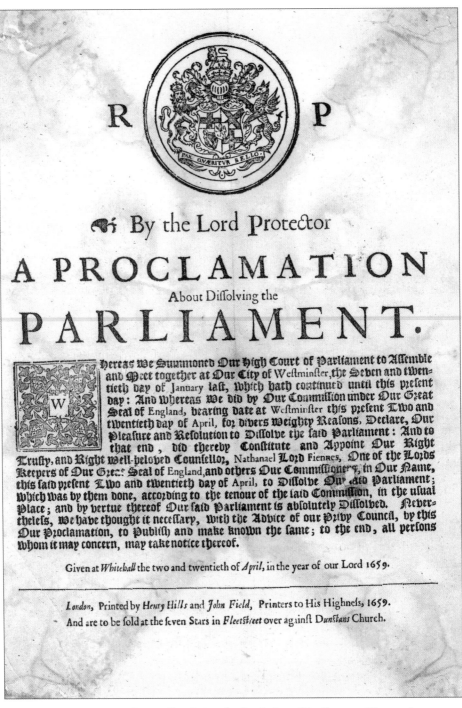

R   P

✥ By the Lord Protector

A PROCLAMATION

About Dissolving the

PARLIAMENT.

Hereas We Summoned Our High Court of Parliament to Assemble and Meet together at Our City of Westminster, the Seven and twentieth day of January last, which hath continued until this present day: And whereas We did by Our Commission under Our Great Seal of England, bearing date at Westminster this present Two and twentieth day of April, for divers weighty Reasons, Declare, Our Pleasure and Resolution to Dissolve the said Parliament: And to that end, did thereby Constitute and Appoint Our Right Trusty, and Right well-beloved Counsellor, Nathanael Lord Fiennes, One of the Lords Keepers of Our Great Seal of England, and others Our Commissioners, in Our Name, this said present Two and twentieth day of April, to Dissolve Our said Parliament; Which was by them done, according to the tenour of the said Commission, in the usual place; and by vertue thereof Our said Parliament is absolutely Dissolved. Nevertheless, We have thought it necessary, with the Advice of our Privy Council, by this Our Proclamation, to Publish and make known the same; to the end, all persons whom it may concern, may take notice thereof.

Given at *Whitehall* the two and twentieth of *April*, in the year of our Lord 1659.

London, Printed by *Henry Hills* and *John Field*, Printers to His Highness, 1659. And are to be sold at the seven Stars in *Fleetstreet* over against *Dunstans* Church.

Proclamation by Richard Cromwell ordering the dissolution of Parliament. The royal Protectoral arms are now accompanied by the regal device of the letters R and P. Soon after the dissolution the Cromwellian Protectorate royal collapsed.

opera. The diarist found the performance pretty inferior 'but what was prodigious', he remarked, was 'that in a time of such a public consternation such a vanity should be kept up or permitted'.[2]

When Parliament's Humble Petition and Advice that he should accept the crown was originally presented to Oliver Cromwell it was on condition that the new constitution must be assented to in its entirety, which included the title of King, or not at all – 'if he [Cromwell] take not all, no part should bind'. This was intended to obviate any possibility of Oliver agreeing to everything in the Humble Petition and Advice except the kingly title. It was with this in mind that the Speaker of the House of Commons told the Protector that all the articles of the new constitution 'are bound up in one link or chain, or, like a building, well knit and cemented. If one stone be taken out it loosens the whole. The rejection of one may make all the rest unsuitable and unpracticable.' But Cromwell refused the royal title even though he had no objection to occupying the actual office of King. The original conditions notwithstanding, Oliver was still permitted to rule under the Humble Petition and Advice, the office of Protector having been made conformable to the kingly dignity. It was a compromise arrangement, and for all its assimilation to kingship, including a coronation without a crown, the Cromwellian Protectorship royal was no substitute for traditional monarchical rule and was therefore not seen as constituting a permanent settlement. Which is why it was expected that Oliver would grasp the nettle and formalise completely his already regal status by adopting the title of King right up until death intervened. Had he done so Richard would truly have succeeded to 'his royal father's throne' as 'Richard the Fourth'. But the removal of that one stone, the kingly title, had loosened the whole, creating a fragile structure liable to collapse. That mighty magnate, Algernon Percy, tenth Earl of Northumberland, was possibly not speaking only for himself when he refused to sit in Protector Richard's Parliament 'till the government was such as his predecessors have served under', which was, of course, traditional monarchical rule. 'But that granted', the new Protector ruling as King in name as well as in fact, Richard would have seen Northumberland's 'willingness to serve him with his life and fortune'.[3]

Within days of the collapse of the Protectorate the successor regime, in the form of a restored pre-Protectorate Commonwealth, set about demolishing what was arguably the most potent symbol of what had gone before, Oliver's royal catafalque or monument:

> The stately and magnificent monument of the late Lord Protector, set up at the upper end of the chancel in the Abbey at Westminster, is taken down by order of the Council of State and public sale made of the crown, sceptre and other of the royal ornaments after they were broken. The inscription set upon the wall is said to be thus: 'Great in policy but matchless in tyranny.' It was put up by one of the royal party but pulled down by one of the soldiery.[4]

Not just the effigy's regal accoutrements were sold off but also practically the entire catafalque, from the expensive fabrics, ironwork and 'six leaden crowns' which adorned it right down to the wooden frame and boards which constituted its basic structure. The sale of these items realised £88 11s. 6d., from which £8 had to be deducted to cover the cost of dismantling the catafalque. Banners were to be disposed of as soon as buyers could be found for them. In the normal course of events the catafalque would have remained in position for longer and have been replaced by a more durable memorial. And this is what was supposed to have happened in Cromwell's case: 'a stately monument was intended to be erected but the alteration of the times saved that expense'.[5]

A year later Cromwellian grandees had effected a restoration of the Stuart line. Sixteen days after Charles II's return 'there was exposed to public view out of one of the windows of Whitehall . . . the effigy (which was made and shown with so much pomp at Somerset House) in wax of Oliver Cromwell, lately so well known by the name of Protector, with a cord about his neck which was tied unto one of the bars of the windows'.[6] A similar fate would befall the disinterred corpse on 30 January 1661, the twelfth anniversary of Charles I's execution. In an act of vengeful barbarism it too was exposed to public view, in this instance on the gallows at Tyburn prior to mutilation at the hands of the public executioner, who once again wore for this special occasion the regal Protectoral arms he had worn as a badge under the Cromwellian regime,[7] which was no doubt meant to be ironically appropriate. It was, however, a highly predictable fate according to the perceptive observation of one Royalist, Thomas Rugg. An entry in this obscure Covent Garden barber's journal, made immediately after the Restoration, tells of the manufacture of a large number of tobacco boxes at this time. The lids of the boxes carried a representation of Charles I on the outside and Charles II on the inside. On the inside of the bottom of the boxes Oliver Cromwell was depicted leaning against a post. Around his neck was a noose attached to a gallows above his head and 'by him a picture of the devil, wide mouthed, so that men in great power (right or wrong gotten) are admired but once fallen from that are the most despisable men that are.'[8] And so it was with Oliver Cromwell, Andrew Marvell's 'great Prince', who not only seemed 'a King by long succession born' but had, moreover, surpassed the most legendary of his royal predecessors:[9]

> And in a valour less'ning Arthur's deeds,
> For Holiness the Confessor exceeds.

Notes

Abbreviations

CJ	*The Journals of the House of Commons*
CSPD	*Calendar of State Papers: Domestic Series*
CSP Ven	*Calendar of State Papers: Venetian*
DNB	*The Dictionary of National Biography*
HMC	Historical Manuscripts Commission
Merc. Pol.	*Mercurius Politicus*
Mod. Intel.	*Moderate Intelligencer*
Perf. Diurn.	*Perfect Diurnal*
Perf. Proc.	*Perfect Proceedings of State Affairs*
Pub. Intel.	*Public Intelligencer*
Sev. Proc.	*Several Proceedings of State Affairs in England, Scotland and Ireland*
SP	State Papers
Weekly Intel.	*Weekly Intelligencer*

1. More Than Sovereign Authority

1. Mark Noble, *Memoirs of the Protectoral House of Cromwell* (Birmingham, 1787), vol. I, p. 119
2. *The Government of the Commonwealth of England, Scotland and Ireland, and the Dominions thereunto belonging, as it was publicly declared at Westminster the 16th day of December, 1653* (London, 1653)
3. *Monarchy Asserted to be the best, most Ancient and legal form of Government, in a conference had at Whitehall with Oliver, late Lord Protector, & a Committee of Parliament*, attrib. Bulstrode Whitelocke (London, 1660), p. 83; Charles Caleb Colton, *Lacon* (London, 1820), verse CCCCVIII; Baschet Transcripts PRO 31/3/92, fols 107–8
4. *CSP Ven.*, 1653–4, p. 164; James Orchard Halliwell, *The Nursery Rhymes of England Collected chiefly from Oral Tradition* (5th edn, reissued, London, 1970), p. 97; *CSPD*, 1653–4, pp. 298, 299; Baschet PRO 31/3/92, fol. 104
5. Harleian MSS 991, p. 22; Samuel Carrington, *The History of the Life and Death of his most Serene Highness Oliver Late Lord Protector* (London, 1659), p. 3
6. Bulstrode Whitelocke, *Memorials of the English Affairs* (London, 1682), pp. 491–2; *The Nicholas Papers*, ed. George F. Warner (Camden Society, 1886), vol. I, p. 310

7. John Lilburne, *Apologetical Narration* (Amsterdam, 1652), p. 20; Whitelocke, *Memorials*, p. 524; *The Unparalleled Monarch: or the Portraiture of a Matchless Prince Exprest in some Shadows of His Highness My Lord Protector* (London, 1656)

2. With Sound Of Trumpets, In Most Solemn Manner

1. *CJ*, vol. VI, pp. 664–5, vol. VII, p. 15

2. *Merc. Pol.*, 16–22 December 1653; *The Memoirs of Edmund Ludlow, 1625–1672*, ed. C.H. Firth (Oxford 1894), vol. I, pp. 372–3; *CSP Ven.*, 1653–4, p. 164; Harleian MSS 991, p. 17

3. *Merc. Pol.*, 16–22 December 1653; Ludlow, *Memoirs*, vol. I, pp. 372–3; *CSP Ven.*, 1653–4, p. 164; Harleian MSS 991, p. 17

4. Clarendon, *The History of the Rebellion and Civil Wars in England*, ed. W. Dunn Macray (Oxford, 1888), vol. V, p. 287; HMC (1905), *Earl of Egmont MSS*, vol. I, part II, p. 532

5. John Campbell, *The Lives of the Lord Chancellors and Keepers of the Great Seal of England, from the earliest times till the reign of King George IV* (London, 1845), vol. I, p. 22

6. Reginald R. Sharpe, *London and the Kingdom* (London, 1894), vol. I, pp. 212–13

7. *Mod. Intel.*, 5–12 July 1649

8. Roy Sherwood, *The Court of Oliver Cromwell* (Willingham Press edn, Cambridge, 1989), pp. 80–1

9. David Cressy, *Bonfires and Bells: National Memory and the Protestant Calendar in Elizabethan and Stuart England* (London, 1989), p. 92; John Thurloe, *A Collection of State Papers of J.T. To which is prefixed the life of Mr Thurloe by Thomas Birch* (London, 1742), vol. I, p. 645; *A Calendar of the Inner Temple Records*, ed. F.A. Inderwick (London, 1898), vol. II, p. 311; *CSPD*, 1653–4, pp. 298, 299; *Sev. Proc.*, 15–22 December 1653; *Perf. Diurn.*, 26 December 1653–2 January 1654; Whitelocke, *Memorials*, p. 561; Sir William Dugdale, *A Short View of the Late Troubles in England* (Oxford, 1681), p. 417; HMC, *Eighth Report*, Appendix, part I (1881), Corporation of the City of Leicester MSS, p. 429

10. *An Ordinance for uniting Scotland into one Commonwealth with England, April 12 1654* (London, 1654); Dugdale, *A Short View*, p. 421

11. *CSPD*, 1653–4, p. 299; Whitelocke, *Memorials*, pp. 561, 565; Ludlow, *Memoirs*, vol. I, pp. 374–5

12. *Government of the Commonwealth, etc.; A Proclamation of his Highness, with the consent of his Council, for continuing all persons being in office for the execution of public justice at the time of the late change of government, until his Highness's further direction*, 21 December 1653 (London, 1653); Whitelocke, *Memorials*, pp. 561, 564; *Stuart Royal Proclamations*, vol. I, Royal Proclamations of King James I, 1603–1625, eds James F. Larkin and Paul L. Hughes (Oxford, 1973), p. 4, vol. II, Royal Proclamations of King Charles I, 1625–1646, ed. James F. Larkin (1983), p. 4; *CSP Ven.*, 1653–4, p. 168; 'A Declaration for alteration of several names and forms heretofore used in courts, &c.' in *A copy of a letter from His Excellency the Lord General Cromwell ... with several transactions since that time* (London, 1656); 'London Sessions Records, 1605–1685', ed. Dom Hugh Bowler, *Publications of the Catholic Record Society*, vol. XXXIV (London, 1934)

13. W.C. Abbott, *The Writings and Speeches of Oliver Cromwell* (Cambridge, Massachusetts, 1945), vol. III, p. 139; *The Stuart Constitution, 1603–1688: Documents and Commentary*, ed. J.P. Kenyon, 2nd edn (Cambridge, 1986), p. 307; *Acts and Ordinances of the Interregnum, 1642–1660*, eds C.H. Firth and R.S. Rait (HMSO, 1911), vol. II, pp. 830–5; *CSP Ven.*, 1653–4, p. 169; *CSPD*, 1653–4, p. 308

14. Sherwood, *Court of O.C.*, pp. 88–96; *CSPD*, 1651–2, p. 334

15. *Sev. Proc.*, 22–29 December 1653, 29 December 1653–5 January 1654, 5–12 January 1654, 12–19 January 1654; *CSP Ven.*, 1653–4, pp. 168, 173

16. *Perf. Diurn.*, 6–13 February 1654; Dugdale, *A Short View*, p. 417

17. *CSPD*, 1649–50, pp. 166, 174; *CJ*, vol. VI, pp. 220–1; *Perf. Diurn.*, 4–11 June 1649, 8–15 September 1651, 15–23 September 1651; Whitelocke, *Memorials*, pp. 387, 391, 485

18. *Perf. Diurn.*, 6–13 February 1654; Dugdale, *A Short View*, pp. 417–18; Whitelocke, *Memorials*, p. 564; *Britania Triumphalis; A Brief History of the Warres and other State Affairs of Great Britain: From the Death of the late King to the Dissolution of the last Parliament* (London, 1654), pp. 205–6; Carrington, pp. 167–8

19. *Perf. Diurn.*, 6–13 February 1654; Dugdale, *A Short View*, pp. 417–18; Carrington, p. 168; Ilse Hayden, *Symbol and Privilege: The Ritual Context of British Royalty* (Tucson, Arizona, 1987), p. 63; *CSPD*, 1649–50, pp. 174, 175; Whitelocke, *Memorials*, p. 391

20. Cressy, *Bonfires and Bells*, p. 73; Carrington, p. 169; *Perf. Diurn.*, 6–13 February 1654; Dugdale, *A Short View*, pp. 417–18; Whitelocke, *Memorials*, p. 564; *Mr Recorders Speech to the Lord Protector upon Wednesday the eighth Februa. 1653, being the day of his Highnesse entertainment in London* (London, 1654)

21. *Perf. Diurn.*, 6–13 February 1654; Dugdale, *A Short View*, pp. 417–18; Whitelocke, *Memorials*, p. 564; Clarendon, *History*, vol. V, p. 287; *The Diary of John Evelyn*, ed. E.S. de Beer (Oxford, 1959), p. 334; Carrington, p. 170; Harleian MSS 991, p. 21; *Britania Triumphalis*, p. 207

22. *Sev. Proc.*, 2–9 March 1654, 23–30 March 1654; *Perf. Diurn.*, 13–20 March 1654

23. *CSPD*, 1649–50, p. 113; Sherwood, *Court of O.C.*, pp. 54, 98–9

24. Sherwood, *Court of O.C.*, pp. 54–7, 96–100; *Britania Triumphalis*, p. 206; Whitelocke, *Memorials*, p. 609

25. *Sev. Proc.*, 2–9 March 1654; Whitelocke, *Memorials*, pp. 566, 609

26. Sherwood, *Court of O.C.*, p. 60; *Swedish Diplomats at Cromwell's Court, 1655–1656*, translated and edited by Michael Roberts, Camden Fourth Series, vol. 36 (Royal Historical Society, London, 1988), p. 125; *Sev. Proc.*, 2–9 March 1654

27. Clarendon, *History*, vol. V, p. 288; Dugdale, *A Short View*, p. 421

28. *Sev. Proc.*, 23–30 March 1654; Dugdale, *A Short View*, p. 421; James Heath, *Flagellum: or the Life and Death, Birth and Burial of O. Cromwell the Late Usurper* (London, 1672), p. 158

29. Hyder E. Rollins, *Cavalier and Puritan: Ballads and Broadsides Illustrating the Period of the Great Rebellion, 1640–1660* (New York, 1923), pp. 343–4; *Cromwelliana: a chronological detail of the events in which Oliver Cromwell was engaged from the year 1642 to his death 1658* (Westminster, 1810), p. 138

3. Soaring Grandeur

1. Sherwood, *Court of O.C.*, pp. 20–2; *Sev. Proc.*, 22–29 December 1653, 13–20 April 1654; *Weekly Intel.*, 14–21 March 1654
2. *The Diary of Ralph Josselin, 1616–1683*, ed. Alan Macfarlane (British Academy, 1976), p. 321; Alan Macfarlane, *The Family Life of Ralph Josselin, a Seventeenth Century Clergyman: An Essay in Historical Anthropology* (Cambridge, 1970), pp. 18, 185; P.G.Rogers, *The Fifth Monarchy Men* (London, 1966), p. 40
3. Sherwood, *Court of O.C.*, p. 33; *CSP Ven.*, 1653–4, p. 168
4. *CSP Ven.*, 1653–4, p. 168
5. Sherwood, *Court of O.C.*, pp. 84, 136–7; *The New Grove Dictionary of Music and Musicians*, ed. Stanley Sadie (London, 1980), vol. V, pp. 382–3, vol. VIII, pp. 588–9; *The New Oxford Companion to Music*, ed. Denis Arnold (Oxford, 1983), vol. I, pp. 548, 858
6. Sherwood, *Court of O.C.*, pp. 36–7
7. *Sev. Proc.*, 20–27 April 1654
8. Thomas Carlyle, *The Letters and Speeches of Oliver Cromwell*, ed. S.C. Lomas (London, 1904), vol. II, p. 386
9. Sherwood, *Court of O.C.*, pp. 15–22
10. *Swedish Diplomats*, p. 107; *Johan Ekeblads Bref*, ed. N. Sjöberg (Stockholm, 1911), vol. I, pp. 411, 414–15; Sherwood, *Court of O.C.*, pp. 22–3, 55, 60
11. Sherwood, *Court of O.C.*, pp. 25–6, 29–30; Evelyn, *Diary*, p. 357
12. Sherwood, *Court of O.C.*, pp. 25–9, 31, Chapter 5
13. Charles Carlton, 'Three British Revolutions and the Personality of Kingship' in *Three British Revolutions, 1641, 1688, 1776*, ed. J.G.A. Pocock (Princeton, New Jersey, 1980), pp. 188–9; Henry G. Hewlett, 'Charles the First as a Picture Collector', *The Nineteenth Century*, vol. XXVIII, no. 162, August 1890; *CSPD*, 1654, p. 395
14. *Perf. Diurn.*, 24 April–1 May 1654; *Sev. Proc.*, 27 April–4 May 1654; *Ceremonies of Charles I: The Note Books of John Finet, 1628–1641*, ed. Albert J. Loomie (New York, 1987), pp. 94–6; *Thurloe State Papers*, vol. II, p. 257; Cressy, *Bonfires and Bells*, pp. 78, 91, 92; HMC, *Sixth Report*, Appendix (1877), ffarington MSS, p. 426
15. Sherwood, *Court of O.C.*, pp. 77, 78; *Sev. Proc.*, 27 April–4 May 1654; *Britania Triumphalis*, p. 206; Carrington, p. 168
16. Sherwood, *Court of O.C.*, p.78; *A second Narrative of the late Parliament (so called). . .* (1658) in *Harleian Miscellany*, vol. III (London 1745), p. 455
17. *Sev. Proc.*, 27 April–4 May 1654; Evelyn, *Diary*, p. 336; E.A.B. Barnard, *A Seventeenth Century Country Gentleman (Sir Francis Throckmorton, 1640–1680)*, 2nd edn (Cambridge, 1948), pp. 7–8; *The Life, Diary and Correspondence of Sir William Dugdale*, ed. William Hamper (London, 1827), p. 281; *Clarendon State Papers*, vol. III, ed. T. Monkhouse (Oxford, 1786), p. 244
18. *CSPD*, 1654, p. 253; Campbell, *Lives of the Lord Chancellors*, vol. III, p. 57; Lansdowne MSS 745, fol. 7

19. David M. Walker, *The Oxford Companion to Law* (Oxford, 1980), p. 983; Norman Wilding & Philip Laundy, *An Encyclopaedia of Parliament*, 4th rev. edn (London, 1972), p. 603; Theodore F.T. Plucknett, *Taswell-Langmead's English Constitutional History from the Teutonic Conquest to the Present Time*, 11th edn (London 1960), p. 119; *Select Cases in the Court of Requests*, ed. I.S. Leadam (Selden Society, 1898), p. Li; *Sev. Proc.*, 12–19 January 1654; *Perf. Diurn.*, 6–13 February 1654; Whitelocke, *Memorials*, p. 564

20. Josselin, *Diary*, p. 330

21. *Sev. Proc.*, 31 August–7 September 1654; Dugdale, *A Short View*, p. 423; Sherwood, *Court of O.C.*, pp. 60–1, 78, 114–15

22. *Sev. Proc.*, 31 August–7 September 1654; Sherwood, *Court of O.C.*, p. 107

23. *Sev. Proc.*, 31 August–7 September 1654; Carlyle, *Letters and Speeches*, vol. II, p. 339

24. *The Parliamentary or Constitutional History of England*, vol. XX (London, 1757), pp. 333–4; Abbott, *Writings and Speeches*, vol. III, p. 443

25. *The Diary of Thomas Burton*, ed. J.T. Rutt (London, 1828), vol. I, p. xx, vol. III, pp. 209–10; John Rushworth, *Historical Collections*, vol. IV (London, 1692), p. 478; *Verney Papers: Notes of Proceedings in the Long Parliament*, ed. John Bruce (Camden Society, 1845), pp. 138–9; *Sidney Papers*, ed. R.W. Blencowe (London, 1825), pp. 140–1; F.P.G. Guizot, *History of Oliver Cromwell and the English Commonwealth* (London, 1854), vol. I, p. 492; *Rebels no Saints: or a Collection of the Speeches, Private Passages, Letters and Prayers of those Persons lately Executed* (London, 1661), p. 9; HMC, *Twelfth Report*, Appendix, part IX (1891), Records of the Corporation of Gloucester, p. 508; *CJ*, vol. VII, p. 365; HMC (1966), *De L'Isle and Dudley MSS*, vol. VI, Sidney Papers, 1626–1698, p. 615

26. *Thurloe State Papers*, vol. II, p. 614

27. *The Clarke Papers*, ed. C.H. Firth (London, 1899), vol. III, p. 16

28. *CSP Ven.*, 1655–6, p. 4

29. Cressy, *Bonfires and Bells*, p. 78; *The Poems and Letters of Andrew Marvell*, ed. H.M. Margoliouth, 3rd edn revised by P. Legouis with the collaboration of E.E. Duncan-Jones (Oxford, 1971), vol. I, p. 118; John M. Wallace, *Destiny His Choice: The Loyalism of Andrew Marvell* (Cambridge, 1968), p. 136

4. More Soaring Grandeur

1. *CSP Ven.*, 1655–6, p. 5; Josselin, *Diary*, p. 342

2. SP 25/75, p. 713

3. Sherwood, *Court of O.C.*, p. 114

4. SP 25/75, p. 683

5. Arthur Penrhyn Stanley, *Historical Memorials of Westminster Abbey*, 7th edn (London, 1890), p. 141; Thomas Pugh, *Brittish and Out-landish Prophesies* (London, 1657); Josselin, *Diary*, p. 412

6. Harleian MSS 991, p. 16

7. SP 25/75, p. 683; Campbell, *Lives of the Lord Chancellors*, vol. I, p. 22

8. SP 25/75, pp. 690, 713; *Swedish Diplomats*, p. 270 fn; Raymond Phineas Stearns, *The Strenuous Puritan: Hugh Peter, 1598–1660* (Urbana, Illinois, 1954), p. 401

9. *Clarke Papers*, vol. III, p. 38; *Swedish Diplomats*, pp. 98, 109; Landsdowne MSS 745, fol. 7

10. *Perf. Proc.*, 3–10 May 1655; Josselin, *Diary*, p. 347; HMC, *Sixth Report*, Appendix, ffarington MSS, p. 438; Whitelocke, *Memorials*, p. 607

11. *Clarke Papers*, vol. III, pp. 42, 43; HMC, *Sixth Report*, Appendix, ffarington MSS, p. 438; *Nicholas Papers*, vol. II, pp. 295, 353; Josselin, *Diary*, p. 348

12. *Swedish Diplomats*, p. 98; *Clarke Papers*, vol. III, p. 44

13. *Swedish Diplomats*, pp. 98, 122, 124; *Clarke Papers*, vol. III, pp. 48–9; *CSPD, 1655*, pp. 277–8

14. *Clarke Papers*, vol. III, pp. 47, 51; Sherwood, *Court of O.C.*, pp. 65–6, 70–1; *Ekeblads Bref*, vol. I, p. 418

15. *CSP Ven.*, 1655–6, p. 132

16. C.H. Firth, 'The Royalists Under the Protectorate', *English Historical Review*, vol. LII, no. 208, October 1937, p. 635

17. *Perf. Proc.*, 3–10 May 1655; SP 78/113, fol. 220; Hastings MSS, Huntington Library MS HA 1472 (Extract reproduced by permission of The Huntington Library, San Marino, California. My thanks are also due to Mary L. Robertson, Manuscripts Department, Huntington Library, and Joyce Schenk, Torrence, California, and Fritha Winton for obtaining the relevant photocopy.)

18. *CSP Ven.*, 1655–6, p. 77

19. *The Case of Colonel Matthew Alured* (London, 1659); *CSPD, 1658–9*, p. 425; William C. Braithwaite, *The Beginnings of Quakerism* (London, 1912), p .435

20. Lucy Hutchinson, *Memoirs of Colonel Hutchinson*, ed. Rev. Julius Hutchinson (Everyman's Library edn, 1908), p. 294

21. Hutchinson, *Memoirs*, p. 294; George Bate, *Elenchus Motuum Nuperorum in Anglia: or a Short Historical Account of the Rise and Progress of the Late Troubles in England* (London, 1685), part II, p. 191

22. *The Diary of Samuel Pepys*, eds Robert Latham and William Mathews (London, 1970–4), vol. VIII, p. 355

23. *ibid*, vol. VI, p. 78

24. J. Nichols, 'London Pageants in the Reign of King Charles the First', *The Gentleman's Magazine*, vol. XCIV, part II, November 1824, p. 413 and 'London Pageants during the Commonwealth and the Reign of Charles II', *ibid.*, December 1824, p. 514; Robert Withington, *English Pageantry: An Historical Outline* (Cambridge, Massachusetts, 1920), vol. II, p. 44; *DNB*; Alexander Chalmers, *The General Biographical History* (London, 1814), vol. XIV, p. 331; Bruce J. Williamson, *The History of the Temple, London* (London, 1924), pp. 441–2; *A Calendar of the Middle Temple Records*, ed. Charles Henry Hopwood (London, 1930), pp. 164–5; *Oratio Anniversaria* (London, 1655)

5. *Gold And Silver Brave*

1. Joseph Ritson, *Ancient Songs, from the time of King Henry the Third to the Revolution* (London, 1790), pp. 229–33; Evelyn, *Diary*, p. 366; Sherwood, *Court of O.C.*, pp. 23, 30–1, 136; Graham Parry, *The Golden Age restor'd: The Culture of the Stuart Court, 1603–42* (Manchester, 1981), pp. 160–1

2. Sherwood, *Court of O.C.*, pp. 72–3, 83; Samuel Pegge, *Curialia: or an Historical Account of some Branches of the Royal Household* (London, 1791), part III, p. 33; Whitelocke, *Memorials*, p. 609

3. Julian Paget, *The Yeomen of the Guard 1485–1985* (Poole, 1984), p. 34; Harvey Kearsley, *His Majesty's Bodyguard of the Honourable Corps of Gentlemen-at-Arms* (London, 1937), pp. 21, 126; Pegge, *Curialia*, part II, p. 69

4. Sherwood, *Court of O.C.*, pp. 82–3; *Swedish Diplomats*, p. 108

5. Sherwood, *Court of O.C.*, pp. 81–2; *Swedish Diplomats*, p. 108

6. Sherwood, *Court of O.C.*, pp. 81, 141; Noble, vol. II, pp. 210–12; Francis Peck, *Desiderata Curiosa: or, a Collection of Divers Scarce and Curious Pieces (Relating chiefly to Matters of English History)* (London, 1732), Lib. XIII, p. 17

7. HMC, *Sixth Report*, Appendix, ffarington MSS, p. 440; *Swedish Diplomats*, p. 270; Edward Raymond Turner, *The Privy Council of England in the Seventeenth and Eighteenth Centuries, 1603–1784* (Baltimore, Maryland, 1927), vol. I, pp. 313–14

8. Sherwood, *Court of O.C.*, pp. 93, 114; *CSP Ven.*, 1655–6, pp. 215, 218; Finet, *Ceremonies of Charles I*, p. 104

9. A.K.B. Evans, 'St George's Chapel, 1345–1975', *History Today*, vol. XXV, no. 5, May 1975; Sherwood, *Court of O.C.*, p. 136

10. Edmund H. Fellowes, *The Military Knights of Windsor, 1352–1944* (Windsor, 1944)

11. *ibid.; An Ordinance for the Continuance and Maintenance of the Almshouses and Almsmen called Poor Knights and other Charitable and Pious Uses* (London, 1655)

12. *ibid.*

13. Anthony Wagner, *Heralds of England: A History of the Office and College of Arms* (HMSO, 1967), pp. 254, 260

14. Lawrence E. Tanner, *Westminster School*, 2nd edn (Country Life, London, 1951); John D. Carleton, *Westminster School: A History* (London, 1965); John Field, *The King's Nurseries: The Story of Westminster School* (London, 1987)

15. Burton, *Diary*, vol. IV, p. 243; *The Letters of John Dryden*, ed. Charles E. Ward (Durham, North Carolina, 1942), p. 120; C.R.L. Fletcher, *Mr Gladstone at Oxford, 1890* (London, 1908), p. 52; Tanner, *Westminster School*; Carleton, *Westminster School*; Field, *The King's Nurseries*

16. *Swedish Diplomats*, pp. 317–18, 326; *The Poems of Edmund Waller*, ed. George Thorn-Drury (London, 1905), vol. II, p. 27; Burton, *Diary*, vol. II, p. 141 fn

17. Nichols, 'London Pageants', *Gentleman's Magazine*, December 1824, p. 514; Withington, *English Pageantry*, vol. II, pp. 45–6

18. Anthony Highmore, *The History of the Honourable Artillery Company of the City of London* (London, 1804), pp. 42, 79, 180; *The Ancient Vellum Book of the Honourable Artillery Company*, ed. G.A. Raikes (London, 1890), pp. vii, xii, 46; G. Goold Walker, *The Honourable Artillery Company, 1537–1947* (Aldershot, 1954), pp. 60, 62

19. HMC, *Sixth Report*, Appendix, ffarington MSS, p. 441; HMC, *Fifteenth Report*, Appendix, part VII (1898), Ailesbury MSS, p.160; John Aubrey, *'Brief Lives', Chiefly of Contemporaries, set down by John Aubrey, between the Years 1669 and 1696*, ed. Andrew Clark (Oxford, 1898), vol. I, p. 155;

H.C.B. Rogers, *Battles and Generals of the Civil Wars, 1642–1651* (London, 1968), p. 94; Thomas Pomfret, *The Life of the Right Honourable and Religious Lady Christian Late Countess Dowager of Devonshire* (London, 1685), pp. 71–3, 79–80

6. We Have A Crown Made

1. HMC, *Fifteenth Report*, Appendix, part VII, Ailesbury MSS, p. 160; Baschet PRO 31/3/101, fols 43–4; *The Tudor Constitution: Documents and Commentary*, ed. G.R. Elton (Cambridge, 1960), pp. 2, 4–5; *Monarchy Asserted*, p. 27
2. *Thurloe State Papers*, vol. V, p. 705
3. Philip Aubrey, *Mr Secretary Thurloe: Cromwell's Secretary of State, 1652–1660* (London, 1990), pp. 94–5, 116; *Thurloe State Papers*, vol. II, pp. 385–6, 510–14
4. Burton, *Diary*, vol. I, pp. 362–3; Baschet PRO 31/3/101, fol. 43
5. *Thurloe State Papers*, vol. VI, p. 15; Ludlow, *Memoirs*, vol. I, p. 353; Baschet PRO 31/3/101, fol. 43; *Clarke Papers*, vol. III, p. 88
6. *CJ*, vol. VII, p. 496; *Clarke Papers*, vol. III, pp. 91, 94
7. *CSPD*, 1656–7, p. 323; *Thurloe State Papers*, vol. VI, p. 104; Josselin, *Diary*, p. 394
8. *DNB*; William Prynne, *King Richard the Third Revived* (London, 1657); *CSP Ven.*, 1657–9, pp. 33–4
9. *CJ*, vol. VII, p. 511; *The Protectorate of Oliver Cromwell, and the State of Europe during the Reign of Louis XIV*, ed. Robert Vaughan (London, 1838), vol. II, p. 139
10. *A Narrative of the late Parliament (so called)* . . . (1657) in *Harleian Miscellany*, vol. III, pp. 429–48; *Stuart Constitution*, p. 310
11. *A Narrative of the late Parliament* in *Harleian Miscellany*, vol. III, pp. 429–48
12. C.S. Egloff, 'Robert Beake: a Letter concerning the Humble Petition and Advice, 28 March 1657', *Historical Research* (Bulletin of the Institute of Historical Research), vol. 68, no. 166, June 1995, pp. 233–9
13. Carlyle, *Letters and Speeches*, vol. III, pp. 487–8; Egloff, 'Robert Beake', *Historical Research*, vol. 68, no. 166, June 1995, p. 238
14. John Nickolls, *Original Letters and Papers of State addressed to Oliver Cromwell*, Found among the Political Collections of Mr John Milton (London, 1743), pp. 139–43
15. *CSPD*, 1656–7, pp. xii, 322
16. *A Collection of the State Letters of the Right Honourable Roger Boyle, the first Earl of Orrery . . . together with . . . the life of the Earl of Orrery by the Reverend Mr Thomas Morrice* (London, 1742), pp. 21–2; *Bishop Burnet's History of His Own Time*, vol. I (Dublin, 1724), p. 40
17. *ibid.*
18. *ibid.*
19. Additional MSS 32093, fols 348–9
20. Pepys, *Diary*, vol. V, pp. 296–7
21. Clarendon, *History*, vol. VI, p. 34; Noble, vol. II, pp. 388–9; *Thurloe State Papers*, vol. VI, pp. 104, 125, 134

22. Noble, vol. II, pp. 233, 243; S.R. Gardiner, *History of the Commonwealth and Protectorate*, 4 vols (Windrush Press edn, 1988/9), vol. IV, p. 243; Aubrey, *Mr Secretary Thurloe*, p. 116
23. *Thurloe State Papers*, vol. VI, p. 134
24. *CSPD*, 1656–7, p. 386

7. Monarchy Asserted

1. Egloff, 'Robert Beake', *Historical Research*, vol. 68, no. 166, June 1995, p. 238; *Merc. Pol.*, 26 March–2 April 1657; Carlyle, *Letters and Speeches*, vol. III, pp. 27–9
2. Carlyle, *Letters and Speeches*, vol. III, pp. 29–33; Burton, *Diary*, vol. I, p. 411; Egloff, 'Robert Beake', *Historical Research*, vol. 68, no. 166, June 1995, p. 238
3. Carlyle, *Letters and Speeches*, vol. III, pp. 22–38
4. *Monarchy Asserted*, pp. 1–3, 9
5. *ibid.*, pp. 10–13; *CSPD*, 1603–10, pp. 96, 97, 99, 100, 101, 103, 130, 159, 203, 241
6. J.R.S. Whiting, *Commemorative Medals: A Medallic History of Britain, from Tudor times to the present day* (Newton Abbot, 1972), p. 36; *A Guide to the Exhibition of Historical Medals in the British Museum* (British Museum, 1924), p. 25; *Thurloe State Papers*, vol. II, p. 614; *Monarchy Asserted*, pp. 13, 23
7. *Monarchy Asserted*, pp. 19–21
8. *ibid.*, pp. 16–18, 26–8
9. *ibid.*, pp. 28–33
10. *ibid.*, pp. 34–5
11. *ibid.*, pp. 39–44
12. HMC, *Fifth Report*, Appendix (1876), Sutherland MSS, p. 163; *Monarchy Asserted*, pp. 53–4
13. Burton, *Diary*, vol. II, p. 7; Whitelocke, *Memorials*, p. 646; *Thurloe State Papers*, vol. VI, p. 220; HMC, *Fifth Report*, Appendix, Sutherland MSS, p. 163; Harleian MSS 991, p. 22
14. Baschet PRO 31/3/101, fols 160–1; Lansdowne MSS 822, fol. 57
15. *Thurloe State Papers*, vol. VI, p. 261; Whitelocke, *Memorials*, p. 647
16. HMC, *Fifth Report*, Appendix, Sutherland MSS, p. 163; *Thurloe State Papers*, vol. VI, pp. 261, 281; *Merc. Pol.*, 7–14 May 1657; *Monarchy Asserted*, pp. 111–12
17. *Thurloe State Papers*, vol. VI, pp. 219, 261; Ludlow, *Memoirs*, vol. II, p. 24
18. *Thurloe State Papers*, vol. VI, p. 281; Baschet PRO 31/3/101, fol. 189; Ludlow, *Memoirs*, vol. II, pp. 26–7
19. Ludlow, *Memoirs*, vol. II, pp. 27–8; *Thurloe State Papers*, vol. VI, pp. 219–20; *Monarchy Asserted* (Preface)
20. Waller, *Poems*, vol. II, p. 11; Burnet, *History*, vol. I, pp. 44–5
21. Burton, *Diary*, vol. II, pp. 531–2; *Sev. Proc.*, 14–21 September 1654; Additional MSS 32093, fols 399–401

8. Protector Royal

1. *CJ*, vol. VII, pp. 535, 537, 539; *Acts and Ordinances of the Interregnum*, vol. II, pp. 1184–5
2. Lansdowne MSS 822, fol. 75

3. HMC, *Sixth Report*, Appendix, ffarington MSS, p. 441; SP 18/113, fol. 220; HMC, *Earl of Egmont MSS*, vol. I, part II, p. 582

4. *Monarchy Asserted*, p. 44; *Thurloe State Papers*, vol. VI, p. 222; Burton, *Diary*, vol. II, p. 303

5. Abbott, *Writings and Speeches*, vol. IV, p. 542; Henry William Henfrey, *Numismata Cromwelliana* (London, 1877), pp. 91–8

6. Henfrey, *Numismata Cromwelliana*, p. 103

7. *ibid.*, pp. 111–13; Pepys, *Diary*, vol. IV, p. 70

8. Austin Woolrych, *Commonwealth to Protectorate* (Oxford, 1982), p. 360

9. Throughout this chapter the description of Cromwell's second investiture and accompanying quotations are taken from Clarendon, *History*, vol. VI, p. 32; *Merc. Pol.*, 25 June–2 July 1657; Sir John Prestwich, *Respublica* (London, 1787), pp. 3–19; Burton, *Diary*, vol. II, p. 514; Ludlow, *Memoirs*, vol. II, p. 29, unless other references are given

10. SP 25/78, p. 170

11. Stanley, *Historical Memorials*, p. 75

12. *The Complete Peerage of England, Scotland, Ireland and the United Kingdom*, ed. G.E. Cokayne, rev. edn, ed. Vicary Gibbs *et al*, vol. X, p. 713

13. 'The Coronation of their Majesties William IV and Queen Adelaide', *The Gentleman's Magazine*, vol. CI, part II, September 1831, p. 220

14. Kenneth J. Mears, *The Tower of London* (Oxford, 1988), p. 145

15. Robert Ware, *Foxes and Firebrands: or, a specimen of the danger and harmony of Popery and Separation*, 2nd edn, 2 parts (Dublin, 1682), part 2, p. 5

16. Anthony à Wood, *Athenae Oxonienses*, vol. II (London, 1692), col. 768

17. Whitelocke, *Memorials*, p. 524

18. *Clarke Papers*, vol. III, p. 94

19. Voltaire, *Mérope, A Tragedy*, transl. John Theobald (London, 1744)

20. *Thurloe State Papers*, vol. VI, p. 15; HMC, *Sixth Report*, Appendix, ffarington MSS, pp. 441–2; HMC, *Fifth Report*, Appendix, Sutherland MSS, p. 164

21. Cressy, *Bonfires and Bells*, pp. 78, 92; *Merc. Pol.*, 25 June–2 July 1657; HMC, *Twelfth Report*, Appendix, part IX, Records of the Corporation of Gloucester, pp. 512–17; Clarendon, *History*, vol. VI, p. 33

22. Noble, vol. II

23. *ibid.*, vol. I, pp. 439–42; David Masson, *The Life of John Milton* (Gloucester, Massachusetts, 1965 reprint), vol. V, p. 354 fn. 1; *Complete Baronetage*, ed. G.E. Cokayne (Exeter, 1903), vol. III, pp. 1–9

24. Noble, vol. I, pp. 439–42; Masson, *Life of John Milton*, vol. V, p. 354 fn. 1; *Complete Baronetage*, vol. III, pp. 1–9; W.A. Shaw, *The Knights of England* (London, 1906), vol. II, pp. 223–4; *Pub. Intel.*, 13–20 September 1658

25. Sherwood, *Court of O.C.*, pp. 96–8, 165

9. *Much Mirth With Frolics*

1. Sir Philip Warwick, *Memoirs of the Reign of King Charles I with a continuation to the Happy Restoration of King Charles II* (London, 1701), p. 382

2. Baschet PRO 31/3/101, fol. 44; Lansdowne MSS 822, fol. 57; *Thurloe State Papers*, vol. V, p. 146; HMC (1900), *Frankland-Russell-Astley MSS*, pp. 21–2

3. *Thurloe State Papers*, vol. V, p. 146; HMC, *Frankland-Russell-Astley MSS*, p. 22

4. *CSPD*, 1656–7, p. 322; *Thurloe State Papers*, vol. VI, pp. 477, 573

5. *Merc. Pol.*, 5–12 November 1657

6. HMC, *Fifth Report*, Appendix, Sutherland MSS, p. 177

7. Percy A. Scholes, *The Puritans and Music in England and New England* (Oxford, 1934), pp. 144–5

8. Harleian MSS 991, p. 23

9. *Complete Peerage*, vol. IX, pp. 549–52; S.R. Gardiner, *History of the Great Civil War*, 4 vols (Windrush Press edn, 1987), vol. II, p. 212, vol. III, p. 67

10. Prestwich, *Respublica*, p. 188, in conjunction with 'Dering's Diary and Commonplace Book, 1656–1662'. (My thanks to Peter Beal of Sotheby's, London, for entry reproduced in Sotheby Catalogue, Lot 2901, p. 55, 26 June 1974, original now in the Huntington Library, San Marino, California, HM 41536.)

11. Warwick, *Memoirs*, p. 247

12. *Sidney Papers*, p. 139

13. Carrington, p. 168; Warwick, *Memoirs*, p. 248

14. *Clarke Papers*, vol. III, p. 127; Cressy, *Bonfires and Bells*, p. 91

15. HMC, *Fifth Report*, Appendix, Sutherland MSS, pp. 145, 183

16. *Parliamentary or Constitutional History of England*, vol. XX, p. 459; *CSP Ven.*, 1657–9, pp. 38, 70; *CSPD*, 1656–7, p. 349; *The Conway Letters*, ed. Marjorie Hope Nicolson, rev. edn, ed. Sarah Hutton (Oxford, 1992), p. 142 fn. 2

17. *Thurloe State Papers*, vol. VI, p. 600; *Merc. Pol.*, 19–26 November 1657

18. Pierre Legouis, *Andrew Marvell: Poet, Puritan, Patriot*, 2nd edn (Oxford, 1968), p. 110; Marvell, *Poems and Letters*, vol. I, pp. 126, 127, 331; Scholes, *Puritans and Music*, pp. 145–6

19. Marvell, *Poems and Letters*, vol. I, pp. 128–9; Scholes, *Puritans and Music*, p. 146

20. Legouis, *Andrew Marvell*, pp. 110–11

21. Sherwood, *Court of O.C.*, p. 144

22. *Sir William Davenant: The Shorter Poems, and Songs from the Plays and Masques*, ed. A.M. Gibbs (Oxford, 1972), p. xxxiii

23. *Merc. Pol.*, 19–26 November 1657; *Thurloe State Papers*, vol. VI, p. 628; HMC (1903), *Various Collections*, vol. II, Wombwell MSS, p. 115

24. *Acts and Ordinances of the Interregnum*, vol. II, p. 716; HMC, *Fifth Report*, Appendix, Sutherland MSS, p. 177; Clarendon, *History*, vol. VI, p. 34; Geoffrey Ridsdill Smith, *In well beware: The Story of Newburgh Priory and the Belasyse Family, 1145–1977* (Kineton, 1978), p. 39; *DNB*

25. Ronald Hutton, *The Restoration: A Political and Religious History of England and Wales, 1658–1667* (Oxford, 1985), p. 26

26. HMC, *Fifth Report*, Appendix, Sutherland MSS, p. 177; Smith, *In well beware*, p. 39; Hutchinson, *Memoirs*, p. 295; Lansdowne MSS 822, fol. 104; *Complete Peerage*, vol. VIII, p. 371

10. Tempest And Foul Weather

1. *Letters from Dorothy Osborne to Sir William Temple, 1652–54*, ed. Edward Abbott Parry (London, 1903), p. 79
2. Sir George Albert Bonner, *The Office of the King's Remembrancer in England* (London, 1930), pp. 31–6, 141–9; Henfrey, *Numismata Cromwelliana*, pp. 118–23
3. *CSPD*, 1657–8, p. 206; *Merc. Pol.*, 31 December 1657–7 January 1658; *CSPD*, 1619–23, p. 362
4. Warwick, *Memoirs*, p. 382
5. *ibid.*; Sherwood, *Court of O.C.*, p. 65; *A second Narrative* in *Harleian Miscellany*, vol. III, p. 455; *Clarke Papers*, vol. III, p. 141
6. Sherwood, *Court of O.C.*, pp. 41–7
7. *ibid.*, pp. 44, 64–5, 149–50
8. Clarendon, *History*, vol. VI, p. 39; *Clarke Papers*, vol. III, p. 132; Carlyle, *Letters and Speeches*, vol. III, pp. 150, 488; *Thurloe State Papers*, vol. I, p. 766
9. *Complete Peerage*, vol. IV, p. 588
10. *ibid.*, p. 589; *Clarke Papers*, vol. III, pp. 127, 132
11. C.H. Firth, *The House of Lords During the Civil War* (London, 1910), p. 251
12. *Stuart Constitution*, p. 325; *A second Narrative* in *Harleian Miscellany*, vol. III, p. 449
13. Carlyle, *Letters and Speeches*, vol. III, p. 192
14. *ibid.*, vol. III, pp. 187, 188, 504
15. HMC, *Earl of Egmont MSS*, vol. I, part II, p. 593; *CSPD*, 1657–8, pp. 255, 258
16. HMC, *Sixth Report*, Appendix, ffarington MSS, p. 442
17. Clarendon, *History*, vol. VI, p. 38; *Clarke Papers*, vol. III, pp. 141, 142; Lou Taylor, *Mourning Dress: A Costume and Social History* (London, 1983), pp. 73, 259; Pepys, *Diary*, vol. I, pp. 244, 246
18. William Godwin, *History of the Commonwealth of England* (London, 1828), vol. IV, pp. 528–30; Clarendon, *History*, vol. VI, p. 90; Noble, vol. II, p. 161; *Complete Baronetage*, vol. III, p. 7
19. Whitelocke, *Memorials*, p. 674; Humphry William Woolrych, *Lives of Eminent Sergeants-at-Law of the English Bar* (London, 1869), vol. I, pp. 33–41; Campbell, *Lives of the Lord Chancellors*, vol. IV, pp. 7–16
20. Woolrych, *Lives of Eminent Sergeants-at-Law*, vol. I, pp. 33–41; Campbell, *Lives of the Lord Chancellors*, vol. IV, pp. 7–16; Gardiner, *History of the Commonwealth and Protectorate*, vol. III, pp. 299–301
21. Clarendon, *History*, vol. VI, p. 93; Walker, *Oxford Companion to Law*, p. 796
22. Bate, *Elenchus*, part II, pp. 190–1
23. Campbell, *Lives of the Lord Chancellors*, vol. IV, p. 14

11. Moses My Servant Is Dead

1. HMC, *Fifth Report*, Appendix, Sutherland MSS, p. 180; *Clarke Papers*, vol. III, p. 150; SP 25/78, p. 623
2. *The Journal of George Fox*, ed. Norman Penny (London 1924), p. 171; Clarendon, *History*, vol. VI, p. 88
3. *Pub. Intel.*, 2–9 August 1658

4. Masson, *Life of John Milton*, vol. V, p. 352
5. Carrington, pp. 218–19; Noble, vol. I, p. 140; Stanley, *Historical Memorials*, p. 505; HMC, *Fifth Report*, Appendix, Sutherland MSS, p. 146
6. *Merc. Pol.*, 5–12 August 1658; Robert W. Ramsey, *Studies in Cromwell's Family Circle* (London, 1930), p. 17; Antonia Fraser, *Cromwell: Our Chief of Men* (London, 1973), p. 665
7. Marvell, *Poems and Letters*, pp. 129–37
8. *Thurloe State Papers*, vol. VII, p. 320; Baschet PRO 31/3/102, fols 378–9
9. *Thurloe State Papers*, vol. VII, p. 320; Fox, *Journal*, p. 173
10. Walker, *Honourable Artillery Company*, pp. 62–71; Highmore, *History of the Honourable Artillery Company*, pp. 80–2
11. *Thurloe State Papers*, vol. VII, p. 320; *Some Farther Intelligence of the Affairs of England* (London, 1659), p. 2
12. Whitelocke, *Memorials*, p. 675; *Merc. Pol.*, 26 August–2 September 1658; Henfrey, *Numismata Cromwelliana*, p. 128
13. Henry Dawbeny, *Historie and Policie reviewed, in The Heroick Transactions of his Most Serene Highness, Oliver, Late Lord Protector, from his Cradle to his Tomb* (London, 1659)
14. *Some Farther Intelligence*, p. 2
15. *Proclamation of Richard Cromwell as Lord Protector* (London, 1658); *Stuart Royal Proclamations*, vol. II, p. 2
16. *ibid.*
17. *By the Protector. A Proclamation Signifying His Highness Pleasure, That all men being in Office of Government, at the decease of his most dear Father, Oliver, late Lord Protector, shall so continue till his Highness further Direction* (London, 1658); *Stuart Royal Proclamations*, vol. II, pp. 4–5
18. Cressy, *Bonfires and Bells*, pp. 78, 91–2; Ludlow, *Memoirs*, vol. II, p. 46; *A True Catalogue, or, An Account of the several Places and most Eminent Persons in the three Nations, and elsewhere, where, and by whom, Richard Cromwell was Proclaimed Lord Protector of the Commonwealth of England, Scotland and Ireland* (London, 1659), pp. 17, 19
19. *A True Catalogue*, pp. 33, 46–7
20. Dugdale, *A Short View*, pp. 461–2
21. Clarendon, *History*, vol. VI, p. 98
22. *Thurloe State Papers*, vol. VII, p. 374
23. Burton, *Diary*, vol. III, p. 65

12. The Last Act Crowns The Play

1. *The New Oxford Book of Verse, 1250–1950*, ed. Helen Gardner (Oxford, 1989), p. 252; Noble, vol. I, p. 119
2. *Merc. Pol.*, 9–16 September 1658; *CSP Ven.*, 1657–9, pp. 243, 248; *Some Farther Intelligence*, p. 5; *The Pourtraiture of his Royal Highness, Oliver, late Lord Protector &c.* (London, 1659); *The Letters of John Chamberlain*, ed. Norman Egbert McClure (American Philosophical Society, Philadelphia, 1939), vol. II, p. 616
3. SP 18/182, fol. 232

4. *Merc. Pol.*, 14–21 October 1658; Prestwich, *Respublica*, pp. 173–4; John Nichols, *The Progresses, Processions and Magnificent Festivities of King James the First* (London, 1828), vol. IV, p. 1037

5. *Merc. Pol.*, 2–9 September 1658; Privy Council Register of Richard Cromwell, September 3rd 1658 – January 18th 1659, p. 32; Noble, vol. I, pp. 289–90; Prestwich, *Respublica*, p. 172

6. Ernst H. Kantorowicz, *The King's Two Bodies: A Study in Mediaeval Political Theology* (Princeton, New Jersey, 1957), pp. 419–21; Nigel Llewellyn, *The Art of Death: Visual Culture in the English Death Ritual c.1500–c.1800* (London, 1992), pp. 54–5

7. *Monarchy Asserted*, p. 47; *Some Farther Intelligence*, p. 4

8. Privy Council Register of Richard Cromwell, pp. 32–4

9. *Merc. Pol.*, 16–23 September 1658; *Pub. Intel.*, 20–27 September 1658; Nichols, *Progresses*, pp. 1037–8; Chamberlain, *Letters*, vol. II, p. 609; *CSP Ven.*, 1657–9, p. 248

10. Bate, *Elenchus*, part II, p. 236; Sherwood, *Court of O.C.*, pp. 111–12

11. Heath, *Flagellum*, p. 187; *The Life and Times of Anthony Wood, Antiquary, of Oxford, 1632–1695, described by Himself*, collected from his diaries and papers by Andrew Clark, vol. I (Oxford Historical Society, 1891), p. 475; Sherwood, *Court of O.C.*, p. 112

12. *Merc. Pol.*, 9–16 September 1658, 14–21 October 1658; Prestwich, *Respublica*, pp. 174, 188; W.H. St John Hope, 'On the Funeral Effigies of the Kings and Queens of England, with special reference to those in the Abbey Church of Westminster', *Archaeologia*, vol. LX, 1907, p. 557; 'Dering's Diary and Commonplace Book'; Sherwood, *Court of O.C.*, p. 104

13. *Parliamentary or Constitutional History of England*, vol. XXI, p. 240; Prestwich, *Respublica*, pp. 174–5; *Merc. Pol.*, 14–21 October 1658; Nichols, *Progresses*, vol. IV, p. 1039

14. Prestwich, *Respublica*, p. 175; *Memoirs of the Verney Family During the Seventeenth Century*, ed. Frances Parthenope Verney and Margaret M. Verney (London, 1925), vol. II, p. 130; Privy Council Register of Richard Cromwell, p. 119; HMC, *Fifth Report*, Appendix, Sutherland MSS, p. 146; *CSP Ven.*, 1657–9, p. 253

15. *Clarke Papers*, vol. III, pp. 167–8; Verney Family, *Memoirs of*, vol. II, p. 129; *CSP Ven.*, 1657–9, p. 268; Stanley, *Historical Memorials*, p. 160

16. *Merc. Pol.*, 5–12 August 1658

17. Lawrence Stone, *The Crisis of the Aristocracy, 1558–1641* (Oxford, 1965), p. 579

18. Prestwich, *Respublica*, p. 175; Ludlow, *Memoirs*, vol. II, p. 47

19. Ludlow, *Memoirs*, vol. II, pp. 47–8; Sherwood, *Court of O.C.*, pp. 126–7; Edward Burrough, 'A Testimony Against a Great Idolatry' in *The Memorable Works of a Son of Thunder and Consolation* (London, 1672), p. 459

20. Burrough, 'A Testimony Against a Great Idolatry' in *Memorable Works*, p. 459; Fox, *Journal*, p. 176; Prestwich, *Respublica*, p. 175

21. Westminster Abbey MSS 6371 (I am grateful to Mr A.J. Richardson of Church Monuments for drawing my attention to this and other relevant Westminster Abbey manuscripts.)

13. A Great Show

1. Burrough, 'A Testimony Against a Great Idolatry' in *Memorable Works*, p. 457

2. *Merc. Pol.*, 18–25 November 1658; Prestwich, *Republica*, pp. 175–6; Burton, *Diary*, vol. II, p. 518; SP 18/183, fol. 272; Sherwood, *Court of O.C.*, pp. 75–6; *Clarke Papers*, vol. III, p. 168

3. *Merc. Pol.*, 18–25 November 1658; Prestwich, *Republica*, p. 176; Nichols, *Progresses*, p. 1034; Sherwood, *Court of O.C.*, pp. 47–8

4. *Merc. Pol.*, 18–25 November 1658; Burton, *Diary*, vol. II, pp. 519, 594; Nichols, *Progresses*, p. 1040; 'Dering's Diary and Commonplace Book'; SP 18/182, fol. 229; Sherwood, *Court of O.C.*, pp. 138–40

5. Henfrey, *Numismata Cromwelliana*, pp. 164–70

6. *Merc. Pol.*, 18–25 November 1658; Prestwich, *Republica*, pp. 175–8; Burton, *Diary*, vol. II, pp. 518–29; 'Dering's Diary and Commonplace Book'; SP 18/183, fol. 272; SP 18/182, fol. 229; Highmore, *History of the Honourable Artillery Company*, pp. 86–7; Walker, *Honourable Artillery Company*, pp. 71–2

7. Prestwich, *Republica*, pp. 177–8, 182–4; *Merc. Pol.*, 18–25 November 1658; Burton, *Diary*, vol. II, pp. 520, 528; Nichols, *Progresses*, pp. 1041, 1043; SP 18/183, fols 272, 275

8. *Merc. Pol.*, 18–23 November 1658; Prestwich, *Republica*, pp. 177–8, 186–7; Burton, *Diary*, vol. II, pp. 527–8; Nichols, *Progresses*, pp. 1045–7; Noble, vol. I, p. 41; SP 18/183, fol. 275

9. *Merc. Pol.*, 18–23 November 1658; Prestwich, *Republica*, p. 178; Burton, *Diary*, vol. II, p. 528 and fn; Nichols, *Progresses*, p. 1047; *CSP Ven.*, 1657–9, p. 269; Hayden, *Symbol and Privilege*, p. 15

10. *Merc. Pol.*, 18–23 December 1658; Prestwich, *Republica*, p. 178; Burton, *Diary*, vol. II, p. 529; SP 18/183, fol. 274; Nichols, *Progresses*, p. 1047

11. Prestwich, *Republica*, p. 178; Burton, *Diary*, vol. II, p. 529; *Merc. Pol.*, 18–23 November 1658; Taylor, *Mourning Dress*, pp. 22–3, 25

12. Evelyn, *Diary*, pp. 394–5; Clare Gittings, *Death, Burial and the Individual in Early Modern England* (London, 1984), pp. 50–5; Frederick John Varley, *Oliver Cromwell's Latter End* (London, 1939), pp. 37–8

13. Varley, *Cromwell's Latter End*, p. 38; Nichols, 'London Pageants', *Gentleman's Magazine*, December 1824, p. 514

14. Frederick William Fairholt, *Lord Mayor's Pageants* (Percy Society, 1843), pp. 66–7

15. *Merc. Pol.*, 18–23 November 1658; Prestwich, *Republica*, pp. 178–9; Burton, *Diary*, vol. II, p. 529; Westminster Abbey MSS 6372; Barnard, *Seventeenth Century Country Gentleman*, pp. 52–3

16. Ludlow, *Memoirs*, vol. II, p. 48

17. Burrough, 'A Testimony Against a Great Idolatry' in *Memorable Works*, pp. 457–9

18. Arthur H. Nethercot, *Abraham Cowley: The Muse's Hannibal* (Oxford, 1931)

19. Abraham Cowley, *A Vision, Concerning his late Pretended Highnesse Cromwell, the Wicked* (London, 1661), pp. 1–3

20. *Clarke Papers*, vol. III, p. 168; *CSP Ven.*, 1657–9, p. 248; Stanley, *Historical Memorials*, p. 160 fn. 1; Maurice Ashley, *Financial and Commercial Policy under the Cromwellian Protectorate*, 2nd edn (London, 1962), p. 105; *CSPD*, 1658–9, p. xi; *CSPD*, 1659–60, p. 146; Noble, vol. II, p. 119; *Upon the much Lamented Departure of the High and Mighty Prince, Oliver, Lord Protector of England, Scotland and Ireland, &c. A Funeral Elegie* (London, 1658)

14. Farewell! A Long Farewell To All My Greatness!

1. Whitelocke, *Memorials*, p. 676; *Pub. Intel.*, 24–31 January 1659; *The Speech of His Highness the Lord Protector made to both Houses of Parliament at their first meeting, on Thursday the 27th of January 1658* (London, 1659)
2. Evelyn, *Diary*, p. 397
3. Egloff, 'Robert Beake', *Historical Research*, vol. 68, no. 166, June 1995, p. 238; Burton, *Diary*, vol. I, p. 411; *Clarendon State Papers*, vol. III, p. 432
4. *Weekly Post*, 31 May–7 June 1659
5. Westminster Abbey MSS 6373, 6374, 6375(A), 6375(B); John Davies of Kidwelly, *The Civil Warres of Great Britain and Ireland* (London, 1661), p. 363
6. *Pub. Intel.*, 18–25 June 1660
7. HMC, *Fifth Report*, Appendix, Sutherland MSS, p. 135
8. *The Diurnal of Thomas Rugg, 1659–1661*, ed. William L. Sachse, Camden Third Series, vol. XCI (Royal Historical Society, London, 1961), p. 114
9. Marvell, *Poems and Letters*, vol. I, pp. 118, 133

Bibliography

A. MANUSCRIPT SOURCES

British Library:
  Additional MSS
  Harleian MSS
  Lansdowne MSS
Huntington Library, California:
  'Dering's Diary and Commonplace Book, 1656–1662'
  Hastings MSS
Marquess of Bath, Longleat House:
  Privy Council Register of Richard Cromwell, September 3rd 1658 – January 18th 1659
Public Record Office:
  Baschet Transcripts PRO 31/3/92, 101, 102
  State Papers 18/113, 182, 183
  State Papers 25/75, 78
  State Papers 78/113
Westminster Abbey MSS

B. CONTEMPORARY OR NEAR CONTEMPORARY PRINTED MATTER

Alured, Colonel Matthew, *The Case of* (London, 1659)

Bate, George, *Elenchus Motuum Nuperorum in Anglia: or a Short Historical Account of the Rise and Progress of the Late Troubles in England* (London, 1685)

Boyle, Roger, the Right Honourable, the first Earl of Orrery, *A Collection of the State Letters of, Together with . . . the life of the Earl of Orrery by the Reverend Mr Thomas Morrice* (London 1742)

Britania Triumphalis; A Brief History of the Warres and other State Affairs of Great Britain: From the Death of the late King to the Dissolution of the last Parliament (London, 1654)

Burnet, Bishop, *History of His Own Time*, vol.I (Dublin, 1724)

Burrough, Edward, 'A Testimony Against a Great Idolatry' in *The Memorable Works of a Son of Thunder and Consolation* (London, 1672)

Carrington, Samuel, *The History of the Life and Death of his most Serene Highness Oliver Late Lord Protector* (London, 1659)

A copy of a letter from His Excellency the Lord General Cromwell . . . with several transactions since that time (London, 1656)

Cowley, Abraham, *A Vision, Concerning his late Pretended Highnesse Cromwell, the Wicked* (London, 1661)

Davies, John, of Kidwelly, *The Civil Warres of Great Britain and Ireland* (London, 1661)

Dawbeny, Henry, *Historie and Policie reviewed, in The Heroick Transactions of his Most Serene Highness, Oliver, Late Lord Protector, from his Cradle to his Tomb* (London, 1659)

A Directory for the Publique Worship of God throughout the Three Kingdoms of England, Scotland and Ireland (London, 1644/5)

Dugdale, Sir William, *A Short View of the Late Troubles in England* (Oxford, 1681)

Gand, Louis de, *Parallelum Olivae nec non Olivarii* (London, 1656)

The Government of the Commonwealth of England, Scotland and Ireland, and the Dominions thereunto belonging, as it was publickly declared at Westminster the 16th day of December, 1653 (London, 1653)

Heath, James, *Flagellum: or the Life and Death, Birth and Burial of O. Cromwell the Late Usurper* (London, 1672)

Liber Regalis, A Collection out of a book called (London, 1661)

Lilburne, John, *Apologetical Narration* (Amsterdam, 1652)

Mercurius Politicus

Moderate Intelligencer

Monarchy Asserted to be the best, most Ancient and legal form of Government, in a conference had at Whitehall with Oliver, late Lord Protector, & a Committee of Parliament, attrib. Bulstrode Whitelocke (London, 1660)

Oratio Anniversaria (London, 1655)

An Ordinance for the Continuance and Maintenance of the Almshouses and Almsmen called Poor Knights and other Charitable and Pious Uses (London, 1655)

An Ordinance for uniting Scotland into one Commonwealth with England, April 12 1654 (London, 1654)

Perfect Diurnal

Perfect Proceedings of State Affairs

Pomfret, Thomas, *The Life of the Right Honourable and Religious Lady Christian Late Countess Dowager of Devonshire* (London, 1685)

The Pourtraiture of his Royal Highness, Oliver, late Lord Protector &c. (London, 1659)

A Proclamation of his Highness, with the consent of his Council, for continuing all persons being in office for the execution of public justice at the time of the late change of government, until his Highness's further direction, 21 December 1653 (London, 1653)

Proclamation of Richard Cromwell as Lord Protector (London, 1658)

By the Protector. A Proclamation Signifying His Highness Pleasure, That all men being in Office of Government, at the decease of his most dear Father, Oliver, late Lord Protector, shall so continue till His Highness further Direction (London, 1658)

Prynne, William, *King Richard the Third Revived* (London, 1657)

Public Intelligencer

Pugh, Thomas, *Brittish and Out-landish Prophesies* (London, 1657)

Rebels no Saints: or a Collection of the Speeches, Private Passages, Letters and Prayers of those Persons lately Executed (London, 1661)

Mr Recorders Speech to the Lord Protector upon Wednesday the eighth Februa. 1653, being the day of his Highnesse entertainment in London (London, 1654)

Rushworth, John, *Historical Collections*, vol.IV (London, 1692)

Several Proceedings of State Affairs in England, Scotland and Ireland

Some Farther Intelligence of the Affairs of England (London, 1659)

The Speech of His Highness the Lord Protector made to both Houses of Parliament at their first meeting, on Thursday the 27th of January 1658 (London, 1659)

A True Catalogue, or, An Account of the several Places and most Eminent Persons in the three Nations, and elsewhere, where, and by whom, Richard Cromwell was Proclaimed Lord Protector of the Commonwealth of England, Scotland and Ireland (London, 1659)

The Unparalleled Monarch: or the Portraiture of a Matchless Prince Exprest in some Shadows of His Highness My Lord Protector (London, 1656)

Upon the much Lamented Departure of the High and Mighty Prince, Oliver, Lord Protector of England, Scotland and Ireland, &c. A Funeral Elegie (London, 1658)

Ware, Robert, *Foxes and Firebrands: or, a specimen of the danger and harmony of Popery and Separation*, 2nd edn, 2 parts (Dublin, 1682)

Warwick, Sir Philip, *Memoirs of the Reign of King Charles I with a continuation to the Happy Restoration of King Charles II* (London, 1701)

Weekly Intelligencer

Weekly Post

Whitelocke, Bulstrode, *Memorials of the English Affairs* (London, 1682)

Wood, Anthony à, *Athenae Oxonienses*, vol. II (London, 1692)

C. LATER PUBLICATIONS OF CONTEMPORARY DIARIES, CORRESPONDENCE, HISTORIES, MEMOIRS, OFFICIAL DOCUMENTS, RECORDS AND OTHER WORKS

Abbott, W.C., *The Writings and Speeches of Oliver Cromwell*, 4 vols (Cambridge, Massachusetts, 1937–47)

Acts and Ordinances of the Interregnum, 1642–1660, eds C.H. Firth and R.S. Rait, vol. II (HMSO, London, 1911)

Aubrey, John, *'Brief Lives', Chiefly of Contemporaries, set down by, between the Years 1669 and 1696*, ed. Andrew Clark, vol. I (Oxford, 1898)

Barnard, E.A.B., *A Seventeenth Century Country Gentleman (Sir Francis Throckmorton, 1640–1680)*, 2nd edn (Cambridge, 1948)

Burton, Thomas, *The Diary of*, ed. J. T. Rutt, 4 vols (London, 1828)

Calendar of State Papers: Domestic Series, 1603–10, 1619–23, 1649–50, 1651–2, 1653–4, 1654, 1655, 1656–7, 1657–8, 1658–9, 1659–60

Calendar of State Papers: Venetian, 1653–4, 1655–6, 1657–9

Carlyle, Thomas, *The Letters and Speeches of Oliver Cromwell with elucidations by*, ed. S.C. Lomas, 3 vols (London, 1904)

Chamberlain, John, *The Letters of*, ed. Norman Egbert McClure, vol. II (American Philosophical Society, Philadelphia, 1939)

Clarendon, Edward, Earl of, *The History of the Rebellion and Civil Wars in England*, ed. W. Dunn Macray, vols V and VI (Oxford, 1888)

Clarendon State Papers, vol. III, ed. T. Monkhouse (Oxford, 1786)

The Clarke Papers, ed. C.H. Firth, vol. III (London, 1899)

Commons, Journals of the House of, vols VI, VII

The Conway Letters, ed. Marjorie Hope Nicolson, rev. edn, ed. Sarah Hutton (Oxford, 1992)

Court of Requests, Select Cases in the, ed. I.S. Leadam (Selden Society, 1898)

Cromwelliana: a chronological detail of events in which Oliver Cromwell was engaged from the year 1642 to his death 1658 (Westminster, 1810)

Davenant, Sir William, *The Shorter Poems, and Songs from the Plays and Masques*, ed. A.M. Gibbs (Oxford, 1972)

Dryden, John, *The Letters of*, ed. Charles E. Ward (Durham, North Carolina, 1942)

Dugdale, Sir William, *The Life, Diary and Correspondence of*, ed. William Hamper (London, 1827)

Ekeblad, Johan, *Bref*, ed. N. Sjöberg, vol. I (Stockholm, 1911)

Evelyn, John, *The Diary of*, ed. E.S. de Beer (Oxford, 1959)

Finet, John, *Ceremonies of Charles I: The Note Books of, 1628–1641*, ed. Albert J. Loomie (New York, 1987)

Fox, George, *The Journal of*, ed. Norman Penny (London, 1924)

Halliwell, James Orchard, *The Nursery Rhymes of England Collected chiefly from Oral Tradition* (5th edn, reissued, London, 1970)

Harleian Miscellany, vol. III (London, 1745)

Historical Manuscripts Commission, *Fifth Report*, Appendix (1876), Sutherland MSS

——, *Sixth Report*, Appendix (1877), ffarington MSS

——, *Eighth Report*, Appendix, part I (1881), Corporation of the City of Leicester MSS

——, *Twelfth Report*, Appendix, part IX (1891), Records of the Corporation of Gloucester

——, *Fifteenth Report*, Appendix, part VII (1898), Ailesbury MSS

——, (1900) *Frankland-Russell-Astley MSS*

——, (1903) *Various Collections*, vol. II, Wombwell MSS

——, (1905) *Earl of Egmont MSS*, vol. I, part II

——, (1966) *De L'Isle and Dudley MSS*, vol. VI, Sidney Papers, 1626–1698

Hutchinson, Lucy, *Memoirs of Colonel Hutchinson*, ed. Rev. Julius Hutchinson (Everyman's Library edn, 1908)

Inner Temple Records, A Calendar of the, vol. II, *1 James I – Restoration (1660)*, ed. F.A. Inderwick (London, 1898)

Josselin, Ralph, *The Diary of, 1616–1683*, ed. Alan Macfarlane (British Academy, 1976)

'London Sessions Records, 1605–1685', ed. Dom Hugh Bowler, *Publications of the Catholic Record Society*, vol. XXXIV (London, 1934)

Lords, The Manuscripts of the House of, 1699–1702 (HMSO, London, 1908)

Ludlow, Edmund, *Memoirs of, 1625–1672*, ed. C.H. Firth, 2 vols (Oxford, 1894)

Marvell, Andrew, *The Poems and Letters of*, ed. H.M. Margoliouth, 2 vols, 3rd edn revised by P. Legouis with the collaboration of E.E. Duncan-Jones (Oxford, 1971)

Middle Temple Records, A Calendar of the, ed. Charles Henry Hopwood (London, 1930)

A Narrative of the late Parliament (so called) . . . (1657) in *Harleian Miscellany*, vol. III, (London, 1745)

The New Oxford Book of Verse, 1250–1950, ed. Helen Gardner (Oxford, 1989)

The Nicholas Papers, ed. George F. Warner, vol. I (Camden Society, 1886), vol. II (1892)

Nichols, John, *The Progresses, Processions and Magnificent Festivities of King James the First*, vol. IV (London, 1828)

Nickolls, John, *Original Letters and Papers of State addressed to Oliver Cromwell, Found among the Political Collections of Mr John Milton* (London, 1743)

Nicoll, John, *A Diary of Public Transactions and other occurrences, chiefly in Scotland, From January 1650 to June 1667* (The Bannatyne Club, Edinburgh, 1836)

Osborne, Dorothy, *Letters from, to Sir William Temple, 1652–54*, ed. Edward Abbott Parry (London, 1903)

Peck, Francis, *Desiderata Curiosa: or, a Collection of Divers Scarce and Curious Pieces (Relating chiefly to Matters of English History)* (London, 1732)

Pepys, Samuel, *The Diary of*, eds Robert Latham and William Mathews, vols I, IV, V, VI, VIII (London, 1970–4)

Prestwich, Sir John, *Respublica* (London, 1787)

The Protectorate of Oliver Cromwell, and the State of Europe during the Reign of Louis XIV, ed. Robert Vaughan, vol. II (London, 1838)

Ritson, Joseph, *Ancient Songs, from the time of King Henry the Third to the Revolution* (London, 1790)

Rollins, Hyder E., *Cavalier and Puritan: Ballads and Broadsides Illustrating the Period of the Great Rebellion, 1640–1660* (New York, 1923)

Rugg, Thomas, *The Diurnal of, 1659–1661*, ed. William L. Sachse, Camden Third Series, vol. XCI (Royal Historical Society, London, 1961)

A second Narrative of the late Parliament (so called) . . . (1658) in *Harleian Miscellany*, vol. III (London, 1745)

Sidney Papers, ed. R.W. Blencowe (London, 1825)

The Stuart Constitution, 1603–1688: Documents and Commentary, ed. J.P. Kenyon, 2nd edn (Cambridge, 1986)

Stuart Royal Proclamations, vol.I, Royal Proclamations of King James I, 1603–1625, eds James F. Larkin and Paul L. Hughes (Oxford, 1973), vol. II, Royal Proclamations of King Charles I, 1625–1646, ed. James F. Larkin (Oxford, 1983)

Swedish Diplomats at Cromwell's Court, 1655–1656, translated and edited by Michael Roberts, Camden Fourth Series, vol. 36 (Royal Historical Society, London, 1988)

Thurloe, John, *A Collection of State Papers of J.T. To which is prefixed the life of Mr Thurloe by Thomas Birch*, 7 vols (London, 1742)

The Tudor Constitution: Documents and Commentary, ed. G.R. Elton (Cambridge, 1960)

Verney Family, Memoirs of the, During the Seventeenth Century, ed. Frances Parthenope Verney and Margaret M. Verney, 2 vols (London, 1925)

Verney Papers: Notes of Proceedings in the Long Parliament, ed. John Bruce (Camden Society, 1845)

Waller, Edmund, *The Poems of*, ed. George Thorn-Drury, vol.II (London, 1905)

Wood, Anthony, Antiquary, of Oxford, *The Life and Times of, 1632–1695, described by Himself*, collected from his diaries and papers by Andrew Clark, vol. I (Oxford Historical Society, 1891)

D. SECONDARY SOURCES

Abbott, Wilbur Cortez, *A Bibliography of Oliver Cromwell* (Cambridge, Massachusetts, 1929)

The Ancient Vellum Book of the Honourable Artillery Company, ed. G.A. Raikes (London, 1890)

Ashley, Maurice, *Financial and Commercial Policy under the Cromwellian Protectorate*, 2nd edn (London, 1962)

Aubrey, Philip, *Mr Secretary Thurloe: Cromwell's Secretary of State, 1652–1660* (London, 1990)

Aylmer, G.E., *The State's Servants: The Civil Service of the English Republic, 1649–1660* (London, 1973)

Boehn, Max von, *Modes and Manners*, vol. III: *The Seventeenth Century*, translated by Joan Joshua (London, 1935)

Bonner, Sir George Albert, *The Office of the King's Remembrancer in England* (London, 1930)

Boutells Heraldry, revised by J.P. Brooke-Little (London, 1973 edn)

Braithwaite, William C., *The Beginnings of Quakerism* (London, 1912)

Brentnall, Margaret, *The Old Customs and Ceremonies of London* (London, 1975)

Brewer's Dictionary of Phrase and Fable, 14th edn., revised by Ivor H. Evans (London, 1989)

Brown, Michèle, *Ritual of Royalty: The Ceremony and Pageantry of Britain's Monarchy* (London, 1983)

Butler, Sir Thomas, *The Crown Jewels and Coronation Ritual* (London, 1973)

Campbell, John, *The Lives of the Lord Chancellors and Keepers of the Great Seal of England, from the earliest times till the reign of King George IV*, vols I and III (London, 1845), vol. IV (1846)

Carleton, John D., *Westminster School: A History* (London, 1965)

Carlton, Charles, *Charles I: The Personal Monarch* (London, 1983)

——, 'Three British Revolutions and the Personality of Kingship' in *Three British Revolutions, 1641, 1688, 1776*, ed. J.G.A. Pocock (Princeton, New Jersey, 1980)

Catterall, R.C.H., 'The Failure of the Humble Petition and Advice', *American Historical Review*, vol. IX, no. 1, 1903

Chalmers, Alexander, *The General Biographical History*, vol. XIV (London, 1814)

Colton, Charles Caleb, *Lacon* (London, 1820)

Complete Baronetage, ed. G.E. Cokayne (Exeter, 1903)

The Complete Peerage of England, Scotland, Ireland and the United Kingdom, ed. G.E. Cokayne, rev. edn, ed. Vicary Gibbs *et al*

The Complete Pelican Shakespeare (London, 1981)

Cook, Chris, *Macmillan Dictionary of Historical Terms*, 2nd edn (London, 1989)

Cooper, Ivy M., 'The Meeting-Places of Parliament in the Ancient Palace of Westminster', *Journal of the British Archaeological Association*, 3rd series, vol. III (1938)

Cormack, Patrick, *Westminster Palace and Parliament* (London, 1981)

'The Coronation of their Majesties William IV and Queen Adelaide', *The Gentleman's Magazine*, vol. CI, part II, September 1831

Coronations: Medieval and Early Modern Monarchic Ritual, ed. János M. Bak (Berkeley, California, 1990)

The Corporation of London: Its Constitution, Powers and Duties (Oxford, 1950)

Cowie, L.W., 'The Old Palace of Westminster', *History Today*, vol. XXIV, no. 8, August 1974

Cressy, David, *Bonfires and Bells: National Memory and the Protestant Calendar in Elizabethan and Stuart England* (London, 1989)

The Culture of English Puritanism, 1560–1700, ed. Christopher Durston and Jacqueline Eales (London, 1996)

Dictionary of National Biography

Dugdale, George S., *Whitehall Through the Centuries* (London, 1950)

Egloff, C.S., 'Robert Beake: a Letter concerning the Humble Petition and Advice, 28 March 1657', *Historical Research* (Bulletin of the Institute of Historical Research), vol. 68, no. 166, June 1995

Evans, A.K.B., 'St George's Chapel, 1345–1975', *History Today*, vol. XXV, no. 5, May 1975

Fairholt, Frederick William, *Lord Mayor's Pageants* (Percy Society, 1843)

Fallon, Robert, *Milton in Government* (University Park, Pennsylvania, 1993)

Fellowes, Edmund H., *The Military Knights of Windsor, 1352–1944* (Windsor, 1944)

Field, John, *The King's Nurseries: The Story of Westminster School* (London, 1987)

Firth, C.H., *The House of Lords During the Civil War* (London, 1910)

——, *The Last Years of the Protectorate, 1656–1658*, 2 vols (London, 1909)

——, 'Cromwell and the Crown', *English Historical Review*, vol. XVII, no. LXVII, July 1902 and vol. XVIII, no. LXIX, January 1903

——, 'The Royalists Under the Protectorate', *English Historical Review*, vol. LII, no. 208, October 1937

Fletcher, C.R.L., *Mr Gladstone at Oxford, 1890* (London, 1908)

Fraser, Antonia, *Cromwell: Our Chief of Men* (London, 1973)

Gardiner, S.R., *History of the Commonwealth and Protectorate*, 4 vols (Windrush Press edn, 1988/9)

——, *History of the Great Civil War*, 4 vols (Windrush Press edn, 1987)

Gaunt, Peter, *Oliver Cromwell* (Oxford, 1996)

Gittings, Clare, *Death, Burial and the Individual in Early Modern England* (London, 1984)

Godwin, William, *History of the Commonwealth of England*, vol. IV (London, 1828)

A Guide to the Exhibition of Historical Medals in the British Museum (British Museum, 1924)

Guizot, F.P.G., *History of Oliver Cromwell and the English Commonwealth*, 2 vols (London, 1854)

Hamilton, Keith, and Langhorne, Richard, *The Practice of Diplomacy: Its Evolution, Theory and Administration* (London, 1995)

Hastings, Maurice, *Parliament House: The Chambers of the House of Commons* (London, 1950)

Hardacre, Paul H., *The Royalists during the Puritan Revolution* (The Hague, 1956)

Hayden, Ilse, *Symbol and Privilege: The Ritual Context of British Royalty* (Tucson, Arizona, 1987)

Henfrey, Henry William, *Numismata Cromwelliana* (London, 1877)

Hewlett, Henry G., 'Charles the First as a Picture Collector', *The Nineteenth Century*, vol. XXVIII, no. 162, August 1890

Highmore, Anthony, *The History of the Honourable Artillery Company of the City of London* (London, 1804)

Hill, C.P., *Who's Who in Stuart Britain* (London, 1988)

Hoey, Brian, *All The Queens Men: Inside the Royal Household* (London, 1992)

Hope, W.H. St John, 'On the Funeral Effigies of the Kings and Queens of England, with special reference to those in the Abbey Church of Westminster', *Archaeologia*, vol. LX, 1907

Hunting, Penelope, *Royal Westminster* (Royal Institution of Chartered Surveyors, London, 1981)

Hutton, Ronald, *The Restoration: A Political and Religious History of England and Wales, 1658–1667* (Oxford, 1985)

Kantorowicz, Ernst H., *The King's Two Bodies: A Study in Mediaeval Political Theology* (Princeton, New Jersey, 1957)

Kearsley, Harvey, *His Majesty's Bodyguard of the Honourable Corps of Gentlemen-at-Arms* (London, 1937)

Korr, Charles P., *Cromwell and the New Model Foreign Policy: England's Policy Toward France, 1649–1658* (Berkeley, California, 1975)

Legg, L.G. Wickham, *English Coronation Records* (Westminster, 1901)

Legouis, Pierre, *Andrew Marvell: Poet, Puritan, Patriot*, 2nd edn (Oxford, 1968)

Llewellyn, Nigel, *The Art of Death: Visual Culture in the English Death Ritual c.1500–c.1800* (London, 1992)

London, H. Stanford, 'The Heralds' Tabards under the Commonwealth', *Notes and Queries*, vol.198, no.7, July 1953

Macfarlane, Alan, *The Family Life of Ralph Josselin, a Seventeenth Century Clergyman: An Essay in Historical Anthropology* (Cambridge, 1970)

Mansel, Philip, *Pillars of Monarchy: An Outline of the Political and Social History of Royal Guards, 1400–1984* (London, 1984)

Masson, David, *The Life of John Milton*, vol. V (Gloucester, Massachusetts, 1965 reprint)

Mears, Kenneth J., *The Tower of London* (Oxford, 1988)

Nenner, Howard, *The Right to be King: The Succession to the Crown of England, 1603–1714* (London, 1995)

Nethercot, Arthur H., *Abraham Cowley: The Muse's Hannibal* (Oxford, 1931)

The New Grove Dictionary of Music and Musicians, ed. Stanley Sadie, vols V and VIII (London, 1980)

The New Oxford Companion to Music, ed. Denis Arnold, vol. I (Oxford, 1983)

Nichols, J., 'London Pageants in the Reign of King Charles the First' and 'London Pageants during the Commonwealth and the Reign of Charles II', *The Gentleman's Magazine*, vol. XCIV, part II, November/December 1824

Noble, Mark, *Memoirs of the Protectoral House of Cromwell*, 2 vols (Birmingham, 1787)

Oxford English Dictionary

Paget, Julian, *Discovering London Ceremonial and Traditions* (Aylesbury, 1989)

——, *The Yeomen of the Guard 1485–1985* (Poole, 1984)

Palme, Per, *Triumph of Peace: A Study of the Whitehall Banqueting House* (London, 1957)

The Parliamentary or Constitutional History of England, vol. XX (London, 1757), vol. XXI (1760)

Parry, Graham, *The Golden Age restor'd: The Culture of the Stuart Court, 1603–42* (Manchester, 1981)

Pegge, Samuel, *Curialia: or an Historical Account of some Branches of the Royal Household* (London, 1791)

Plucknett, Theodore F.T., *Taswell-Langmead's English Constitutional History from the Teutonic Conquest to the Present Time*, 11th edn (London, 1960)

The Protestant Dictionary, eds Charles Sydney Carter and G.E. Alison Weeks, rev. edn (The Harrison Trust, London, 1933)

Ramsey, Robert W., *Henry Cromwell* (London, 1933)

——, *Richard Cromwell, Protector of England* (London, 1935)

——, *Studies in Cromwell's Family Circle* (London, 1930)

Rogers, H.C.B., *Battles and Generals of the Civil Wars, 1642–1651* (London, 1968)

Rogers, P.G., *The Fifth Monarchy Men* (London, 1966)

Roosen, William, 'Early Modern Diplomatic Ceremonial: A Systems Approach', *Journal of Modern History*, vol. 52, no. 3, September 1980

Roots, Ivan, *The Great Rebellion, 1642–1660* (London, 1972)

Round, J. Horace, 'Coronation Peerages', *The Monthly Review*, vol. VI, February 1902

Scholes, Percy A., *The Puritans and Music in England and New England* (Oxford, 1934)

Schramm, P.E., *A History of the English Coronation*, translated by L.G. Wickham Legg (Oxford, 1937)

Scott-Giles, C.W., *The Romance of Heraldry* (London, 1929)

Sharpe, Reginald R., *London and the Kingdom*, vols I and II (London, 1894)

Shaw, W. A., *The Knights of England*, 2 vols (London, 1906)

Sherwood, Roy, *The Court of Oliver Cromwell* (Willingham Press edn, Cambridge, 1989)

Smith, Charlotte Fell, *Mary Rich, Countess of Warwick (1625–1678): Her Family and Friends* (London, 1901)

Smith, Geoffrey Ridsdill, *In well beware: The Story of Newburgh Priory and the Belasyse Family, 1145–1977* (Kineton, 1978)

Stanley, Arthur Penrhyn, *Historical Memorials of Westminster Abbey*, 7th edn (London, 1890)

Stannard, David E., *The Puritan Way of Death: A Study in Religion, Culture, and Social Change* (Oxford, 1977)

Stearns, Raymond Phineas, *The Strenuous Puritan: Hugh Peter, 1598–1660* (Urbana, Illinois, 1954)

Stone, Lawrence, *The Crisis of the Aristocracy, 1558–1641* (Oxford, 1965)

Tanner, Lawrence E., *Westminster School*, 2nd edn (Country Life, London, 1951)

Taylor, Lou, *Mourning Dress: A Costume and Social History* (London, 1983)

Turner, Edward Raymond, *The Privy Council of England in the Seventeenth and Eighteenth Centuries, 1603–1784*, vol. I (Baltimore, Maryland, 1927)

Varley, Frederick John, *Oliver Cromwell's Latter End* (London, 1939)

Voltaire, *Mérope, A Tragedy*, translated by John Theobald (London, 1744)

Vries, Ad de, *Dictionary of Symbols and Imagery* (London, 1974)

Wagner, Sir Anthony, *Heralds of England: A History of the Office and College of Arms* (HMSO, 1967)

——, *Historic Heraldry of Britain*, 2nd impr. reprint (London, 1972)

Walker, David M., *The Oxford Companion to Law* (Oxford, 1980)

Walker, G. Goold, *The Honourable Artillery Company, 1537–1947* (Aldershot, 1954)

Wallace, John M., *Destiny His Choice: The Loyalism of Andrew Marvell* (Cambridge, 1968)

Watney, Marylian, *Royal Cavalcade: A History of the Carriages and Transport of English Kings and Queens from Elizabeth I Onwards* (London, 1987)

Whiting, J.R.S., *Commemorative Medals: A Medallic History of Britain, from Tudor times to the present day* (Newton Abbot, 1972)

Wilding, Norman, and Laundy, Philip, *An Encyclopaedia of Parliament*, 4th rev. edn (London, 1972)

Wilkinson, B., *The Coronation in History* (Historical Association Pamphlet, General Series no. 23, 1953)

Williamson, Bruce J., *The History of the Temple, London* (London, 1924)

Winn, James Anderson, *John Dryden and His World* (New Haven, Connecticut, 1987)

Withington, Robert, *English Pageantry: An Historical Outline*, vol. II (Cambridge, Massachusetts, 1920)

Woodward, John, and Burnett, George, *A Treatise on Heraldry* (David and Charles Reprint, Newton Abbot, 1969)

Woolrych, Austin, *Commonwealth to Protectorate* (Oxford, 1982)

——, 'The Cromwellian Protectorate: A Military Dictatorship?' *History*, vol. 75, no. 244, June 1990

Woolrych, Humphry William, *Lives of Eminent Sergeants-at-Law of the English Bar*, vol. I (London, 1869)

Wyon, A.B., *The Great Seals of England* (London, 1887)

Index

Abraham tapestries, 31, 33

Additional and Explanatory Petition and Advice, 91–2, 97

Alured, Colonel Matthew, 53

ambassadors, foreign, 15–16, 19–20, 157, *see also* France; Genoa; Portugal; Spain; Sweden; United Provinces; Venice

Anabaptists, 75

Anne of Denmark, 144

Arms, Officers of the College of, 12–13, 15, 17, 23, 35, 63, 97, 99, 101, 104, 146, 157, 158

arms, royal, 13, 20, 45, 107

arms of the pre-Protectorate Commonwealth, 12–13, 14, 17, 20, 43, 63, 94, 106

arms of the Protectorate, 45–8, 93, 94, 95, 107, 136, 145, 149, 166, 168

army, 4, 6, 7, 9, 10, 11, 16–17, 18, 21, 50, 51, 58–9, 71, 73, 74, 75, 80, 86, 88–90, 104, 124, 138, 142, 156, 157, 158, 165

Arthur, King, 46, 168

Artillery Company, 65–6, 134–5, 157
  Captain of *see* Skippon, Philip

Arundel House, 19

Ashe, John, 70, 71, 109

Aubrey, John, 68

Bampfield, Colonel Joseph, 70, 78, 113

bargemasters *see* watermen

Bate, Dr George, 55, 129, 146–7, 150

Bath, Order of the, 60–1

Beake, Robert, 74, 75, 80

Bedchamber, Gentlemen of the, 50, 51, 146, 155

Beke, Major Richard, Captain of the Life Guard, 59, 126

Belasyse, Lord John, 77

Beverley, 140, 142

Black Rod, Usher of the, 123

Blake, Robert, 151

Blondeau, Peter, 95

Bonde, Count Christer, *see* Sweden, ambassador of

Bordeaux, Antoine de, *see* France, ambassador of

Bradford, Captain William, 75

Bradshaw, Richard, 36, 49, 59, 92, 126

Brandenburg agent, 93

Bristol, 11

Broghill, Roger Boyle, Baron, 69, 75–6, 77, 81, 83, 87

Bruce, Lord, 66, 69

Buckingham, George Villiers, first Duke of, 123

Buckingham, George Villiers, second Duke of, 114–15

Burgoyne, Roger, 150

Burnet, Gilbert, Bishop of Salisbury, 75, 90

Burrough, Edward, 153, 154, 155, 163, 164

Burton, Thomas, 85

Busby, Dr Richard, 64, 157

Bysshe, Edward, Garter, Principal King of Arms, 63, 158

Cadwallader, 45–6

Cambridge University, 63
  Sidney Sussex College, 4

Canterbury, Archbishop of, 97, 99, 103

Carrington, Samuel, 4, 17, 19, 113, 131, 132

Cassillis, Earl of, 124

Cavendish, Charles, 68, 111

Ceremonies, Master of, 15, 19, 20, 36, *see also* Fleming, Sir Oliver

Chancery, High Court of, 9

Charing Cross, 11

Charles I, 1, 2, 4, 7, 10, 11, 12, 13, 15, 18, 19, 20, 21, 22, 23, 27, 28, 29, 31, 33, 34–6, 38, 40, 41, 42, 43, 44, 48, 51, 53, 54, 55, 57 and n, 58, 60, 61, 63, 66, 70, 72, 76, 77, 78, 84, 86, 94, 95, 106, 107, 109, 114, 120, 123, 126, 130, 136, 138, 139, 140, 143, 146, 157, 160, 168
Charles II, 4, 12, 36, 38, 52, 53, 54, 55, 57n, 61, 62, 63, 68, 69, 70, 72, 74, 75–7, 78, 81, 83, 88, 94, 95, 108, 111, 112, 113, 115, 116, 117, 118, 125, 126, 129, 131, 132, 135, 140, 146, 147, 164, 168
Charleton, Stephen, 86
Chelsea College, 90
Chesterfield, Philip Stanhope, second Earl of, 114–15
Civil War, 1, 2, 10, 12, 23, 37, 38, 40, 54, 55, 61, 65, 68, 72, 77, 84, 85, 109, 111, 113, 119, 120, 123, 128, 163
Clarenceux King of Arms, 158, see also Kings of Arms
Clarendon, Edward Hyde, Earl of, 9, 18, 19, 23, 40, 78, 95, 102, 105, 109, 113, 115, 118, 126, 127, 129, 131, 142
Clarke, William, 150
Claypole, Elizabeth, 20, 114, 118, 131–4, 135, 151
Claypole, John, Master of the Horse, 20, 21, 28, 31, 40, 54, 59, 99, 101, 106, 123, 131, 133, 136, 160
Clifton, Alice, 52
Cofferer of the Household, 121, 123
coinage, 93–5, 135
College of the Propaganda, 90
Cologne, 42
Commons, House of, 10, 16, 40, 41, 43, 70, 71, 72, 74, 80, 86, 87, 89, 96, 113, 123–6, 165
Speaker of, 16, 18, 43, 70, see also Lenthall, William; Widdrington, Sir Thomas
Commonwealth, pre–Protectorate, 1, 11, 12, 13 and n, 15, 16–17, 18, 20, 23, 27, 28, 30, 37, 41, 42, 43, 44, 45, 48, 63, 64, 70, 71, 72, 78, 84, 85, 94, 106, 109, 120, 151, 167
Council of State, 16, 120, 167

Comptroller of the Household see Jones, Colonel Philip
Conway, Lady Elizabeth, 92
Conway, Lord, 72
Cony, George, 52, 128–9
Cooper, Sir Anthony Ashley, 42
Copenhagen, 36, 49, 59, 92
Coronation Chair, 96, 99, 100, 102
Council, his Highness's, 2, 7, 9, 10, 12, 13, 15, 16, 18, 21, 26, 37, 42, 48, 50, 51, 59, 62, 65, 66, 73, 74, 81, 83, 88, 91–2, 96, 97, 99, 104, 106, 112, 120, 123, 129, 130, 136, 138, 144, 156
President of, 31
Council for the Protestant Religion, 90
court, Protectoral, see Cromwell, Oliver
court, royal, 21, 28–9, 36, 37, 50–1, 52, 117, 146
court party, 40, 42
Cowley, Abraham, 163–4
Coyet, Peter Julias, see Sweden, ambassador of
Cranmer, Thomas, 103
Cromwell, Elizabeth (Oliver's mother), 103, 132, 158
Cromwell, Elizabeth, the Lady Protectress, 4, 5, 26, 35–6, 53, 76, 109, 112, 113, 115, 158
Cromwell, Frances, 29, 75–6, 77, 86, 101, 108, 109–12, 114, 115, 116, 118, 119, 126–7, 147
Cromwell, Henry, 18, 42, 53, 54, 85, 86, 89, 92, 93, 106, 109, 111, 115, 117, 120, 142, 158
Cromwell, Katherine (Oliver's great-great grandmother), 46
Cromwell, Mary, 29, 77–9, 108, 109, 111, 114–18, 119, 130
Cromwell, Oliver
Colonel, 68, 111
Lord General of the Army, 1, 4, 6, 7, 11, 17, 103, 113, 120, 135
Lord Lieutenant of Ireland, 11, 17, 26
Lord Protector:
assassination plots and risings against, 52, 70, 77, 130, 163–4
baronets created by, 106, 119, 135
caps of estate made for, 130, 147
champions Protestantism, 38, 90

Charles I's personal effects put at disposal of, 33–5
City of London reception for, 16–19
comparisons with past kings and Biblical and classical heroes, 136, 142, 168
corpse disinterred, 145, 168
court, 28–9, 31, 36, 37, 50–1, 61, 117, 118, 126–7
court, splendour of, 30, 51, 52–5
court fashion, 52
court life, Chapter 9
crown made for, 75
death, 1, 135–6, 138, 140, 142
dress, 7, 17, 18, 53, 113–14, 126–7, 147
ejects Rump, 41–2, 71, 74, 113, 120
entertained by Lord Mayor and Corporation of London, 16–19
establishes Arabian breed of horse in England, 20
ex–royal palaces put at disposal of, 26, 27, 28
feared and respected by foreign powers, 23–5
first investiture as Lord Protector, 6, 7–11, 12, 16, 17, 18, 40, 95, 99, 136
funeral, 1, Chapters 12 and 13
gift to Oxford University, 90
hereditary peerages created by, 105–6, 119, 127, 135
household, 28–9, 40, 50–1, 121–3, 136, 138, 146, 155, 157
kingship and emperorship, 3, 4, 6, 27, 34, 36, 38, 39, 42, 43, 48–51, 52, 59, 64, 65, 66, Chapters 6, 7 and 8, 109, 111–12, 118–19, 120–1, 124, 125–6, 129, 130–1, 132, 134, 145, 167
knights created by, 18, 19, 60–1, 106, 119
love of hawking and stag hunting, 31
opens first Protectorate Parliament, 39–41, 42
pleasure boat for, 53
proposals for endowing new colleges, 90
receives and entertains ambassadors, 15–16, 19, 20–3, 33, 35–6
religious toleration, 48, 118
sceptre made for, 96, 102
second investiture as Lord Protector, 93, 95–104, 107, 109, 121, 123, 136, 167

Cromwell, Sir Oliver (Oliver's uncle), 158
Cromwell, Richard, 53, 54, 99, 101, 120–1
    as Lord Protector, 136–43, 145, 155, 156, 158, 160, 164, 165–7
    Parliament of, 165–6, 167
Cromwell, Sir Richard (Oliver's great-grandfather), 58
Cromwell, Thomas, 46, 109

Davenant, Sir William, 116, 117
Dawbeny, Henry, 136
De facto Act, 69
Dering, Richard, 29
Desborough, Colonel John, 74, 88–9, 165
Devonshire, Christiana Cavendish, Dowager Countess of, 66–8, 69, 70, 111, 112, 113, 114, 118, 119
Devonshire, first Earl of, 113
Directory for the Publique Worship of God, 150–1, 161
Divine Right of Kings, 11, 21
Dobbins, William, 125
Dryden, John, 64, 156, 157
Dublin, 13, 106
Dugdale, Sir William, 23, 112, 142
Dunbar, Battle of, 135
Dunch, Edmund, 127
Dunkirk, 131, 132, 134
Durham College, 90

East Friesland, 31
East Indies, 90
Edgar, King, 101
Edward the Confessor, 40, 46, 168
Edward I, 96, 120
Edward II, 96, 145
Edward III, 61, 62
Edward V, 2
Edward VI, 103, 132, 144
Egloff, C.S., 74
Ekeblad, Johan, 51
Elizabeth I, 9n, 37, 44, 45, 48, 84, 132, 145
Elizabeth II, 136
Engagement, the, 15
Essex, Robert Devereux, third Earl of, 151
Eton College, Provost and Fellows of, 62
Evelyn, John, 19, 33, 38, 57, 160, 164, 165, 167
Exeter, 140

Fairfax, Lord, 77
Fairfax, Mary, 115
Fairfax, Sir Thomas, 17, 77, 115
Fanelli, Francis, 57
Fauconberg, Thomas Belasyse, second
    Viscount, 77–9, 114–18, 119, 160
Feake, Christopher, 15
Fergus, King, 96
Fiennes, Nathaniel, 50, 82
Fifth Monarchy Men, 27–8
Firth, C.H., 124
Fisher, Payne, 56
Fitzgerald, William, 93
Fleetwood, Bridget, 54
Fleetwood, Charles, 33, 74, 88–9, 99, 158,
    160, 165
Fleming, Sir Oliver, 15, 16, 20, 36, 71,
    138
Fox, George, 130, 134, 135, 153
France, 24, 48, 70, 72, 75, 82, 92, 126,
    134
    ambassador of, 4, 19, 20, 23, 24, 26, 69,
        71, 86, 89, 99, 109, 134, 165
    King of see Louis XIV

Gardiner, S.R., 78
Garland, Augustine, 42
Garter, Order of the, 60–1, 62, 63, 106,
    157, 158
Garter, Principal King of Arms, 63, 97,
    104, see also Bysshe, Edward; Kings
    of Arms; Walker, Sir Edward
Genoa, 38, 49
    ambassadors of, 52
George III, 29
George IV, 95
Gerard, Colonel John, 70
Gibbons, Orlando, 29
Gloucester, City of, 104–5
Gloucester, Henry, Duke of, 4, 126
Glynne, John, Lord Chief Justice, 129
Goodwin, Dr Thomas, 40
Gravesend, 19, 20
Greencloth, Board of, 121, 123
Greenwich House, 19, 20
Grocers' Company, 16
Grocers' Hall, 16, 18, 19
Guernsey, 43
Guildford, Mayor and Corporation of,
    29–30, 58

Hague, The, 71
Hamilton, Duke of, 31, 123
Hampton Court Palace, 30–3, 49, 57, 115,
    117, 132, 134, 135
Harold II, 40
Harvey, Charles, Groom of the
    Bedchamber to his Highness, 134
Hayden, Ilse, 17, 160
Heath, James, 23, 146
Henrietta Maria, Queen, 29, 35–6, 60, 114
Henry V, 63
Henry VII, 36, 46, 69, 72, 132, 147
Henry VIII, 2, 33, 46, 58, 63, 65, 109
heralds, 12, 17, 35, 99, 104, 146, 157, 158,
    see also Lancaster; Somerset; York
Hertford, William Seymour, Marquess of,
    76–7
Hewett, Dr John, 118, 130
High Court of Justice, 130
Hinchingbrooke House, 158
Hingston, John, Master of the Music, 29, 116
Hobart, Lady, 150
Holland, Earl of, 109
Honourable Artillery Company see
    Artillery Company
Horse, Master of the, see Claypole, John
Household, Gentlemen of the, 155, 161
household, Protectoral, see Cromwell,
    Oliver
household, royal, 12, 15, 28–9, 31, 50–1,
    123, 155, 157
Howard, Charles, Captain of the Life
    Guard, 12, 40, 59, 69
    created Viscount Morpeth and Baron
        Gilsland, 105, 124
Howes, William, Gentleman of his
    Highness's Music, 61
Humble Address and Remonstrance, 71,
    72–3
Humble Petition and Advice, 73, Chapter
    7, 91–3, 96, 97, 103, 104, 124, 125,
    136, 138, 167
Huntingdon, Earl of, 52
Hutchinson, Colonel John, 53–5
Hutchinson, Lucy, 53–5, 119
Hyde Park, 37, 38

Inner Temple, 12
Inns of Court see Inner Temple; Middle
    Temple

Instrument of Government, 1, 2, 9, 13, 43, 73, 74, 81, 128
Ireland, 11, 13, 17, 26, 40, 43, 45, 48, 50, 54, 82, 93, 96, 97, 104, 106, 125
Ireton, Henry, 151

James I, 1, 4, 11, 13, 21, 29, 36, 37, 46, 82, 84, 96, 106, 120, 132, 138, 140, 143–5, 146, 147, 148, 149, 150, 155–60, 162–3
Jersey, 43
Jones, Inigo, 11, 22, 57, 163
Jones, Colonel Philip, Comptroller of the Household, 121–3, 138, 146
Josselin, Rev. Ralph, 27, 39, 43, 46, 49, 50, 72

Kenneth, King, 96
Kilkenny, 140
King's two bodies, 145
Kings of Arms, 12, 157, 158, see also Clarenceux; Garter, Principal; Norroy
kingship see Cromwell, Oliver
Kinnersley, Clement, Wardrobe Keeper, 33
Kinnersley, John, Assistant Wardrobe Keeper, 33
Knight Marshal, 156
   deputy, 156
Knights Bachelor, 60–1

lacqueys, 17, 20, 28, 36, 40, 107, 121, 135, 145
Lambert, John, 1, 7, 9, 10, 40, 64, 73, 89, 92, 97
Lancaster Herald, 158, see also heralds
Leicester, 12
Lenthall, William, Speaker of the House of Commons, 16, 41–2
Levellers, 28, 52
Leveson, Sir Richard, 86
Life Guard, 7, 11–12, 17, 36, 40, 58–9, 101, 104, 105, 126, 134, 146
   for Captain of see Beke, Major Richard; Howard, Charles
Lilburne, John, 6
Lisle, John, 50
Lisle, Robert Sidney, Viscount, 99, 101, 160

Livery Companies, 16, 55, see also Grocers; Mercers; Merchant Taylors; Skinners
Llywelyn the Great, 46
Lockhart, Sir William, 78–9, 114, 126
Lockyer, Nicholas, 11
London, 9 and n, 10–11, 12, 16–19, 27, 36, 41, 55, 65, 71, 101, 104, 114, 134–5, 136, 138, 142, 161
   Aldermen of, 7, 10, 12, 104, 135, 138
   Common Council, 10
   Corporation, 10, 16, 17
   Lord Mayor of, 7, 9, 10–11, 12, 16, 17, 18, 19, 33, 49, 55, 65, 97, 99, 104, 135, 138, 161
   Lord Mayor's Show, 55–6, 65, 135, 161
   mace bearer, 104
   Recorder, 17–18, 104
   sword bearer, 104
   Tower of, 2, 36, 37, 48, 113, 114, 128, 129, 157
      gentlemen porters, 160
      Yeomen Warders, 36, 40, 160
   trained bands, 65, 157
Lord Chamberlain see Pickering, Sir Gilbert
Lords, House of, 10, 15, 41, 71, 96, 109, 123–6, 158, 165, see also Other House
Lords Chief Justice, 81, 83, see also Rolle, Henry
Louis XIV, 23, 53, 78, 112, 131, 132
Ludlow, Edmund, 89, 140, 153, 163, 164
Ludlow Castle, 116

Magna Carta, 129
Major Generals, rule of, 52
Man, Isle of, 43
Manchester, Earl of, 119, 124
Mantegna, Andrea, 33–4
Manton, Thomas, 99
Marriages Act (1653), 118
Marvell, Andrew, 42, 43, 56, 115–17, 134, 156, 168
Mary Queen of Scots, 132
Mary Tudor, 103, 132
masques, 21, 23, 116–17
Masson, David, 131
master carver, his Highness's, 147
May Day, 37–8

Maynard, John, his Highness's Sergeant, 128–9
Mazarin, Cardinal, 70
Mercers' Company, 55
Merchant Taylors' Hall, 135
Middle Temple, 56
Millenarianism see Fifth Monarchy Men
Milton, John, 65, 116, 156
Mint, the, 45, 95
Mompesson, Thomas, 125
Monck, George, 77
Montague, Edward, 99, 101
Morrice, Thomas, 75
Mulgrave, Edmund Sheffield, Earl of, 59, 124
Music, Gentlemen of his Highness's, 28–9, 61, 116
music, lads brought up to, 29, 116
Music, Master of the, see Hingston, John

National Covenant, 64
navy, 43, 73, 109, 124, 142, 157
Naylor, James, 124
Nedham, Marchamont, 126
Newport, Countess of, 113
Newport, Mountjoy Blount, first Earl of, 112, 113, 118
Newport, Rachel, 132
Nicholas, Sir Edward, 115, 125
Noble, Mark, 77
Norroy King of Arms, 97, 104, 158, see also Kings of Arms
Northumberland, Algernon Percy, tenth Earl of, 167
Norwich, Bishop of, 72
Nova Scotia, Plantation of, 106

opera, 165, 167
Osborne, Dorothy, 120
Other House see Parliament, second Protectorate
Oxford, City of, 140
Oxford University, 63, 90
   Magdalen College, 33, 40, 57
   St Mary's Hall, 90

Packe, Sir Christopher, 71, 74
Paris, 69, 70, 72, 75, 78, 112, 114
Parliament, 2, 7, 9, 128
   first Protectorate, 30, 39–42, 43, 78, 82, 132

Long, 11, 12, 37, 38, 40, 41, 61, 64, 70, 75, 106, 109, 113, 128, 150
Rump, 15, 41, 71, 74, 113, 120, 165
second Protectorate, 64, 69, 70, 71, 72, 73, 74, 75, Chapter 7, 91, 93, 96, 104, 123–6, 167
   Other House, 97, 123–6, 158
Pearson, Anthony, 53
Pensioners, Gentlemen/Ordinary, 12, 58–9, 146
Pepys, Samuel, 55, 77, 95, 126
Percivall, John, 93, 125
Peter, Hugh, 48, 136
Philip II of Spain, 153
Pickering, Sir Gilbert, Lord Chamberlain of the Household, 50–1, 121, 123, 136, 138, 146, 158
Portugal, ambassador of, 23
Powell, Vavasour, 15
Powis, 46
prerogative courts, 38–9
Presbyterians, 109
Preston, Battle of, 78
Pride, Colonel Thomas, 86
Printers to his Highness, 13, 14
Privy Chamber, Gentlemen of the, 30, 58, 104, 146
Privy Council see Council, his Highness's
Providence Plantation, New England, President of, 31
Prynne, William, 72
Pugh, Thomas, 46
Pursuivants, 12, 157
Pyx, Trial of the, 120

Quakers, 118, 130, 134

Raleigh, Sir Walter, 37
Raphael, 33
Read, Sir John, 106
Republicans, 28, 71, 73, 125
Requests, Court of, 39
Requests, Masters of, 39
Rich, Richard, 109
Rich, Robert (grandson of the Earl of Warwick), 75, 86, 99, 101, 108, 109–12, 116, 118, 119, 126–7
Rich, Robert (son of the Earl of Warwick), 112
Richard II, 10

Richard III, 2, 46, 72, 109
Richmond, Duke of, 151
Robartes of Truro, Baron, 101 and n
Robinson, Hum., 75
Roehampton, 68
Rolle, Henry, Chief Justice, 129
Rolls, Master of the, 81, 82
Royalists, 28, 49, 52, 66, 68, 69, 70, 74, 77, 114–15, 125, 130, 163
Rubens, 11
Rugg, Thomas, 168
Russell, Elizabeth, 120
Russell, Sir Francis, 86, 92

St Edward's Chair, 96, 99, 100, 102
St Gregory by St Pauls, church of, 118
St James's Park, 88, 150
St Margaret's, Westminster, church of, 154
St Martin in the Fields, Westminster, church of, 140
St Paul's Cathedral, 135
St Peter Mancroft, Norwich, church of, 140
Savoy, Duke of, 60
Saye and Sele, Viscount, 83, 124
Scobell, Henry, 112, 118
Scotland, 13n, 40, 45, 46, 48, 50, 70, 73, 82, 96, 97, 104, 124, 157, 158
Seal, Great, 9, 10, 38, 40, 43–50, 52, 93, 94, 95, 141
Seal, Privy, 48
Sealed Knot, 77
Secretary of State see Thurloe, John
Sergeants-at-Arms, 9, 40
Sergeants-at-Law, 13, 104, 128
Sewster, Robina, 78
Sherard of Leitram, Baron, 101
Shirley, James, 23
Simon, Thomas, 45, 95, 147, 156
Simpson, John, 15
Skinners' Company, 65
Skippon, Philip, Captain of the Artillery Company, 66
Society of Friends see Quakers
Somerset, Edward Seymour, Duke of, 144
Somerset Herald, 158, see also heralds
Somerset House, 57, 144, 145–6, 147, 150, 151–3, 155, 161, 163, 168
Southampton, 140

Spain, 35, 64, 86, 93, 96, 131, 134
ambassador of, 24, 36, 52
Star Chamber, 38
Stone of Scone, 96, 99n
Stoupe, Jean Baptiste, 90
Strickland, Walter, Captain of the Yeomen of the Guard, 37, 40, 123, 138
Sweden, 48
ambassador of, 21, 33, 48, 50, 58, 59, 60, 64
King of, 50, 59, 60
Swift, William, 126
Symonds, Richard, 4, 19, 48, 86

Temple Bar, 17, 18, 104
Thames, River, 36, 65, 146
Thistle, Order of the, 60
Throckmorton, Sir Francis, 38, 163
Thurloe, John, Secretary of State, 21, 69, 70, 71, 72, 73, 78, 85, 87, 89, 92, 97, 104, 112, 115, 117, 134, 135, 142
Titian, 33, 57
Tower of London see London
Tower Wharf, 19, 20
treasons act, 15
Turkey, 90
Tyburn, 168

Ulster, Plantation of, 106
United Provinces, 23, 35–6, 37, 70
ambassadors of, 19, 20–1, 24, 26, 36, 99

Vane, Sir Henry (the younger), 71, 104
Venice, ambassador of, 51, 52–3
envoy of, 2, 9, 13, 15, 16, 28, 42, 43, 72, 115, 143, 146, 150, 160
Verney, Ralph, 150
Voltaire, 104
Vyner, Thomas, 18, 33

Wales, 45
Walker, Sir Edward, Garter, Principal King of Arms, 63
Waller, Edmund, 64–5, 90, 96
Warbeck, Perkin, 48
Wardrobe, Keepers of, see Kinnersley, Clement; Kinnersley, John
Wars of the Roses, 46, 69, 109
Warwick, Sir Philip, 113–14, 121
Warwick, Richard Neville, Earl of, 109

Warwick, Robert Rich, second Earl of, 75, 97, 99, 101 and n, 108–12, 113, 114, 119, 124, 126–7, 140, 160
watermen, his Highness's, 20, 106–7, 157
Waynwright, James, 36, 49, 59, 66, 126
West Indies, 90
Westminster, 12, 17, 48, 49, 51, 101, 136
    poor men of, 156
Westminster, Palace of, 7, 11, 19, 40–1, 96, 125, 132, 165
    Painted Chamber, 40–1, 87, 89, 96, 132
Westminster Abbey, 1, 7, 39, 63, 96, 100, 102, 132, 145, 150, 151, 153–4, 155, 156, 160, 161–3, 167
    dean and chapter of, 63
    Henry VII's Chapel, 1, 132, 142, 150, 151, 161–3, 167
Westminster Hall, 7–11, 40, 95–102
Westminster School, 63–4, 90, 157, 161
Wharton, Lord, 124
Whetstone, Lavinia, 59, 108, 126
White, Dr Jeremiah, 77
Whitehall, Palace of, 1, 7, 9, 11, 16, 17, 19, 26, 27, 28, 29–31, 33, 35–6, 39, 41, 53, 57–8, 59, 65, 89, 101, 104, 108, 112, 113, 114, 115, 117, 119, 123, 126, 132, 135, 136, 143, 144, 145, 147, 165, 168
    Banqueting House, 11, 19, 20–1, 22, 57, 72, 80, 87, 89
    Cockpit lodgings, 26
    Cockpit theatre, 57

Whitelocke, Bulstrode, 4, 6, 33, 49, 52, 64, 85, 87, 89, 97, 99, 101, 103, 135, 165
Widdrington, Sir Thomas, 49, 52, 80, 81, 96, 97, 167
William the Conqueror, 46
William III, 45
    and Mary, 101
William IV, 101
Williams, Sir Abraham, 19, 20
Williamson, Jos., 75
Windsor, 63
    dean and canons of, 61, 62, 63
    Mayor of, 62
Windsor, Poor Knights of, 61–3, 157
Windsor Castle, 30, 61, 63
    governors of the almshouses of, 62, 63
    St George's Chapel at, 61, 62
Wolseley, Sir Charles, 83
Wood, Anthony à, 103
Woolwich, 17
Worcester, Battle of, 4, 12, 17, 78, 135
Wyndham, William, 135

Yeomen of the Guard, 12, 36–7, 40, 58, 101, 102, 107, 121, 136, 144, 145, 146, 160
    for Captain of see Strickland, Walter
York, James, Duke of, 70, 86
York, Richard, Duke of, 2, 48
York Herald, 158, see also heralds